WORLD OF ANIMALS

30

INSECTS
AND OTHER INVERTEBRATES

MOLLUSKS AND ECHINODERMS

Slugs, Snails, Starfish...

ANDREW CAMPBELL

GROLIER

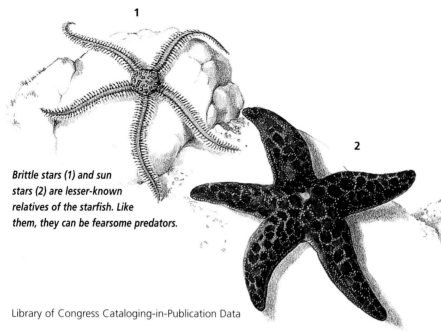

Brittle stars (1) and sun stars (2) are lesser-known relatives of the starfish. Like them, they can be fearsome predators.

Published 2004 by Grolier, an imprint of Scholastic Library Publishing Danbury, CT 06816

This edition published exclusively for the school and library market

The Brown Reference Group plc.
(incorporating Andromeda Oxford Limited)
8 Chapel Place
Rivington Street
London
EC2A 3DQ

Library of Congress Cataloging-in-Publication Data

Insects and other invertebrates.
    p. cm. -- (World of animals ; 21-30)
    Contents: v. 21. Simple and wormlike animals -- v. 22. Insects 1: millipedes and unusual insects -- v. 23. Insects 2: crickets, grasshoppers, and flies -- v. 24. Insects 3: true bugs -- v. 25. Insects 4: beetles -- v. 26. Insects 5: butterflies and moths -- v. 27. Insects 6: wasps, bees, and ants -- v. 28. Crustaceans -- v. 29. Arachnids -- v. 30. Mollusks and echinoderms.
    ISBN 0-7172-5894-7 (set) -- ISBN 0-7172-5895-5 (v. 21) -- ISBN 0-7172-5896-3 (v. 22) -- ISBN 0-7172-5897-1 (v. 23) -- ISBN 0-7172-5898-X (v. 24) -- ISBN 0-7172-5899-8 (v. 25) -- ISBN 0-7172-5900-5 (v. 26) -- ISBN 0-7172-5901-3 (v. 27) -- ISBN 0-7172-5902-1 (v. 28) -- ISBN 0-7172-5903-X (v. 29) -- ISBN 0-7172-5904-8 (v. 30)
    1. Insects--Juvenile literature. 2. Invertebrates--Juvenile literature. [1. Insects. 2. Invertebrates.] I. Grolier (Firm) II. World of animals (Danbury, Conn.) ; v. 21-30.

QL467.2 .15875 2004
595.7--dc22

2003063100   Set ISBN 0-7172-5894-7

Project Director: Graham Bateman
Editors: Virginia Carter, Angela Davies
Art Editor and Designer: Steve McCurdy
Editorial Assistants: Marian Dreier, Rita Demetriou
Picture Manager: Claire Turner
Picture Researcher: Vickie Walters
Production: Clive Sparling

Origination: Unifoto International, South Africa

Printed in China

About This Volume

Two major groups of invertebrate are dealt with in this volume, the mollusks and the echinoderms. Superficially they appear to have little in common, the mollusks being frequently shelled and either snail-, slug-, clam-, or squidlike, while the echinoderms are star shaped or round and often protected by a spiny skin. But underlying these apparent dissimilarities of shape and form are a number of common features.

Mollusks are predominantly aquatic, many are marine, and the echinoderms are exclusively sea dwelling. Mollusks and echinoderms make up a large part of the fauna of the seabed worldwide. The majority of these bottom-living sea dwellers have microscopic development stages in their life cycles known as larvae. These larvae drift in the plankton communities of the surface layers of the sea, where they grow and develop without any parental care.

Both groups have a considerable effect on the environments in which they live. Some, like terrestrial slugs and snails, graze on vegetation and have economic significance as agricultural pests. Freshwater snails can be significant as carriers of disease both of humans and domesticated animals. Sea urchins graze on seaweeds and often control the development of marine plants. Squids and octopuses are powerful carnivores, pursuing their victims and overwhelming them with an array of tentacles, suckers, and venomous saliva. Starfish are also stealthy predators capable of trapping their prey and consuming it slowly. Many mollusks are of economic importance as seafood, especially clams, scallops, mussels, squid, and octopus, while even the rather inedible-looking echinoderms are popular items on the menu in some parts of the world.

Contents

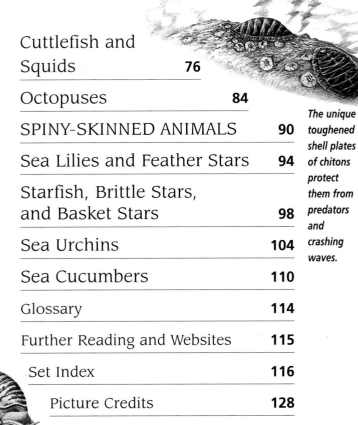

How to Use This Set	4
Find the Animal	6
MOLLUSKS	8
Neopilina	12
Chitons	14
Elephant's Tusk Shells	16
GASTROPODS	18
Limpets and Top Shells	22
Winkles and Relatives	26
Whelks and Cone Shells	32
Bubble Shells and Allies	36
Sea Slugs	38
Snails and Slugs	44
BIVALVES	50
Mussels	54
Oysters	56
Scallops and Allies	58
Freshwater Mussels	60
Cockles, Clams, and Razor Shells	62
CEPHALOPODS	72
Nautiluses	74
Cuttlefish and Squids	76
Octopuses	84
SPINY-SKINNED ANIMALS	90
Sea Lilies and Feather Stars	94
Starfish, Brittle Stars, and Basket Stars	98
Sea Urchins	104
Sea Cucumbers	110
Glossary	114
Further Reading and Websites	115
Set Index	116
Picture Credits	128

The unique toughened shell plates of chitons protect them from predators and crashing waves.

Nautiluses are known mainly as fossils and are represented by just a handful of living species.

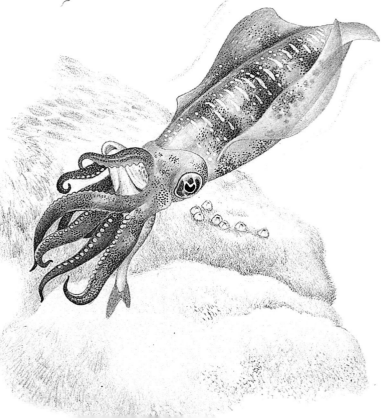

Squids are formidable hunters. This Loligo species paralyzes its prey with venom from its salivary glands.

How to Use This Set

World of Animals: Insects and Other Invertebrates is a 10-volume set that describes in detail creatures from all corners of the globe. Each volume brings together those groups that share similar characteristics or have similar lifestyles. This set contains a huge diversity of animal types. To help you find the volumes containing animals that interest you, look at pages 6 to 7 (Find the Animal). A brief introduction to each volume is also given on page 2 (About This Volume).

Article Styles

Each volume contains two types of article. The first kind introduces major groups (such as the animal kingdom, mollusks, insects, or flies). It presents a general overview of the subject. The second type of article makes up most of each volume. It concentrates on describing in detail important groups often with familiar names, such as tarantulas, octopuses, or seed bugs. Each such article starts with a fact-filled data panel to help you gather information at a glance. Used together, the two styles of article enable you to become familiar with animals in the context of their evolutionary history and biological relationships.

A number of other features help you navigate through the volumes and present you with helpful

---

Data panel presents basic statistics of each animal group

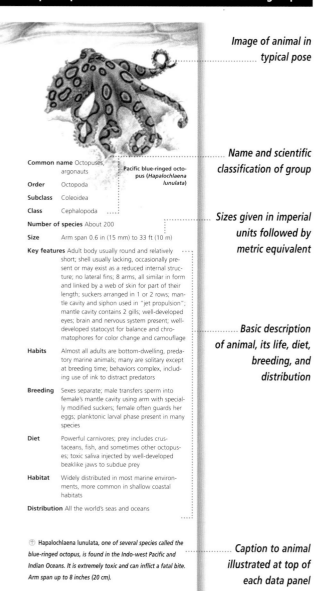

Image of animal in typical pose

Name and scientific classification of group

Common name Octopuses, argonauts

Pacific blue-ringed octopus (Hapalochlaena lunulata)

Order Octopoda

Subclass Coleoidea

Class Cephalopoda

Number of species About 200

Size Arm span 0.6 in (15 mm) to 33 ft (10 m)

Sizes given in imperial units followed by metric equivalent

Key features Adult body usually round and relatively short; shell usually lacking, occasionally present or may exist as a reduced internal structure; no lateral fins; 8 arms, all similar in form and linked by a web of skin for part of their length; suckers arranged in 1 or 2 rows; mantle cavity and siphon used in "jet propulsion"; mantle cavity contains 2 gills; well-developed eyes; brain and nervous system present; well-developed statocyst for balance and chromatophores for color change and camouflage

Habits Almost all adults are bottom-dwelling, predatory marine animals; many are solitary except at breeding time; behaviors complex, including use of ink to distract predators

Breeding Sexes separate; male transfers sperm into female's mantle cavity using arm with specially modified suckers; female often guards her eggs; planktonic larval phase present in many species

Diet Powerful carnivores; prey includes crustaceans, fish, and sometimes other octopuses; toxic saliva injected by well-developed beaklike jaws to subdue prey

Habitat Widely distributed in most marine environments, more common in shallow coastal habitats

Distribution All the world's seas and oceans

Basic description of animal, its life, diet, breeding, and distribution

ⓉHapalochlaena lunulata, one of several species called the blue-ringed octopus, is found in the Indo-west Pacific and Indian Oceans. It is extremely toxic and can inflict a fatal bite. Arm span up to 8 inches (20 cm).

Caption to animal illustrated at top of each data panel

Article describes important groups with familiar names

Scientific name of group

Common name of group

Captions to photographs provide additional information about each animal's lifestyle

TRUE BUGS   Lygaeidae

Seed Bugs

Seed bugs is an appropriate common name for the Lygaeidae, since the majority feed on seeds of a range of plant species, including trees. They are also called ground bugs because they feed on seeds that have fallen from the plant onto the ground.

Trapezonotus arenarius

Lygaeus kalmii

Common name Seed bugs (ground bugs)

Family Lygaeidae

Suborder Heteroptera

Order Hemiptera

Number of species About 3,000 (295 U.S.)

Size From about 0.09 in (2.2 mm) to 0.8 in (20 mm)

Key features Rather tough-bodied bugs, mostly oval in shape, some longer and thinner species; body usually appears flat topped; ocelli present; fully and partially winged as well as wingless forms and species; front femurs enlarged in many species, most are combinations of black and brown; a few are brightly colored

Habits Found either on the plant that produces seeds on which they feed or running around on the ground beneath

Breeding Sound production is involved in courtship in many seed bugs; eggs usually laid on or into food plants

Diet The vast majority are seed feeders; others specialize in insect eggs and larvae; a few are blood suckers

Habitat Forests, grasslands, meadows, gardens, marshes, seashore, and deserts

Distribution Worldwide

SEED BUGS ARE AMONG the drabbest-colored bugs, with most being shades of brown to black. There are, however, notable exceptions such as the warningly colored, distasteful large milkweed bugs of the genus Oncopeltus, which have black-and-orange patterning.

While most seed bugs live away from the coast, a few species are found on the seashore, including salt marshes. Henestaris species from Europe and Asia live in such habitats, as well as inland alongside salt pans. Henestaris halophilus is widespread in the region and is also found in sea salt marshes, where it feeds on the seeds of sea purslane, Atriplex portulacoides. As the tide comes in, the nymphs remain submerged on the food plant without coming to harm.

Saliva Injection

Seed-feeding Lygaeidae inject saliva into the seed to digest it before sucking up the liquid that results. Those that do not feed on seeds but on the plants themselves puncture single groups of plant cells and suck the sap out of them. With around 3,000 species in the family a number have become pests by attacking the seed crops on which humans depend.

Perhaps the most important seed bug pests in North America are the chinch bugs of the genus Blissus. Blissus leucopterus, a very widespread species, is a particular problem. The adults overwinter in bunches of wild grasses, but on emerging in spring they then move into fields of cultivated crops such as wheat, barley, and other small-grained cereals. As these ripen and dry out, further generations of the bug move onto crops such as corn and

ⓉThe small eastern milkweed bug, Lygaeus kalmii from the United States, feeds and lays its eggs on milkweed plants. The bug is immune to the toxic chemicals in milkweed but is itself toxic to other insect predators. Length 0.4–0.5 inches (10–13 mm). Trapezonotus arenarius is a less common species from the Northern Hemisphere, where it lives on savanna. Length 0.15–0.2 inches (4–5 mm).

A mating
Neacoryphy
ragweed
Great Sm
of Tenni
seed k
wear
"wa

Cross-references to relevant pages in this and other volumes

44   SEE ALSO Whiteflies 24:08. Aphids 24:100

Easy-to-read and comprehensive text

extra information. At the bottom of many pages are cross-references to other articles of interest. They may be to related animals, animals that live in similar places, or that have similar behavior, predators (or prey), lifestyles, and much more. Each volume also contains a Set Index to the complete *World of Animals: Insects and Other Invertebrates*. Animals mentioned in the text are indexed by common and scientific name, and many topics are also covered. Since this set contains such a diverse group of animals, there are many unfamiliar words that need to be used. There is, therefore, a Glossary that will help you understand them. Each volume includes lists of useful Further Reading and Websites that help you take your research further.

Introductory article describes lesser groups, such as orders

Graphic full-color photographs bring text to life

Meticulous drawings illustrate details of structure and anatomy

Tables summarize classification of invertebrate groups and give scientific names of groups mentioned in the text

Who's Who tables summarize classification of each major group and give scientific names of animals mentioned in the text

Introductory article describes major groups of animals

At-a-glance boxes cover topics of special interest

5

Find the Animal

World of Animals: Insects and Other Invertebrates is the third part of a library that describes all groups of living animals. Each cluster of volumes in World of Animals will cover a familiar group of animals—mammals, birds, reptiles and amphibians, fish, and insects and other invertebrates.

The Animal Kingdon

The living world is divided into five kingdoms, one of which (kingdom Animalia) is the main subject of the World of Animals. Kingdom Animalia is divided into major groups called phyla, but only one of them (Chordata) contains those animals that have a backbone. Chordates, or vertebrates, include all the animals familiar to us and those most studied by scientists—mammals, birds, reptiles, amiphibians, and fish. There are about 38,000 species of vertebrates; but the animals without backbones (so-called invertebrates, such as insects, spiders, mollusks, and crustaceans) number at least 1 million species, probably many more. To find which set of volumes in the World of Animals you need, see the chart below.

Invertebrates in Particular

World of Animals: Insects and Other Invertebrates provides a broad survey of the most varied and numerous creatures on our planet. The only common factor linking all the animals described here is the lack of a backbone. We start by describing single-celled life forms (kingdom Protista), which are not regarded as true animals at all because the group includes both animal-like and plantlike forms and some that have both sets of characteristics.

There are 33 invertebrate phyla recognized here in the kingdom Animalia. Each one is quite distinct, so the diversity of animals described is immense. Mostly they are small, even microscopic; but monsters of the deep, such as the giant squid, can reach 65 feet (20 m) long.

Rank	Scientific name	Common name
Kingdom	Animalia	Animals
Phylum	Arthropoda	Animals with an external skeleton and jointed limbs
Class	Insecta	Six-legged arthropods
Order	Lepidoptera	Butterflies and moths
Family	Danaidae	Milkweed butterflies
Genus	*Danaus*	
Species	*Danaus plexppus*	

The kingdom Animalia is subdivided into phyla, classes, orders, families, genera, and species. Above is the classification for the monarch butterfly.

An important point must be made about the current scientific knowledge of these animals. New discoveries are being made every day, from the biology of individual creatures to the finding of new species. Knowledge is changing all the time, particularly regarding relationships between groups, and the number of species (and even phyla) increases all the time. Many of the figures given here are estimates based on the latest knowledge.

The greatest range of phyla is in Volume 21, where we describe single-celled life and 16 separate phyla of animals. The biggest phylum within the animal kingdom is the Arthropoda, which is made up of crustaceans, insects, spiders, and other familiar groups. They are covered in Volumes 22–29. Finally, there are the mainly marine phyla of mollusks and echinoderms in Volume 30.

➔ *This chart lists the phyla in two of the five kingdoms. The phylum Arthropoda makes up a high proportion of all invertebrate animals.*

⊕ *The main groups of animals alive today. Volumes that cover each major group are indicated below.*

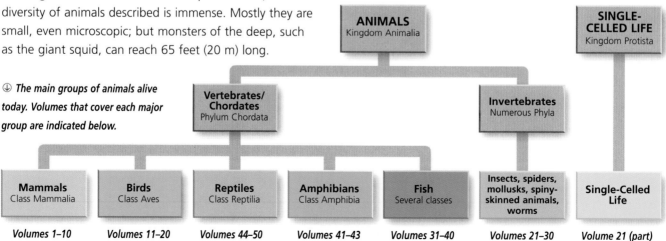

ANIMALS Kingdom Animalia

SINGLE-CELLED LIFE Kingdom Protista

Vertebrates/ Chordates Phylum Chordata

Invertebrates Numerous Phyla

Mammals Class Mammalia	**Birds** Class Aves	**Reptiles** Class Reptilia	**Amphibians** Class Amphibia	**Fish** Several classes	**Insects, spiders, mollusks, spiny-skinned animals, worms**	**Single-Celled Life**
Volumes 1–10	*Volumes 11–20*	*Volumes 44–50*	*Volumes 41–43*	*Volumes 31–40*	*Volumes 21–30*	*Volume 21 (part)*

KINGDOM PROTISTA	single-celled animals
Phylum: Sarcomastigophora **(Vol. 21)**	flagellates, amebas
Phylum: Ciliophora **(Vol.21)**	ciliates
Phylum: Apicomplexa **(Vol. 21)**	malaria, etc.
Phylum: Microspora **(Vol. 21)**	single-celled parasites

KINGDOM ANIMALIA	animals
Phylum: Porifera **(Vol. 21)**	sponges
Phylum: Placozoa **(Vol. 21)**	plate animals
Phylum: Orthonectida **(Vol. 21)**	marine invertebrates
Phylum: Rhombozoa **(Vol. 21)**	parasitic invertebrates
Phylum: Cnidaria **(Vol. 21)**	jelly animals (hydrozoans, jellyfish, corals, and sea anemones)
Phylum: Ctenophora **(Vol. 21)**	comb jellies
Phylum: Gnathostomulida **(Vol. 21)**	no common name
Phylum: Gastrotricha **(Vol. 21)**	aquatic wormlike animals
Phylum: Rotifera **(Vol. 21)**	rotifers or wheel animalcules
Phylum: Acanthocephala **(Vol. 21)**	spiny-headed worms
Phylum: Cycliophora **(Vol. 21)**	microscopic animals
Phylum: Phoronida **(Vol. 21)**	horseshoe worms
Phylum: Bryozoa **(Vol. 21)**	moss animals

Phylum: Brachiopoda **(Vol. 21)**	lampshells
Phylum: Endoprocta **(Vol. 21)**	endoprocts
Phylum: Platyhelminthes **(Vol. 21)**	flatworms, tapeworms, and flukes
Phylum: Nemertea **(Vol. 21)**	ribbon worms
Phylum: Sipuncula **(Vol. 21)**	peanut worms
Phylum: Echiura **(Vol. 21)**	spoonworms
Phylum: Annelida **(Vol. 21)**	segmented worms
Phylum: Pogonophora **(Vol. 21)**	beard worms
Phylum: Kinorhyncha **(Vol. 21)**	spiny-crown worms
Phylum: Loricifera **(Vol. 21)**	loriciferans
Phylum: Nematoda **(Vol. 21)**	roundworms
Phylum: Nematomorpha **(Vol. 21)**	horsehair worms
Phylum: Priapulida **(Vol. 21)**	cactus worms
Phylum: Tardigrada **(Vol. 22)**	water bears
Phylum: Onychophora **(Vol. 22)**	velvet worms
Phylum: Arthropoda (Vols. 22–29)	jointed-limbed invertebrates
Phylum: Mollusca **(Vol. 30)**	mollusks, slugs, snails, etc.
Phylum: Echinodermata **(Vol. 30)**	echinoderms
Phylum: Chaetognatha **(Vol. 21)**	arrowworms
Phylum: Hemichordata **(Vol. 21)**	acorn worms

Phylum: Arthropoda

Subphylum: Pycnogonida **(Vol. 29)**	sea spiders
Subphylum: Chelicerata **(Vol. 29)**	spiders, scorpions, horseshoe crabs
Subphylum: Myriapoda **(Vol. 22)**	centipedes, millipedes, etc.
Subphylum: Crustacea **(Vol. 28)**	crustaceans
Subphylum: Hexapoda (Vol. 22)	Diplura, Protura, springtails, and insects

Subphylum: Hexapoda

Class: Collembola **(Vol. 22)**	springtails
Class: Protura **(Vol. 22)**	proturans
Class: Diplura **(Vol. 22)**	diplurans
Class: Insecta (Vols. 22–26)	insects

Class: Insecta

Order: Thysanura **(Vol. 22)**	silverfish
Order: Archeognatha **(Vol. 22)**	bristletails
Order: Ephemeroptera **(Vol. 22)**	mayflies
Order: Odonata **(Vol. 22)**	dragonflies and damselflies
Order: Phasmatodea **(Vol. 22)**	walkingsticks and leaf insects
Order: Dermaptera **(Vol. 22)**	earwigs
Order: Isoptera **(Vol. 22)**	termites
Order: Blattodea **(Vol. 22)**	cockroaches
Order: Mantodea **(Vol. 22)**	mantids
Order: Plecoptera **(Vol. 22)**	stoneflies
Order: Embioptera **(Vol. 22)**	web spinners
Order: Zoraptera **(Vol. 22)**	zorapterans
Order: Thysanoptera **(Vol. 22)**	thrips
Order: Psocoptera **(Vol. 22)**	booklice and barklice

Order: Phthiraptera **(Vol. 22)**	lice
Order: Neuroptera **(Vol. 22)**	lacewings
Order: Megaloptera **(Vol. 22)**	alderflies and dobsonflies
Order: Raphidioptera **(Vol. 22)**	snakeflies
Order: Trichoptera **(Vol. 22)**	caddisflies
Order: Mecoptera **(Vol. 22)**	scorpionflies and hangingflies
Order: Siphonaptera **(Vol. 22)**	fleas
Order: Strepsiptera **(Vol. 25)**	strepsipterans
Order: Orthoptera **(Vol. 23)**	crickets and grasshoppers
Order: Hemiptera **(Vol. 24)**	true bugs
Order: Coleoptera **(Vol. 25)**	beetles
Order: Diptera **(Vol. 23)**	flies
Order: Lepidoptera **(Vol. 26)**	butterflies and moths
Order: Hymenoptera **(Vol. 27)**	wasps, ants, bees, and sawflies

MOLLUSKS

There are many different types of mollusk, and no one type gives a good general body plan for all the other members of the phylum. Mollusks are essentially bilaterally symmetrical animals, meaning they have a head at the front end, a rear, and distinct left and right sides—but coiling and twisting of the body may obscure this. In some the anus is at the rear, but in others it is located elsewhere. Their bodies are unsegmented—unlike annelids, insects, and crustaceans. The head is often well developed and usually bears sensory structures, eyes, tentacles or palps, and a mouth. Inside the mouth there is a toothed, ribbonlike tongue called the radula. The radula is a key feature of mollusks, and it is used for a variety of tasks, such as scraping algae from rocks, cutting vegetation, drilling into the shells of prey, and sometimes for injecting poison.

The body mass (the visceral hump) is covered for the most part with specialized skin known as the mantle. The mantle secretes the shell (if one is present) by a process involving the formation of calcium carbonate crystals. The mantle also encloses a space (the mantle cavity) where in many species the gills lie, and into which the anus and reproductive ducts discharge. On the under surface there is a foot for creeping or digging. In the squids and octopuses it is divided up to form the suckered tentacles. Active mollusks generally have a well-developed central nervous system and sensory organs, including organs of

balance, vision, and smell. The brain is made up of groups of nerve cell bodies organized into masses called ganglia in the head and positioned close to the sensory organs.

Mollusks may be hermaphrodites or live as separate males and females. In marine forms the fertilized egg generally develops into a planktonic drifting larva, which later metamorphoses. However, some species such as whelks may lay their eggs in tough egg cases in which the embryo develops before hatching out as a fully formed juvenile. Terrestrial mollusks normally lay their eggs in masses that can be buried in the soil and from which young snails and slugs hatch.

Mollusk Success

After the arthropods the mollusks form one of the largest groups of invertebrates in terms of their species diversity,

↩ *A much-enlarged colored scanning electron micrograph of the surface of a slug's radula. The radula is a tonguelike organ studded with horny teeth used to pick up food particles, among other things.*

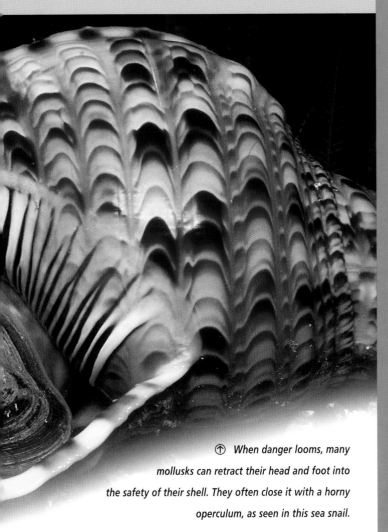

① *When danger looms, many mollusks can retract their head and foot into the safety of their shell. They often close it with a horny operculum, as seen in this sea snail.*

Who's Who among the Mollusks?
Phylum Mollusca

Class: Monoplacophora—monoplacophorans
25 species

Class: Aplacophora—solenogasters, chaetoderms
2 subclasses, about 370 species

Class: Polyplacophora—chitons
About 1,000 species

Class: Scaphopoda—elephant's tusk shells
About 900 species

Class: Gastropoda—slugs and snails
3 subclasses, 15 orders, about 150 families, about 70,000 species
    Subclass Prosobranchia—3 orders of limpets, winkles, slipper limpets, sea snails, whelks, and cone shells
    Subclass Opisthobranchia—9 orders of bubble shells, sea slugs, and saccoglossans
    Subclass Pulmonata—3 orders of pond snails, tropical slugs, and land snails and slugs

Class: Bivalvia—clams and mussels (bivalves)
7 orders, about 50 families, about 15,000 species, including:
    Order: Dysodonta—about 250 species of mussels
    Order: Ostreiformes—about 40 species of oysters
    Order: Pseudolamellibranchia—about 60 species of scallops
    Order: Schizodonta—about 1,000 species of freshwater mussels
    Order: Eulamellibranchia—about 4,000 species of cockles, clams, and razor shells

Class: Cephalopoda—cephalopods
2 subclasses, 4 orders, 30 families, about 900 species
    Subclass Nautiloidea—1 order of nautiluses
    Subclass Coleoidea—3 orders of cuttlefish, squids, and octopuses

population sizes, and commercial and agricultural importance. Most mollusks are aquatic, and many of them are marine; but a number of species (the terrestrial snails and slugs) have very successfully conquered land. The basic body plan of these animals has been adapted in a particular fashion by each of the seven classes of mollusks so that when viewed overall, the group has members that can appear quite dissimilar.

The Shell

The most familiar feature of the mollusks is the shell, although in some groups it is internal or lacking. The shell provides support and protection for the soft internal parts of the body and may perform other functions such as regulating buoyancy in swimming species. The shape of the shell is adapted to that of the animal that occupies it. Although mollusks are usually bilaterally symmetrical, many of the gastropods (winkles, whelks, and snails) are asymmetrical as adults. That is due to two separate processes—coiling and torsion.

Coiling of the visceral hump and the shell allows an increase in the size of the gut and other organs. Torsion, a peculiar twisting of the body, results in an unequal development of the left- and right-hand sides of the body. It leads to an apparent rotation of the visceral hump and the ducts and organs it houses. The anus and the gills, which originally develop behind the hump, now come to lie in front of it. The ducts associated with the anus and gills also become twisted.

The forms and habits of the various classes of mollusks vary greatly. The chitons (Polyplacophora) are relatively inconspicuous and creep slowly over rocks and shells in search of their algal food. They number about 1,000 species. Two other classes—the Monoplacophora and the Aplacophora—are obscure marine forms that nevertheless have considerable evolutionary significance.

The Mollusk Shell

The shell is arranged in four layers. The outermost is normally the horny periostracum, which is made of protein and is usually the thinnest. It is missing in some types, such as cowries, and can be very thick and even hairy, as in certain whelks. Below it are three layers made from calcium carbonate: First is the prismatic, made up of individual calcium carbonate crystals. Each crystal is surrounded by a thin protein layer. The innermost layers are the calcareous layer, made up of calcium carbonate laid down in sheets, and the nacreous layer, which resembles mother-of-pearl, but is not always present. The shell color comes either from the periostracum or one of the other layers.

The gastropod shell can be thought of as a coiled tube. If it is held upright—with the mouth facing down and the tip pointing upward—the coil is right-handed (dextral) if the mouth is on the right, and left-handed (sinistral) if the mouth is on the left. As the snail grows, the tube is made longer and wider so that the newest part is always nearest the mouth.

The shells of bivalve mollusks, such as clams and mussels, are also formed of about four layers, the outer one being the periostracum. The most obvious difference between the shells of gastropods and those of bivalve mollusks is that bivalve shells are made up of two valves, or halves, joined together at the top by a special hinge and by a rubbery ligament. When the bivalve shells are pulled shut by the special adductor (closing) muscles, the ligament is squeezed and compressed. When the muscles relax again, the ligament expands and forces the shells open.

The secretion and maintenance of the shell is one function of the mantle. Unlike the exoskeleton of insects and the "shells" of crustaceans, which must be molted and then replaced to permit growth, the molluskan shell grows continually and is not molted.

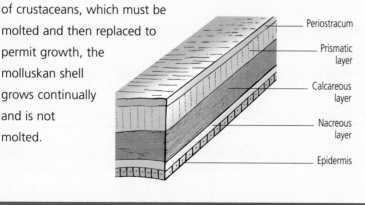

Periostracum

Prismatic layer

Calcareous layer

Nacreous layer

Epidermis

The Gastropoda (marine, freshwater, and terrestrial snails and slugs) is the largest class, consisting of roughly 70,000 known species. It is divided into three subclasses, all of which creep on a flattened foot. The first of them is the Prosobranchia (limpets, winkles, whelks, and others). They are familiar seashore animals; although not swiftly moving, they search actively for their food, which is taken with the help of their radulae.

The subclass Opisthobranchia includes the sea slugs. The adults have undergone detorsion of their bodies and are frequently colorful and attractive, unlike their terrestrial namesakes. They are usually carnivorous. In a third subclass (the Pulmonata) the mantle cavity has developed into a lung that breathes air. The Pulmonata includes the familiar land snails and slugs. Very few species of Pulmonata are marine, but some freshwater and brackish species are found.

The Scaphopoda (elephant's tusk shells) is a small class of about 350 species. They are partly buried in sand and mud in tusk-shaped shells. The class Bivalvia (mussels, oysters, and clams) numbers about 15,000 species. Most of them are marine, and many are burrowers. Almost all use their gills to filter seawater in order to collect particles of food, as well as for respiration. In this group the foot is frequently developed to form an efficient digging organ.

In the class Cephalopoda (octopuses, squids, and cuttlefish) the foot has been greatly modified to form eight or 10 suckered tentacles. The head merges with them and houses the highly developed brain and sensory organs. These animals are active predators and rapid movers. There are about 900 species. Only in the nautiluses and their relatives has the external shell been retained. In the squids and cuttlefish the shell has become internal, and in the octopuses it is missing.

⊙ *Hermissenda crassicornis, the opalescent sea slug, is found in a variety of habitats, including mud flats, rocky shores, and wharf pilings. This pair was seen in Barkley Sound, British Columbia, Canada.*

⊙ *Cross-section of a mollusk shell. Molluskan shells show great variation in shape, thickness, and texture. Marine examples are often thick and heavy, while land snails tend to have thinner shells.*

Neopilina galatheae

Common name Monoplacophorans (*Neopilina*)

Class Monoplacophora

Phylum Mollusca

Number of species About 25

Size 0.04 in (1 mm) to about 1.2 in (3 cm)

Key features Limpetlike mollusks with a single, slightly cap-shaped unhinged shell; body flat and not spiral; creeping solelike foot; clear bilateral symmetry with some structures such as gills, retractor muscles, parts of the heart, reproductive, and excretory organs repeated one behind the other along the body; head reduced; few species alive today, many fossil examples

Habits Adults are marine bottom dwellers living in deep water

Breeding Little known; larval stage exists

Diet Unicellular organisms and organic detritus on the deep seabed

Habitat Limited distribution, mainly in very deep marine habitats

Distribution Restricted, usually in the deep ocean

⬆ *In 1952 the Danish research ship* Galathea *dredged up the first specimens of* Neopilina galatheae *from the Pacific Ocean. The species was thought to be restricted to the oceans around Central and South America, but in 1967 a specimen was caught in the Gulf of Aden in the Indian Ocean, revealing a much wider distribution. Size 0.04–1.2 inches (1 mm–3 cm).*

Neopilina

Monoplacophora

The monoplacophorans were once thought to be a missing link between the mollusks and other segmented invertebrates. Little is known about the habits of these rare, ancient deep-sea animals.

IN 1952 A DANISH MARINE biology expedition was investigating animals that live in the deep trenches of the ocean at around 16,500 feet (5,000 m). Many important scientific discoveries were made, but the significance of what was found only became apparent when the samples were analyzed by specialists.

One set of samples included 10 small limpetlike forms collected from the deep seabed around the Pacific coastal region of Central America. The animals had a single shell on the upper surface and a flat, creeping foot on the underside. There was a mouth at the front on the underside and an anus at the rear. The shell was secreted by a mantle covering the upper surface of the body.

Living Proof

It turned out that these animals were not true limpets—they were the first living representatives of a group of mollusks previously known only from fossils and believed to be extinct. This group was known as the class Monoplacophora. The samples from the expedition fitted in remarkably well with the characteristics of the class Monoplacophora as established from fossil studies and caused a lot of excitement in zoological circles. The animals were named *Neopilina galatheae* and immediately became zoological celebrities.

It is thought that many of the shallow-water monoplacophorans became extinct because they could not compete with the evolving range of other shallow-water organisms. However, *Neopilina* probably survived because it inhabited very deep parts of the ocean where there were few competitors or suitable predators.

⊙ *Epimenia, a solenogaster, lives and feeds on soft coral. This wormlike animal is from the seas around northern Australia.*

SEE ALSO Hydrozoans **21**:46; Corals **21**:62; Worms, Segmented **21**:94; Limpets and Top Shells **30**:22

Examination of *Neopilina galatheae* at first suggested that the six pairs of gills that lie in a groove running around the underside of the shell might be arranged on a segmental basis. There are eight pairs of foot retractor muscles (muscles that pull the foot inside the shell). The excretory organs are also arranged in six pairs located on each side of the body. Each pair discharges into the groove just inside the shell edge. The sexes are separate, and there are two pairs of reproductive organs.

Missing Link?

Segmentation is a characteristic of annelid worms, insects, and crustaceans, but it is not a typical molluskan trait. Scientists wondered whether *Neopilina* was evidence of an evolutionary link between the segmented groups and the mollusks. After the discovery of *Neopilina* a second monoplacophoran genus, named *Vema*, was found in shallower water, and today about eight different species are known from these two genera.

A more detailed examination of the internal organs of monoplacophorans revealed a lack of true segmentation. A connection with the annelids and arthropods was therefore ruled out. Scientists now believe that the Monoplacophora are surviving deep-water representatives of a much larger group of mollusks that existed in Cambrian times (a period of the Paleozoic era) about 500 million years ago.

Solenogasters

The solenogasters belong to the class Aplacophora and are strange-looking, wormlike animals. The 370 or so species are poorly known, partly because of their small size and shy habits. The average size is less than 0.2 inches (5 mm) in length. They occur in seas and oceans down to extreme depths of 29,500 feet (9,000 m). Some live freely on the seabed, while others live on the surfaces of other organisms such as hydroids and corals.

They lack the typical molluskan features of a head, mantle, and foot. In most cases the body appears wormlike because its edges are rolled toward the underside. At the rear of the body there is a small chamber into which the anus opens. Some scientists think that the chamber may be the remnants of a mantle cavity. There is no shell, but chalky plates are embedded in the outer skin.

Solenogasters are hermaphrodites, but little is known about the way they reproduce. They appear to feed mainly on cnidarians such as hydroids and corals.

Chiton

Common name Chitons
(coat-of-mail shells)

Class Polyplacophora

Phylum Mollusca

Number of species About 1,000

Size About 0.1 in (3 mm) to 5 in (13 cm)

Key features Adult body appears segmented with 8
overlapping shell plates; body not divided into
segments underneath; head is simple and
lacks eyes and tentacles; wide creeping foot
on the underside; microscopic light receptors
in the shell plates

Habits Marine, attached to and creeping on rocks
and shells on the seashore and seabed

Breeding Sexes separate; sperm and eggs released into
seawater, where fertilization occurs; forms a
microscopic planktonic larva; larva matures
and grows in the plankton, and at
metamorphosis settles on suitable surfaces on
the seabed

Diet Mainly herbivores, feeding on algae and tiny
organisms; a few are carnivores; food scraped
off rocks and hard surfaces using the radula

Habitat Seashore and bottom dwelling

Distribution All the world's seas, but better represented
in tropical waters

↑ *Chitons tend to hide in crevices and underneath boulders,
and are well camouflaged among the surrounding rocks.
Their primitive "eyes" are embedded within their shell and
are capable of detecting light and dark. Chitons will scurry
away from the light when a boulder is overturned. Length
0.1 inches (3 mm) to 5 inches (13 cm).*

Chitons

Polyplacophora

*Chitons are sometimes called coat-of-mail
shells—a reference to their armored
appearance. Their unique shell plates protect
them from predators and crashing waves.*

THE MOST CONSPICUOUS FEATURE of chitons is their
shell, which is made up of eight plates and is
unlike that of any other mollusk. Chitons are
perfectly adapted for life on the seabed. The
shell plates, which cover most of the upper
body surface, move with each other, allowing
flexibility as the animal moves over uneven
surfaces, such as rocks. If a chiton is knocked
off its rock or pebble, it will roll up defensively.
From this position it is also able to turn itself the
right way up.

When viewed from above, only the eight
shells and the fleshy girdle in which they are
embedded can be seen. The shells are secreted
by the underlying mantle and are covered at
their edges by the girdle, an extension of the
mantle. The girdle often has spines, hard plates,
or other calcareous decorations that can be
useful in identifying different chiton species.

On the underside of the body is a typical
broad, flat molluskan foot that acts as an organ
of attachment and locomotion. It sticks to the
substrate by lifting the central area while the
outside remains fixed to the
surface, creating a vacuum.

Night Feeding

Many chitons live between the
tidemarks. When the tide is out,
they rest motionless; but when
the tide returns, they move
around in search of food. They
are most active when high tide
coincides with darkness. Like
some of the limpets, some
chitons appear to return to the
same spot at the end of a
feeding session.

↓ *This chiton,* Loricella
angasi, *has been turned
upside down. Its small
head and large foot can
be clearly seen. The
species is found in the
temperate South Pacific
region, especially around
the south and west
coasts of Australia.*

Sharp-Toothed Tongue

The chiton's head is simple and not well developed. Most species feed on young algae and other minute organisms. The feeding organ is the radula, a toothed tongue that can scrape material from rocks and can cut up plant and animal tissue. Some chitons, for example, *Placiphorella* from the West Coast of the United States, lift up and expand their front ends when hunting in order to be able to seize small crustaceans and other invertebrates. As in other mollusks, the chiton radula bears many crosswise rows of teeth. In chitons there are 17 or so in each row. The tips of the teeth are strengthened by a "cap" of magnetite (iron oxide) to strengthen their cutting surfaces.

At the front of the mouth is a sensory organ, the subradula organ, that tests for the presence and suitability of food. If the food is acceptable, then the radula itself is projected from the mouth and begins to scrape at the food. The waste material is voided from the anus, and the fecal pellets are swept away by water movements.

The surfaces of the shell plates also have special sensory organs, known as esthetes, embedded in them. These organs are thought to play some role in light detection.

Reproduction without Mating

Although chitons occur as separate males and females, reproduction does not involve mating. Each individual has a single reproductive organ; when it is ripe, the gametes (sperm or eggs) move out through paired gonoducts to the seawater. Fertilization occurs in the sea or within the female's mantle cavity. In most species a drifting planktonic larva of the trochophore type develops (like that of the segmented worms), as opposed to a veliger-type larva (the typical mollusk form).

Beneath the shell there is one gill lying on each side close to the edge of the foot. The gills supply oxygenated blood to the heart. From there the blood is distributed around the chiton's body through vessels and blood spaces.

⬆ *Tonicella lineata, the lined chiton, exhibits a range of colors, from brownish-black to lavender or pink. The zigzagging lines help camouflage the chiton against its background. It is usually found feeding on algae on coral reefs from Alaska to Japan.*

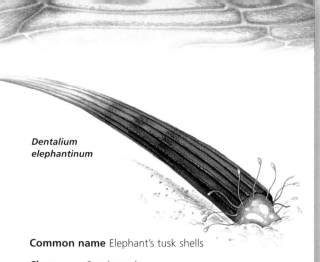

*Dentalium
elephantinum*

Common name Elephant's tusk shells

Class Scaphopoda

Phylum Mollusca

Number of species About 900

Size 0.2 in (5 mm) to about 6 in (15 cm)

Key features Tubular tusk-shaped shell open at both narrower (hind) and wider (head) ends; simple head with feeding tentacles; lacks gills; digging foot; mantle performs gas exchange

Habits Bottom-dwelling marine animals found at most depths; burrow in sediments

Breeding Sexes separate; microscopic planktonic larva forms after fertilization; settles on suitable sediments at metamorphosis

Diet Microscopic marine algae (diatoms) and larval and small juvenile invertebrates such as bivalves occurring in or on the sediment

Habitat Widely distributed marine sediments

Distribution All the world's seas and oceans

ⓣ *The elephant's tusk shell* Dentalium elephantinum *lies with its head buried in the sand. Its feeding tentacles are exposed. The animal's distribution ranges from Japan to the Philippines. Length up to 3 inches (8 cm).*

Elephant's Tusk Shells

Scaphopoda

Found in all the world's seas and oceans, sometimes at great depths, the distinctive elephant's tusk shells burrow into the sediment. Their specially adapted body features make them suited for such a lifestyle.

THE CLASS SCAPHOPODA contains a number of species—about 900—that have evolved a particular body plan quite unlike that of any other mollusk. These animals live in tubular, tapering shells that resemble an elephant's tusk. All the body organs as well as the head are completely encircled by the mantle and the shell, the free edges of which are fused on the underside to form a tubular mantle and a tubular shell. The animal is broader at the bottom, where the head and foot are located, and narrower at the top, where the reproductive organs are situated. The concave side of the shell forms the animal's back.

Elephant's tusk shells first appeared in the Devonian period, some 395 million years ago. *Dentalium*, *Antalis*, and *Cadulus* are bottom-dwelling burrowers, usually found in deeper water down to 10,000 feet (3,000 m).

Unusual Anatomy

Because the body organs are completely enclosed by the mantle and shell, the internal anatomy of the scaphopods is unusual. It probably has more in common with bivalves than any other group of mollusks. The molluskan head is usually at the front, and the foot is usually turned toward the ground, so in these animals they generally point in the same direction. Both can be extended from the wider opening of the shell or drawn back into it.

The head carries a snoutlike, muscular proboscis on which the mouth opens, and there are a number of club-tipped tentacles arranged around the base of the proboscis. These tentacles are sometimes called the captacula,

⊙ *Diagram showing the general anatomy of a scaphopod. Unusually for a mollusk, the head and foot are together at the wide end of the tubular, tapering shell. The narrow end protrudes above the surface of the sediment, allowing for respiration.*

⊕ *An elephant's tusk shell,* Dentalium elephantinum, *washed up on the sand in the Philippines.*

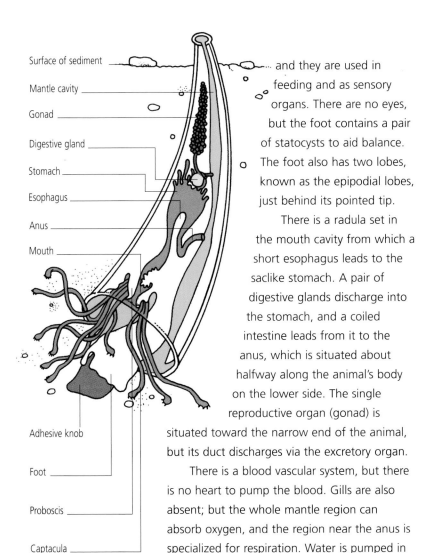

Surface of sediment

Mantle cavity

Gonad

Digestive gland

Stomach

Esophagus

Anus

Mouth

Adhesive knob

Foot

Proboscis

Captacula

and they are used in feeding and as sensory organs. There are no eyes, but the foot contains a pair of statocysts to aid balance. The foot also has two lobes, known as the epipodial lobes, just behind its pointed tip.

There is a radula set in the mouth cavity from which a short esophagus leads to the saclike stomach. A pair of digestive glands discharge into the stomach, and a coiled intestine leads from it to the anus, which is situated about halfway along the animal's body on the lower side. The single reproductive organ (gonad) is situated toward the narrow end of the animal, but its duct discharges via the excretory organ.

There is a blood vascular system, but there is no heart to pump the blood. Gills are also absent; but the whole mantle region can absorb oxygen, and the region near the anus is specialized for respiration. Water is pumped in and out through the small opening of the shell by ciliated areas of the mantle and by periodic movements of the foot in the lower part of the tubular shell.

Eggs and Larvae

The sexes are separate; males release sperm, and females release eggs into the water, where fertilization takes place. Typical molluskan larvae (trochophores and veligers) form and develop during a free-swimming stage. When the larvae are almost fully grown, they metamorphose and settle on the seabed as juvenile tusk shells.

Scaphopods burrow into the sediment by exploring it with the pointed foot. When the foot tip reaches a suitable depth in the sand, the epipodial lobes fold out and expand to form an anchor. The retractor muscles in the foot contract and pull the animal into the sand. The cycle is repeated until the animal is almost buried with just the narrow tip of the shell protruding above the level of the sediment.

Digging for Food

Scaphopods feed on organisms living in the sediment. Buried in the sand, the expanded end of the foot digs a small space around the wide end of the shell. The foot moves around in a circle, pushing sand away in all directions. The tentacles around the proboscis then stretch out and feel the walls of the chamber to detect food items—usually minute single-celled animals with chalky shells.

The tentacles, bearing cilia and sticky with mucus, carry the food particles to the mouth, where the hard shells are crushed by the sharp radula. Digestion takes place as the food moves along the alimentary canal. The feces are passed through the anus into the mantle cavity and from there through the narrow opening of the shell that is situated above the surface of the sediment.

Gastropods

Common name Gastropods **Class** Gastropoda

MAIN GROUPS

Subclass Prosobranchia: 3 orders:

Archaeogastropoda	Abalones, limpets, top shells
Mesogastropoda	Winkles, slipper limpets, violet seasnails
Neogastropoda	Whelks, cone shells

Subclass Opisthobranchia: 9 orders including:

Bullomorpha	Shelled sea slugs
Thecosomata	Shelled pteropods
Gymnosomata	Naked pteropods
Aplysiomorpha	Sea hares
Sacoglossa	Bivalve gastropods
Nudibranchia	Shell-less sea slugs

Subclass Pulmonata: 3 orders:

Basommatophora	Water snails
Systelommatophora	Tropical slugs
Stylommatophora	Terrestrial snails and slugs

Number of species About 70,000

Size 0.04 in (1 mm) to 18 in (45 cm)

Key features Adult body usually asymmetrical and spiral, arranged in coils; head normally well developed, with 1 or 2 pairs of sensory tentacles, usually with eyes, statocyst, mouth, and radula; well-developed creeping foot with sole; during development and growth body organs and mantle may rotate 90–180 degrees in relation to foot (known as torsion); bearing 1 cone-shaped (limpets) or spiral shell (snails) into which the head, body, and foot may be withdrawn; shell reduced or absent (slugs); body has 1 or 2 nephridia (excretory organs) and well-developed mantle cavity housing the ctenidia (gills) and osphradium (organ of scent detection in marine forms); terrestrial and freshwater snails may evolve an air-breathing lung; many sea slugs have no mantle cavity

Habits Almost all adults bottom-dwelling marine or freshwater animals found at all depths or on land; some marine forms have planktonic adults; creeping locomotion is by means of the foot (snails and slugs); a few swim using flaplike extensions of the foot (sea butterflies)

Diet Herbivorous, carnivorous, or suspension feeding; often specialists consuming one particular prey type

Habitat Widely distributed in most aquatic and terrestrial environments

Distribution All the world's seas and oceans at all depths; widely distributed in lakes and rivers, and on almost all landmasses

Today five out of every six mollusks is a gastropod. It is difficult to estimate exactly how many gastropod species exist in the world, but it must be about 70,000. Present-day gastropods are classified into three subclasses: the Prosobranchia, which includes the seasnails; the Opisthobranchia, which includes the sea slugs and their allies; and the Pulmonata, which includes the terrestrial snails and slugs.

The Main Orders

The prosobranchs are divided into three orders: Archaeogastropoda (the oldest surviving group), Mesogastropoda, and the newest group, Neogastropoda. They represent ascending levels of evolutionary attainment. Many prosobranchs have heavy, stout shells, a result of the high levels of calcium carbonate in the sea.

The opisthobranchs include nine orders. The Bullomorpha are the shelled sea slugs with internal gills, and the Nudibranchia are the shell-less sea slugs with external gills and brightly colored skin. The remaining orders include the Thecosomata (shelled pteropods) and Gymnosomata (naked pteropods), which are important swimming groups, and some minor orders.

Finally, there are the pulmonates, the three orders of air-breathing gastropods that have lost their gills. They breathe using the mantle cavity, which is modified as a lung. The shell is conspicuously present in the terrestrial snails, but reduced or lacking in the slugs. Consequently, the snails are dependent on soils with a high calcium content, whereas slugs can manage in less limey habitats.

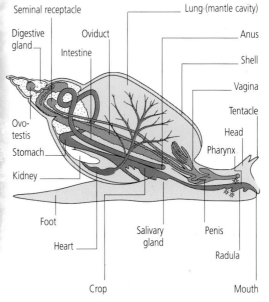

⬅ *The European grove snail,* Caepaea nemoralis, *is found in gardens, fields, and on roadsides. Its shell color ranges from pale yellow to dark red or brown.*

Seminal receptacle

Lung (mantle cavity)

Digestive gland

Oviduct

Anus

Intestine

Shell

Vagina

Ovo-testis

Tentacle

Head

Stomach

Pharynx

Kidney

Foot

Salivary gland

Penis

Heart

Radula

Crop

Mouth

⬆ *This body plan of an air-breathing freshwater snail shows the main characteristics of a gastropod—a creeping foot, head with tentacles, mantle, coiled single shell, and well-developed digestive, reproductive, circulatory, nervous, and excretory systems.*

⬅ Buccinum undatum, *the common northern Atlantic whelk, is carnivorous. It is edible and forms the basis of a modest fishing industry.*

a horny, rough tongue known as the radula. The head may contain a balance organ, the statocyst, and the external male reproductive organs may be carried on one side of the head, too.

In some species such as the neogastropod whelks there is a well-developed proboscis, which carries the radula and mouth at its tip. It is used for attacking prey and sucking flesh out of shells and cavities when feeding. The head merges with the foot, which is flattened and muscular, and is used for locomotion. A creeping movement is achieved by contracting and relaxing the muscles on the sole of the foot. The foot usually has mucus glands whose secretions aid movement and adhesion. The body contains the gut, digestive organs, excretory organs, male and female reproductive organs,

The Gastropod Body Plan

The gastropod body is complex. In many cases it undergoes two distinct processes as the animal grows, which can change its outward appearance. These processes are known as coiling and torsion. The basic gastropod body plan is made up of a head, a foot, and a well-developed body (visceral mass). The head contains the brain and sensory organs. They include the eyes, sensory tentacles, the mouth with the salivary glands, and

and their associated ducts, and is enclosed in a mantle—a wrap of skin frequently specialized for secreting the shell.

Inside the mantle is the mantle cavity, a major molluskan feature with various functions. In many aquatic species the gills are located in the mantle cavity, and water currents flow in and out. The anus and excretory and reproductive ducts also open into the mantle cavity. In the prosobranchs there is a special scent organ, the osphradium, situated close to where water enters the cavity from the siphon. This organ detects scents of prey or predators in the water. In the terrestrial forms the mantle cavity may become adapted to breathe air and functions like a lung. There is a well-developed blood vascular system with blood vessels and a heart. Blood,

usually containing a pigment called hemocyanin, is pumped away from the heart in arteries but returns to the heart through blood spaces that surround the tissues.

The prosobranchs usually have a strong external shell; but only some opisthobranchs, such as the Bullomorpha, show this feature. In the Aplysiomorpha the shell is internal, and it is absent in the Nudibranchia. In the terrestrial snails the shell is a typical external feature, although not as large as in the prosobranchs. It is reduced and carried internally or absent in the terrestrial slugs.

Twists and Turns

The developmental processes known as coiling and torsion are particularly apparent in the shelled sea-

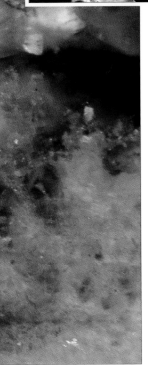

⬆ *This nudibranch sea slug, a species of Hermissenda, is characterized by numerous feathery gills, or cerata, running along its back.*

⬅ *The black-lined nudibranch,* Casella astromarginata, *grazing on a reef in Mayanmar (formerly Burma). The black line bordering the wavy mantle edge is characteristic of this common species.*

dwelling and terrestrial snails. Much of their body remains inside the shell, and only the head and foot protrude to enable the animal to creep around. When danger threatens, these parts may be withdrawn inside the shell. The purpose of coiling is to increase the volume of the body without unbalancing the animal. A coiled body also allows for a longer gut—an important feature in species that feed on vegetation, which is slow to digest.

Torsion is a separate process. It involves twisting the body mass through 180 degrees so that the gills are brought nearer the front of the body. As a result, they benefit from a fresh stream of water passing over them, which sweeps away excrement that could foul the gills. Torsion also affects the excretory and reproductive organs.

Different body forms adopt different methods of reproduction. Primitive forms like the limpets have

separate sexes, and fertilization takes place in seawater. In more advanced types such as the periwinkles internal fertilization has evolved because the arrangement of the reproductive ducts after torsion has made it possible.

A number of gastropods, such as the sea slugs, have evolved torsion and then laid it aside by undergoing detorsion as they have advanced farther along the path of evolution. The sea slugs have also abandoned coiling as adults; and unlike their terrestrial counterparts, many species have totally lost their shell.

Diverse and Beautiful

Gastropods are amazingly diverse. They occur in almost all habitats, apart from the air, in virtually every part of the globe. While they are mainly thought of as slow moving and clumsy, a number, like the sea slugs, are delicate and exceedingly beautiful to look at.

Gastropods have a considerable impact as pests, especially terrestrial slugs, which are serious pests of seeded crops. Gastropods also have economic significance. Snails are harvested and farmed for their flesh, and seashore snails, such as winkles and whelks, are collected in many parts of the world as shellfish. Some snail species act as carriers (vectors) in the transmission of various parasites of humans and domestic animals. For example, bilharzia, a human disease caused by parasitic worms called schistosomes, is transmitted for part of its life cycle by water snails.

Despite their negative image in parts of the world where they are pests or carry diseases, gastropods are the subject of conservation projects elsewhere, an example being the *Partula* snails of the Polynesian Islands.

➡ *In most gastropods torsion of the body in the developing embryo (1–3) brings the opening of the mantle cavity, anus, and other organs to the front. The nervous system also becomes twisted. Sea slugs and bubble shells lose torsion in adult life.*

Gills

Gut

Nerves

1

2

3

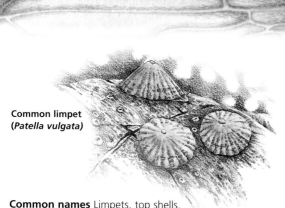

Common limpet
(Patella vulgata)

Common names Limpets, top shells, turban shells, keyhole limpets, abalones

Order Archaeogastropoda

Subclass Prosobranchia

Class Gastropoda

Number of species Unknown

Size 0.08 in (2 mm) to about 16 in (40 cm)

Key features Adult body usually asymmetrical and spiral (not obviously so in abalones and limpets); head normally with 1 or 2 pairs of sensory tentacles, usually with eyes, statocyst, mouth, and radula; well-developed creeping foot with sole; during development body organs and mantle may undergo torsion; bearing 1 flattened shell with apertures arranged in a row (abalones), a cone-shaped shell (limpets), or a spiral shell (top shells, etc.); shell usually lined with mother-of-pearl; head, body, and foot may be withdrawn into shell or covered by it; in top shells shell may be closed by an operculum; no operculum in abalones and limpets; 2 nephridia (excretory organs); well-developed mantle cavity housing ctenidia (gills) and osphradium (organ of scent detection in some marine species)

Habits Adults bottom-dwelling marine or freshwater animals; found in all depths in aquatic environments; foot used for creeping

Breeding Sexes separate; copulation may occur; fertilized egg develops into microscopic planktonic larva in marine forms

Diet Generally herbivores

Habitat Almost all marine, generally living on rocks, reefs, or other hard surfaces

Distribution All the world's seas and oceans; most common between the tidemarks and in shallow water

⬆ Patella vulgata, *the common limpet, is slow growing and can live for 15 years. It is found from northern Norway to the Mediterranean Sea. Length 2.4 inches (6 cm).*

Limpets and Top Shells

Archaeogastropoda

The limpets, top shells, and relatives are creatures of the rocky shore. Their highly specialized body structure prevents them from colonizing freshwater, land, or even mud or sand habitats.

THE ORDER ARCHAEOGASTROPODA includes the abalones, keyhole limpets, common limpets, top shells, and turban shells. These marine gastropods have a number of relatively primitive features in common relating to the layout and function of the gills inside the mantle cavity, as well as to their reproductive processes.

Although there are some exceptions, in the course of evolution many archaeogastropods have lost the right-hand gill but have retained the one on the left. Under a microscope the gill looks a bit like a two-dimensional tree. It is attached to both the roof and the floor of the mantle cavity. Unfortunately, there are pockets between it and the mantle wall on either side that can become blocked by sediments drawn in with the inhaled water stream.

➔ *A shimmering limpet browses algae from rocks in Cape province, South Africa.*

Stuck on Rocks

Because archaeogastropods risk accumulating sediments in their mantle cavity and gills, their gill structure has had an important effect on the type of habitats they can tolerate. They have become restricted to rocky and reefal habitats. The familiar limpet of the rocky shore is a classic example—clinging to the rocks with its well-developed muscular foot but not venturing onto sands and muds. On the rocks they graze on developing young encrusting algae. The effects of the animals have been shown in experiments in which limpets have been removed from the rocks, resulting in the luxuriant growth of seaweeds.

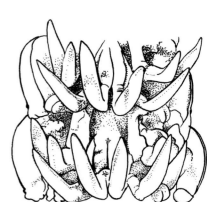

Because of the effects of torsion (twisting of the body organs during development), only the right-hand reproductive organ is functional, and it shares a duct with the right-hand kidney. Since the duct has dual use, it cannot be specialized in the male for the transmission of sperm (there is no penis) and in the female cannot be modified to store sperm. Therefore there is no copulation; sperm is released into seawater to meet the eggs that are laid directly into the water. As a result, archaeogastropods have not been able to invade fresh water or land, since they need seawater to reproduce. After fertilization a planktonic larva develops and spends a while feeding on zooplankton before settling on the seabed and metamorphosing into a juvenile.

⬅ Diagram of the radula of Patella vulgata, *the common limpet, showing the teeth, which are all similar, unlike those of more advanced gastropods.*

Conveyor-Belt Tongue

The radula of the common European limpet, *Patella vulgata,* is the simplest type of radula found in archaeogastropods. It consists of a tough ribbon of tissue studded with teeth, which can be pulled back and forth over a structure known as the odontophore. The odontophore acts a bit like a pulley. As this pulling takes place, driven by special muscles in the head, the teeth of the radula rasp away at rocks and remove particles of vegetation. The teeth are arranged in rows. Each row has a central tooth; on either side of it are the lateral teeth, and there may also be marginals.

Despite their limited distribution, there are well-developed fisheries for some archaeogastropods. This is true in particular for the abalones, which are highly regarded as food items in California, France, southern Arabia, and Australasia. They are usually collected by divers. In the Channel Islands in the British Isles, however, abalones are regarded as endangered, and strict controls govern their fishing. In southern Arabia abalones are collected because it is believed that they have aphrodisiac qualities, and they are traded in local markets at considerable prices. The tall pyramidal shells of the Red Sea *Trochus niloticus,* a large top shell found on coral reefs, were once harvested for their flat lower surface. The shell is lined with mother-of-pearl and was used to make shirt buttons. Today plastic is mainly used.

Top Shells

The top shells (family Trochidae) are another conspicuous group of archaeogastropods. They are all characterized by their cone-shaped shells. This shape is very clearly seen in *Trochus niloticus, Calliostoma zizyphinum*, and to a lesser extent in *Monodonta* and *Gibbula*.

The top shells are so-called because of the similarity between the shape of their shells and that of a Victorian child's spinning top. Like the limpets, top shells are herbivores, rasping at

⊙ *A giant keyhole limpet,* Megathura crenulata, *on a rocky coast of southern California. "Keyhole" refers to the central hole at the top that is used to expel the respiratory current.*

plant material growing on rocks. Unlike the limpets, however, their shells are coiled, and the animals' feet do not form such powerful suckers. They are less able to grip the rocks and so are more easily dislodged by wave action. They may roll around in the water until they get lodged in a crevice or between some pebbles.

⊕ *A wavy top shell,* Astraea undosa, *on rocks. Its common name probably comes from the wavy ornamentation at the far edges of its shell.*

They are able to emerge from such positions when the conditions become calmer. In a way that makes them less suitable for life between the tidemarks, and they are found in shallow water as well as on the shore.

Safe Retreat

Another feature distinguishes top shells from the limpets. It is the operculum—a horny or calcareous disk carried on the rear of the animal's foot. When the animal withdraws into its shell, the tip of the foot is pulled in last, and the operculum closes the aperture of the shell. The operculum is important because it restricts water loss when the animals are left behind by the falling tide. It also helps in defense by keeping out predators.

Top shells flourish most of all on horizontal surfaces such as gently sloping shores and reefs, and in warm temperate and tropical areas. *Trochus niloticus*, from the Red Sea and the Great Barrier Reef, is an example of a top shell that can grow to about 4.5 inches (11 cm) in height and width.

Turban Shells

Closely related to the top shells are members of the family Turbinidae, or turban shells. They have relatively few representatives in colder water, but they are conspicuous in the tropics. A good example is *Turbo marmoratus* from East Africa. It has a green-colored shell that reaches a height and width of 8 inches (20 cm). The turban shells of the genus *Turbo* are often very attractively patterned, like the tapestry turban, *Turbo petholatus* from the reefs of the Red Sea. These shells also have attractively marked, thick opercula, known as cat's eyes.

The pheasant shells form another small group of archaeogastropods, which some people include within the turban shells. These animals have shells whose marks resemble the coloration of a pheasant's plumage. The temperate European pheasant shell, *Phasianella*, has a conspicuous white operculum.

Limpets—Familiar Archaeogastropods

The most familiar archaeogastropods are the limpets, which belong to the family Patellidae. They abound on almost all rocky shores. Good examples are species of *Patella* and *Acmaea* found on both sides of the Atlantic. Although the animals are not very large, rarely exceeding 2 inches (5 cm) in length, their creeping, suckerlike feet are very large in proportion to the rest of their bodies. They are well adapted to serve as suckers, holding the animal firmly against rocks, as well as providing the means of locomotion.

Their reputation for clinging to surfaces has made limpets famous. If you steal up on a limpet, making no vibration on the rocks, it is possible to dislodge the animal by giving it a hard tap with the heel or toe of your shoe or boot. However, if the animal is forewarned of your approach by vibrations in the rocks, it will be impossible to dislodge without causing damage because the sucker will clamp down very hard on the rocks. In that way limpets are able to preserve their positions on the rocky shore even in the presence of very rough seas and huge waves. The conical shape of the shell is ideal for dispersing the energy of the waves as they crash over the animals. When firmly anchored, the edges of the shell fit exactly against the rocks, almost making a complete seal against the surface. Apart from protecting the animal from damage by physical forces and predators, the precise fit is an advantage when the tide is out, since it means that the animal inside the shell will not dehydrate through water loss. The shell, which is not coiled but is a simple cone, holds water inside because of its near-perfect fit against the rocks.

Underside of the shell of the blue limpet, Patella coerulea, showing the foot, mouth, and sensory head tentacles, and the tentacles at the edge of the mantle.

After a while the limpet generates a "homing scar," where the edge of the shell rubs repeatedly against the same piece of rock. The fit of a limpet's shell against the rocks has led to the idea of "homing" (the notion that individuals return to the same place each time they have finished feeding) in limpets. However, other research shows that very few limpets return to the same spot over a period of time, and that many limpets settle down when they cease feeding, moving around a bit until they find the best position for the shell to fit against the rocks.

Food for limpets is growing vegetation, mainly young developing algae. However, as they rasp away at the rocks with the radula, the limpets will also pick up and ingest a variety of organic remains. The grazing pressure of limpets on the rocky shore is a major force in keeping the algae from growing too quickly.

Flat periwinkle
(*Littorina
obtusata*)

Common name
Periwinkles,
tower shells, conches,
cowries, tuns, helmet shells, seasnails,
slipper limpets

Order   Mesogastropoda

Subclass   Prosobranchia

Class   Gastropoda

Number of species Unknown

Size   0.04 in (1 mm) to 18 in (45 cm)

Key features Adult body usually asymmetrical with spiral
shell arranged in coils; head quite well
developed, with 1 or 2 pairs of sensory
tentacles, usually with eyes, statocyst, mouth,
and radula; well-developed creeping foot
with sole; during development body organs
and mantle may rotate between 90 and 180
degrees in relation to the foot (known as
torsion); shell may be closed by a horny
stopper (the operculum) attached to tail of
foot; body has 2 nephridia (excretory organs)
and a well-developed mantle cavity housing
ctenidia (gills) and an osphradium (organ of
scent detection) in some marine species

Habits   Adults mainly bottom-dwelling marine
animals; some float on a raft of bubbles;
locomotion is by creeping, using the foot

Breeding   Sexes separate or hermaphrodites; mating
may occur; fertilized egg develops into tiny
planktonic larva in most marine forms

Diet   Herbivorous and carnivorous

Habitat   Almost all marine, generally living on rocks,
reefs, or other hard surfaces

Distribution All the world's seas and oceans, most
common in shallow water

⊕ *Littorina obtusata is known as the flat periwinkle. Its
body shape is oval and flattened on top. It feeds on brown
seaweed and is found across northwestern Europe from
Norway to Spain. Diameter 0.4 inches (10 mm).*

Winkles and Relatives

Mesogastropoda

*The Mesogastropoda is one of the more highly evolved
orders of gastropods. The twisted figure-eight shape of
many of them results from the rotation of the mantle
and body organs during development.*

MANY MEMBERS OF THE Mesogastropoda have
made evolutionary advances in their respiratory
and reproductive systems allowing them to
exploit a wider range of marine environments.

The gill is simplified, and its axis is fused to
the mantle wall so that there is no pocket
behind it where sediments can accumulate. The
animals can therefore venture into water that
has more sediment. The right-hand excretory
duct in many male mesogastropods is
specialized for reproduction—its opening leads
into a groove that travels along the side of the
head to deliver sperm to the penis, which is
situated on the right-hand side of the head. The
female's reproductive duct (the oviduct) is also
modified. It is thicker and extends to the edge
of the mantle just to the right of the anus, so
that it can be accessed easily by the male's
penis. The oviduct has internal pockets where
sperm received during mating can be held until
it is needed to fertilize the eggs. Because the
transfer of sperm takes place inside the female's
body, seawater is not needed for sperm to
reach the eggs. That has allowed several types
of mesogastropod snails to emigrate—*Viviparus
viviparous* from seawater to fresh water, and
Pomatias elegans from seawater to land.

Sex Change
Although the sexes are separate in many
mesogastropods, there is a trend toward
hermaphroditism. Individuals of *Crepidula
fornicata,* for example, start life as males. Later
they lose their penis, their sexual parts are
rearranged, and they become females.

Two families of snails—the nerites and the
periwinkles—are considered "typical"

⊖ *The Pacific partridge
tun, Tonna perdix, from
Indonesia. Its brilliant
colors and shiny outer
shell make it a favorite
among collectors.*

⊕ *The triton trumpet,
Charonia tritonis from
the Indo-Pacific region,
devours a starfish. It uses
the radula to penetrate
the skin of its victim,
which is then
immobilized by the
trumpet's toxic saliva.*

high temperatures and desiccation typical of rocky shores in arid zones. The heavy, calcified operculum on the back of the foot can close off the shell after the animal has withdrawn inside, acting as a stopper and keeping the animal inside from drying out.

The periwinkles in the family Littorinidae include a wealth of small- to medium-sized shore-dwelling snails. They live as herbivores on rocks, seaweeds, and mangrove trees in temperate and tropical seas.

Members of the family Hydrobiidae have successfully conquered new habitats. The family includes the small mud snails, *Hydrobia*, from northwestern Europe. Several species can be

mesogastropods. The nerites (family Neritidae) are almost exclusively found in the tropics. Generally, they are small, but the first whorl of the shell is quite large. The nerite shell usually has a depressed spire and a semicircular opening ornamented with teeth, granules, and grooves. *Nerita textilis* and *Nerita albicilla* inhabit the rocky shores of the Indian Ocean, but they also live in fresh water and on land. *Theodoxus fluviatilis*, one of the few northern temperate nerites, lives in estuaries. Some species are adapted to cope with the extreme

Conches and Cowries

Conch shells and cowries are well known in the tropics, but they also have relatives in colder temperate climates, such as the European pelican-foot shell, *Aporrhais pes-pelecani*. The lip of this animal's shell opening has a winglike extension that allows it to breathe as it lies burrowed in the sediment, where it feeds on organic material in the mud and water column. *Strombus gigas* is a tropical conch found in the Caribbean Sea. The conches are herbivorous and eat tufts of delicate red algae. Using their foot, they move forward in a characteristic lurching fashion. They rely heavily on eyesight, and their eyes are carried on long eyestalks that are often more conspicuous than their head tentacles.

The cowries are a large group with many tropical representatives, such as *Cypraea*, which is widely distributed in the Indo-west Pacific. The cowries' finest feature is the beautifully polished appearance of the shell surface. The shell is covered by mantle flaps, so it is protected from knocks and scratches. Many cowries have specific dietary requirements, and some feed on just one species of (usually sedentary) animal prey, such as octocorals or colonial sea squirts.

The "Littorinid Zone"

In northwestern Europe periwinkles in the family Littorinidae are so abundant that the upper shore is sometimes called the "littorinid zone." At the very top of many rocky shores—the highest position where truly marine animals can exist—lives the minute crevice-dwelling snail *Melaraphe neritoides*. It has counterparts in other regions, such as *Nodilittorina tuberculata* from the Red Sea and Indian Ocean. *Melaraphe neritoides* lives in a zone dominated by lichens and shared by a few other tiny insects and crustaceans. It has evolved a respiratory system that can breathe air. Although it lives so high on the shore, it has a seagoing larval phase, and maturing individuals have to climb back up the shore when they arrive on land.

Farther down the rocky shore in Europe is a second zone containing *Littorina saxatilis*, the rough periwinkle. These snails are often very variable in appearance. There are in fact several species, or possibly subspecies, included under this name, each with its own distinctive shell characteristics. The preservation of individual local types is maintained because this snail lacks a sea-going larva, and the various subforms do not appear to interbreed.

Below the level occupied by the rough periwinkle are three more species. The first, conspicuous because of its greater size, is the so-called edible periwinkle, *Littorina littorea*. Great numbers are collected annually as seafood, but the reproductive rate seems able to cope with such pressures. Below this are *L. obtusata* and *L. mariae*, which share the same zone. *Littorina littorea* and *L. saxatilis* also occur on the Northeast coast of the United States.

The littorinid zone is a good example of the way in which closely related species can evolve very different physiological adaptations and behaviors in response to different physical conditions.

Left: Littorina saxatilis, the rough periwinkle, is usually restricted to the eastern and western Atlantic, but has been seen in San Francisco Bay. *Right:* Littorina peruviana on a rocky shore in Chile.

found on marine mud flats at incredible densities—over 30,000 per square yard (25,000 per sq. m). They can live in soft mud because their respiratory system does not get blocked by sediment particles. At low tide they can burrow under the mud to feed on a rich supply of diatoms and organic debris. When the tide returns to cover the mud again, they drift around on the surface film of water and collect incoming phytoplankton.

The family Potamididae has begun to lose its dependence on seawater—some members are almost terrestrial. *Telescopium telescopium* is a remarkable snail that inhabits the leaves and branches of mangrove trees in the Indo-west Pacific region. It breathes air and can produce long sticky "ropes" of mucus from glands beneath its skin by which it can rapidly lower itself to the mud. One of its more interesting relatives is *Triphora perversa*, found in southwestern Britain, which is notable for its left-hand coiling shell (the shells of most seasnails coil to the right) and also because it is a carnivore. There is a distinct trend toward carnivory among the more advanced species of mesogastropods.

Floating on Bubbles

The floating purple seasnail, *Janthina*, with its beautiful and delicate violet shell, is a true oceanic mesogastropod. Only a dozen or so species are known, and they are widely distributed in warm seas. Their entire life cycle is seagoing, which is unusual for a gastropod. The animal produces a raft of bubbles that act as a buoyancy aid, enabling it to drift across vast ocean spaces, feeding on surface-living animals such as jellyfish. *Janthina* is seldom seen except when washed ashore after violent gales and storms.

Two other genera, *Calyptraea* and *Crepidula*, contrast sharply with *Janthina*. They belong to the family Calyptraeidae. Their shell

⤻ *As in many animals that live near the surface of the sea, the color pattern of the violet seasnail, Janthina species, is designed to protect it. The underside of the shell (which is on top when the animal is floating) is much darker than the upper side. This provides camouflage from above and below.*

⊕ *A helmet shell,*
Semicassis labiata,
crawling along the sand
in Sydney, Australia.

has a shelf that protects the body mass beneath it, giving *Crepidula* the common name of slipper limpet (the shelf looks like the toe end of a slipper). These animals do not creep around in search of food. Instead, they draw in currents of water bearing suspended food particles such as phytoplankton. The currents are created by the beating cilia around their gills.

Crepidula fornicata was introduced accidentally to Europe from the United States. It is widely regarded as a pest in shellfish beds because it competes for food with commercial shellfish. It is a bottom-dwelling hermaphrodite and lives in groups, with the younger males attached to the upper surfaces of the older females. The attached individual begins as a male and changes to a female as it ages and as more individuals settle on top of it. The younger males fertilize the older females below, using their remarkably long penises.

Violent Predators

Some mesogastropods pursue moving prey. *Natica*, the necklace shell, burrows under sand in pursuit of burrowing invertebrates, which it can detect by their scent. *Cassis cornuta*, the helmet shell, is one of the more advanced mesogastropods and has developed sophisticated predatory behaviors. It has been observed attacking a variety of invertebrate prey species, including spiny sea urchins such as *Diadema setosum*. These animals are difficult to handle, but *C. cornuta* subdues them by smashing their spines with a blow from its heavy shell. It then uses its saliva, which contains a neurotoxin, to paralyze the victim. The snail can then open the urchin's shell with its biting radula and proceed to suck out the animal's soft body tissues.

⊙ *A stack of* **Crepidula fornicata** *slipper limpets off the coast of Devon, England. The younger males attach themselves to the older female limpets below, gradually turning into females as they age.*

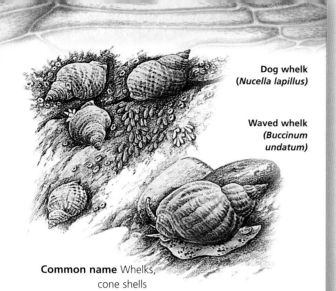

Dog whelk
(*Nucella lapillus*)

Waved whelk
(*Buccinum undatum*)

Common name Whelks, cone shells

Order Neogastropoda

Subclass Prosobranchia

Class Gastropoda

Number of species Unknown

Size 0.04 in (1 mm) to 18 in (45 cm)

Key features Adult body usually asymmetrical with a spiral, coiled shell; head quite well developed, with 1 or 2 pairs of sensory tentacles, usually with eyes, statocyst, mouth, and radula; well-developed creeping foot with sole; during development and growth the body organs and mantle covering them may rotate between 90 and 180 degrees in relation to the foot (known as torsion); head, body, and foot may be withdrawn into shell or at least covered by it; shell may be closed by a horny stopper (the operculum) attached to tail of foot; body has 2 nephridia (excretory organs), a well-developed mantle cavity housing ctenidia (gills), and an osphradium (organ of scent detection)

Habits Adults mainly bottom-dwelling marine animals; locomotion is by creeping foot

Breeding Sexes separate; mating may occur; fertilized egg develops into microscopic planktonic larva in most marine forms

Diet Generally carnivores, preying on various invertebrates; some cone shells can catch fish

Habitat Almost all marine, generally living on rocks, reefs, or other hard surfaces

Distribution All the world's seas and oceans; most common in shallow water

⤴ Nucella lapillus, *a dog whelk, is found on rocky shores in northwestern Europe. Height 1.2 inches (3 cm). The waved whelk,* Buccinum undatum, *is often found in waters of the eastern United States and Europe. Height 3 inches (8 cm).*

Whelks and Cone Shells Neogastropoda

The neogastropods are a large and varied group of seasnails. Among the most evolved of gastropods, they are sophisticated hunters, and some of their beautiful or rare shells are valuable collectors' items.

THE WHELKS AND CONE SHELLS in the order Neogastropoda probably evolved from ancestors similar to the archaeogastropods (limpets and top shells). Neogastropods have radulae that never have more than three rows of teeth. The teeth are large and curved, and are adapted for seizing prey. Although the animals cannot move very fast, they can suddenly shoot out a highly extended proboscis that rapidly overtakes their victim. The mouth and the radulae are carried on the end of the proboscis. The animal can cut or drill its way into the victim's body using the radula teeth and suck out the food tissues with the mouth. In some species the proboscis can extend forward a very long way—longer than the overall length of its owner.

Scent Detectives

Neogastropods hunt carrion and live prey. To help locate suitable food, they have an efficient scent organ called the osphradium. The siphon at the opening of the mantle cavity draws in water for respiration. As the water enters the

⤵ *The common whelk (genus Buccinum) is often caught in traps and exported to the Far East. Masses of lentil-shaped eggs are often found attached to subtidal rocks, stones, or shells in the whelk's habitat. Empty egg masses can be seen on the strandline and are sometimes mistaken for sponges.*

mantle cavity, it passes over the osphradium, and any scent in the water is detected.

Neogastropods occur as separate sexes. When the females lay their eggs, they usually deposit them in horny capsules, the size varying depending on species. In whelks of the genus *Buccinum* each capsule is linked by a string that can be rolled up into a ball-like mass containing several hundreds of embryos. In *Neptunea* the eggs are carried on the female's shell.

Both *Buccinum* and *Neptunea* feed as scavengers on dead and dying invertebrates. On the Atlantic coast of North America the large whelk *Busycon carica* is common. It has a right-handed coiling shell. There is also a left-handed coiled species, *B. contrarium,* which occurs in the same region. Both species prey on bivalves and manage to open their prey by inserting the lip of their shell opening between the two bivalve shells. Bivalve shells with their edges chipped by such activity are often found.

Many species of smaller whelks can be found on the rocky shore and in the shallow sea. One of the best-known species from northwestern Europe is the common dog

Cone Shells

Perhaps the most famous tropical neogastropods are those belonging to the family Conidae, the cone shells. These shells are unmistakable in shape and appearance, and about 500 species are known. The shells are broad toward the tip and have a very low spire. The opening near the base is long and stiltlike. There is a great range of color and patterns in the cone shells, and in some species this only becomes clear when the horny outer layer (the periostracum) has been removed from the shell. Certain species of cone, such as *Conus gloriamaris* from the Philippines, have become extremely rare due partly to small natural populations and partly to the trading in their shells.

The beautiful appearance of some of the shells created by these animals disguises some of the most predatory mollusks. Some cones feed on marine worms, some on other gastropods such as the mesogastropod strombids, while others feed on fish. The radula teeth that harpoon the victim vary in form depending on the preferred prey type. In some cases the prey is as large as the hunter, and sizable victims are quickly broken down by powerful enzymes secreted in the cone shell gut. Some species can even kill a human!

One species that has a particular reputation for its toxicity is the fish-eating geography cone, *Conus geographicus* from the Indo-west Pacific. *Conus textilis*, the textile cone from the same region, is another fish eater. Like all gastropods, these animals cannot move swiftly, but they can spear active prey with a hollow tooth from the radula. This tooth is coated with venom and is barbed so that it holds fast to its target. It is hurled forward by the sudden extension of the proboscis, which emerges from the front of the animal, and which may be as long as the shell itself. The base of the tooth is broad and is retained in the mouth, so that both the tooth and the impaled victim can be dragged back to the hunting cone to be eaten. The animal keeps in readiness a supply of teeth suitable for use as poisoned projectiles in a special sac near the radula.

↥ *The harp shell,* Harpa articularis, *lives in a burrow in the sand by day. By night it preys on crustaceans. To subdue and kill its prey, it wraps its foot around the victim and secretes a special asphyxiating mucus. This individual was photographed in Indonesia.*

whelk, *Nucella lapillus*. It inhabits the middle zone of the rocky shore and is often found among barnacles, which form an important part of its diet. It also attacks limpets and mussels, using its radula to drill through their shells in order to get at the soft flesh within. This can be a laborious process—it takes about two days to get through a really thick shell.

Shell color varies according to environment. Whelks that live on shores exposed to strong winds and waves are generally yellow in color. If the animals feed a lot on mussels, they tend to have bands of brown pigment in the shell.

If the animals change to a different diet, the new part of the shell grows white.

Other small whelks such as the netted dog whelk, *Nassarius reticulatus*, and the thick-lipped dog whelk, *N. incrassatus*, occur on European rocky shores. They are scavengers and pick over carcasses left by other predators. In terms of movement they rank among the most rapid of all whelks. Typically, they glide along with their external siphon fully extended, sampling the seawater for food scents. Their speed also helps them avoid falling victim to predators such as starfish. All members of the genus *Nassarius* can swing their whole body around on the foot as they move, so that the siphon can sample water behind as well as in front. In this way they can avoid animals that might attack from behind.

In the northwestern Atlantic *Nassarius obsoletus* browses on accumulations of microscopic plants called diatoms that collect in shallow pools on the muddy flats where it lives.

One notable family of whelks is the Muricidae, which contains a number of attractive and remarkably shaped shells. They are often decorated with rows of spines or leaf-shaped extensions and have long anterior siphonal canals. Many come from warmer waters. They are carnivorous and use their radulae to penetrate

⬆ The attractive volute, Amorena undulata, feeds on the sand flats of southeastern Australia. The colors and patterns of this species are variable.

⬅ Nucella lapillus, the dog whelk, in South Wales (United Kingdom), surrounded by eggs that look rather like grains of wheat or barley.

the shells of their victims. They secrete a poison known as purpurin, which is used to relax and kill their prey. Purpurin is also used by *Nucella* to kill barnacles.

Within the neogastropods the olive shells (Olividae), the harp shells (Harpidae), the miter shells (Mitridae), and the volutes (Volutidae) form a group that is closely related to the whelks. Most members are found in the tropics, but a few genera are found in warm temperate waters. The olive shells are aptly named, since their polished shells are similar in size to an olive. They hunt their prey under coral rubble and sand. Their eyes are buried in their skin, and the outer surface of their shell is protected by mantle flaps that the animal extends as it moves around. The olive shells have some representatives on the West Coast of the United States, but they do not extend as far north on the eastern side of the Atlantic.

The harp shells are another group of sand dwellers. They are also scavengers and carnivores, and lie almost completely buried in the sand, often escaping detection. Their shells are usually highly colored, conspicuously ribbed, thick, and glossy. There is a large opening from which the animal's moon-shaped foot protrudes when it is moving. Strangely, the foot can be broken off if the animal is disturbed and can be

seen moving independently in the sand. This is possibly a defense reaction to distract or confuse predators.

The miter shells are so-called because of the supposed resemblance to a bishop's pointed miter. The shells are never closed by an operculum. The animals live in sand and coral rubble, generally in reef areas. The inner lip of the miter shell opening is usually ornamented with several ridges, which spiral up the central pillar (columella) of the shell.

Finally, the volutes form a large family of tropical carnivores. Generally, their shells are very attractive, making them popular with collectors. They thrive in coral reef habitats, and many species have exceptionally large final whorls and shell openings. In one genus, *Melo*, the opening is so large that it was used by Australian aboriginals to bale out their canoes.

Spires and Anchors

The auger shells belong to the family Terebridae. They form very long shells that have highly pointed tips, or spires. Their name was doubtless coined from a resemblance to the screw of an auger (a type of tool). The auger shells are carnivores and live in sandy deposits in warm tropical regions. They are excellent diggers, and the way in which they burrow is reminiscent of the bivalves. The foot is long, active, and powerful. It can be extended rapidly down into the sand, where the tip dilates and widens to form an anchor. When secure, the shaft of the foot contracts, pulling the animal down into the sand. The snail has a long siphon so it can remain in contact with seawater above the sand's surface and obtain a supply of oxygen for breathing.

Many neogastropod shells are in demand by collectors. Snorkeling and scuba diving have increased the pressure on beautiful and rare shells. Fortunately, conservation policies in some parts of the world and the international regulation of traffic in endangered species have helped in safeguarding vulnerable species, but the attractive and rare seashell will always be a temptation to some collectors.

Eloise's acteon (*Acteon eloiseae*)

Common name Bubble shells, sea hares, sea butterflies

Orders Bullomorpha, Gymnosomata, Thecosomata, Aplysiomorpha, and Pleurobranchomorpha

Subclass Opisthobranchia

Class Gastropoda

Number of species Unknown

Size From 0.04 in (1 mm) to 8 in (20 cm)

Key features A diverse group; adult body snail-like or sluglike, usually with some coiling; may have a delicate external shell, but shell is sometimes internal or absent; radula usually present; external gill sometimes present; body may be narrow or broad, often wedge shaped with a broad, solelike foot on the underside; edge of foot may be drawn out on either side to form a flap or winglike outgrowths known as parapodia; front of body usually bears 2 tentaclelike sensory structures, but head structures often appear reduced; some shelled forms have an operculum

Habits Marine, generally bottom dwellers; often live in shallow coastal waters and on shores, burrowing in or living on the surface of sediments

Breeding Hermaphrodites; sperm transferred from the male organs of one individual to the female organs of another by copulation; after fertilization larval animals emerge to develop in plankton before settling on appropriate substrate, e.g., alga, shell, or rock

Diet: Generally carnivorous, feeding on a range of bottom-dwelling invertebrates

Habitat Widely distributed in most marine environments, especially coastal ones

Distribution Worldwide in seas and oceans

⊕ *The attractive bubble shell* Acteon eloiseae, *Eloise's acteon, is found only in the Arabian Sea around the Sultanate of Oman. Length up to 1.5 inches (3.8 cm).*

Bubble Shells and Allies

Opisthobranchia

Bubble shells in the subclass Opisthobranchia are a diverse group, with varying lifestyles and body forms. With or without shells, swimmers or nonswimmers, they are all well adapted to their own environment.

THE OPISTHOBRANCHIA is a complex group of interesting, often beautiful sluglike marine animals. Generally speaking, there are three types. Some are burrowers with bodies that are protected by a thin external shell—the bubble shells. Then there are the swimming opisthobranchs. The most important of them are the pteropods, which include the sea butterflies. Finally, there are the somewhat flattened sluglike forms—often brightly colored and conspicuous—which as adults may lack a shell, internal gills, and a mantle cavity. They include the pleurobranchomorphs. Members of the Aplysiomorpha, which are sluglike and only slightly flattened, are often called sea hares.

Built for Burrowing

Bullomorpha such as *Acteon tornatilis*, *Scaphander lignarius*, and *Philine aperta* from the North Atlantic have streamlined bodies protected by shells. They have a broad, almost rectangular foot, and the head is expanded to form a "shield." Outgrowths called parapodia on either side of the body make it wedgelike—an ideal shape for burrowing. *Acteon* is the only genus that has a strong sculptured shell and retains an operculum (stopper). In *Scaphander* the shell is lighter, and in *Philine* it is transparent and internal. These bubblelike animals are carnivores, feeding on a range of bottom-dwelling invertebrates.

The grayish-white body of the European species *Philine aperta* can be found at very low tide on muddy sand. It usually lives just offshore and feeds on other invertebrates burrowing in the sediment. A related form of *Philine* can be found living in the sea-grass beds of California.

⊕ *The sea hare* Aplysia punctata *is found in the northeast Atlantic from Greenland to the Mediterranean. Its body color is very variable, from olive-green, brown, red, to purplish-black. Its shape is long and sluglike, and it produces purple or white secretions when disturbed.*

This species secretes a slime envelope through which it moves, and its relatively unprotected body has a remarkable quality: The surface of its skin can secrete sulfuric acid—an effective way of warding off predatory attacks.

The European species *Retusa pertenuis* is remarkable in that it lies in the mud and ambushes the fast-moving mud snail, *Hydrobia ulvae*. *Haminea navicula* is an herbivorous European species that moves along the surface like a plow, making a furrow as it goes. It has wide, flaplike growths on either side of the body that work like the runners of a sled, as

⊖ *The bubble shell Hydatina amplustrum, photographed in Australia, burrows into the sand. A coiled ribbon of eggs can be seen on the mantle.*

⊕ *Sea butterflies, such as this one swimming in the Atlantic Ocean, have evolved to live without shells. This means that they do not sink too quickly, enabling them to feed in the water column by trapping food particles in a mucous web.*

well as keeping particles from entering the mantle cavity and clogging its contents.

Sea Butterflies and Sea Hares

Swimming is a key feature in two opisthobranch groups—the naked and shelled pteropods. The naked pteropods belong to the order Gymnosomata and are sometimes known as sea butterflies. These shell-less carnivores spend their lives swimming in the ocean quite close to the surface. The sole of the foot is reduced and is made up of two flaps that beat continuously, driving and lifting the animal through the water. They feed largely on the shelled pteropods (order Thecosomata), which they catch with suckered tentacles. The shelled thecosomes are herbivorous. Their parapodia are covered with beating cilia that help trap the phytoplankton that forms their diet.

The sea hares (order Aplysiomorpha) are often large, sluglike animals that come inshore seasonally to feed on green algae. The shell is reduced and covered by mantle flaps. They appear very fleshy and vulnerable, but they defend themselves from predators by secretions from glands in the mantle area. The European *Aplysia punctata* can reach a length of 8 inches (20 cm), but some of the warmer water and tropical species are even larger.

The order Pleurobranchomorpha also has members with smooth, streamlined bodies, for example, *Pleurobranchus membranaceus* from the northeastern Atlantic. It can grow up to 4.5 inches (12 cm) in length, and it swims by undulating movements that lift it into the water current where it is swept about. Like *Philine*, it secretes sulfuric acid to protect itself from predators. It also has a gland at the rear of the foot that secretes a chemical important for sexual attraction. It feeds on solitary sea squirts, which it attacks with its radula.

Sea Slugs

Nudibranchia

The Nudibranchia are some of the most vivid and beautiful of all mollusks. Most are bottom dwelling, but some species live in drifting communities both as larvae and adults.

Common name Sea slugs	
Order Nudibranchia	**Sea lemon** *(Archidoris pseudoargus)*
Subclass Opisthobranchia	
Class Gastropoda	

Number of species About 1,700

Size 0.04 in (1 mm) to 8 in (20 cm)

Key features Adult body sluglike; uncoiled and lacking a shell and operculum, although often bearing exposed tentaclelike structures; body may be narrow or broad, with well-developed, adhesive, solelike foot on the underside, often ornamented by gills and papillae; head bears 1 or 2 pairs of sensory tentacles arranged in various ways; no mantle cavity; there may be a ring of gills around the posterior anus or the upper body surface; sides may bear tentaclelike cerata; torsion reversed in adults

Habits Marine, generally bottom dwellers; often in shallow coastal waters and on shores, especially among rocks and algae; sometimes in deeper water; a few are pelagic

Breeding Hermaphrodites; mating occurs; eggs often laid in elaborate and conspicuous jellylike egg masses; larva emerges to develop in plankton before settling on appropriate substrate such as alga, shell, or rock

Diet Generally carnivorous; often specialists consuming 1 particular prey type or species

Habitat Widely distributed in most marine environments, especially coastal ones; some in oceanic planktonic habitats

Distribution All the world's seas and oceans

⊕ *The sea lemon,* Archidoris pseudoargus, *is commonly found on northwestern European shores. It is a large, warty slug and feeds mainly on sponges. Size up to 5 inches (13 cm).*

THE NUDIBRANCHIA HAVE DONE AWAY with a shell, as well as with the operculum used to close it. The heavy calcareous shell, characteristic of the seasnails, is a major constraint. Building a heavy shell and then carrying it around uses energy. Also, a shell may limit the ability of the animal bearing it to creep into small crevices in search of food or when fleeing from predators.

The nudibranchs provide a good example of how a group of gastropods has managed to flourish without a shell because they have replaced its protective functions with much more sophisticated, proactive means of defense found in the skin.

Pretty Predators

Nudibranchs are very attractive animals and are widely distributed in the marine environment. In the main they can be found browsing on organisms that encrust rocks and plants. They are usually very specific in their dietary requirements, with some feeding exclusively on

⊕ **Glaucus atlanticus (left)** *drifts on the surface of the ocean looking for suitable prey. In this case it is feeding on a* Porpita *species hydrozoan off Bermuda.*

⬅ Notodoris gardineri
laying eggs in the seas off
Sulawesi, Indonesia.

one species of prey. This is reinforced by the remarkable manner in which the metamorphosing planktonic larvae of some types have the ability to identify and settle on organisms that will become their main food species when they become adults.

Brightly Colored Bodies

One striking feature of almost all the nudibranchs is the soft, delicate, flexible body—often brightly colored or patterned and ornamented with special structures both on the head and body. Many species can swim, especially if there are body extensions that increase the animals' surface area to enable them to exert a force on the seawater.

A few tropical species are not flexible and are almost as hard to the touch as the rocks they creep over. One example is the yellow-and-black Indo-west Pacific species *Notodoris gardineri*, which has such a stiff body that it is sometimes mistaken for dead.

Nudibranchs are carnivores. Members of each family tend to consume similar types of prey. Colonies of hydroids are favored by many families, including the Dendronotidae and the Facelinidae. Sea anemones are attacked by the Aeolidiidae, and soft corals such as *Alcyonium* species dead man's fingers are targeted by the Tritoniidae. Sponges are favored by some types of dorid nudibranchs (family Dorididae) and sea mats or polyzoa by others.

A few feed on eggs rather than the adults of other organisms. Some, such as *Calma,* eat the eggs of bony fishes. *Calma glaucoides*, from northwestern Europe and the Mediterranean, manages on this rich diet without a functional anus, since it is closed off during development. Presumably after digestion of the egg material there is little solid matter to dispose of. *Favorinus* consumes the egg masses of other opisthobranchs, but it has a fully functional anus throughout its life, probably because it strays from the strict diet from time to time.

⬆ **Nembrotha rutilans**
feeds on tunicates in the
seas off the Philippines.
The species has a creamy-
white body with large
brown patches and an
orange-red patch on the
tail. The long red
extensions are scent
organs known as
rhinophores.

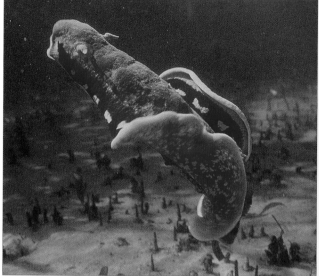

⊕ *The Spanish dancer,* Hexabranchus sanguineus, *swims among mangrove roots along the East African coast. It is a striking red-and-white-colored species.*

⊖ *A pyjama sea slug,* Chromodoris quadricolor, *in the Red Sea. It can grow to 1.5 inches (4 cm) long and is often seen on red sponges, on which it feeds.*

Remarkably, the shape of the nudibranch body often relates to the form of the food material the animals feed on. Those that eat encrusting species, like barnacles, colonial sea squirts, or marine sponges, often have flattened, oval-shaped bodies and broad radulae. Those that feed on plantlike or bushy organisms, such as hydroid colonies of sea anemones, have a long, narrow body with a long foot. The radulae are usually narrow.

Swimming Styles

Swimming is a key skill for many species of nudibranch. The ability to swim has probably been developed as a result of pressure from relatively sluggish bottom-dwelling predators like starfish. The actual mechanism of swimming appears to vary from group to group. For example, swimming is achieved in *Tritonia* by contractions of the muscles in the whole body in a dorsoventral plane (top to bottom). Unlike *Tritonia*, *Dendronotus*, which has a relatively flattened body, swims by

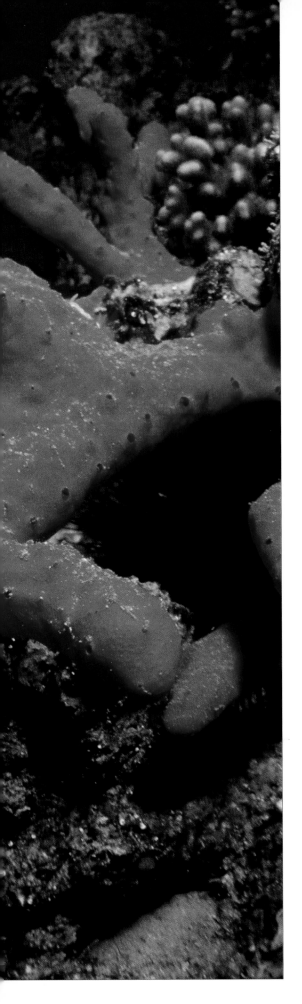

running waves of muscular activity along its body.

Certain types of nudibranch employ specific structures on the outsides of their bodies to assist in swimming. The most remarkable example is *Hexabranchus sanguineus*, a resident of Indo-west Pacific coral reefs. It is brightly colored red and white. When crawling, it can be relatively sluggish and inconspicuous. In this mode the mantle edges are to some extent rolled up. When disturbed, it begins to "dance," unfurling the mantle edges or "skirt." Powerful waves of muscle activity sweep across the skirt, carrying the animal up into the water. The body itself starts making strong bending movements; and they, combined with the skirt

↑ *A pair of* **Hermissenda crassicornis** *sea slugs mating in the seas off California. Since they are hermaphrodites, both partners give and receive sperm.*

Nudibranch Defense

The loss of the shell in the nudibranchs means that other forms of defense must be used to protect their soft bodies from predators. Species like *Discodoris planulata* from northwestern Europe and the Mediterranean spend much of their lives feeding on rock-encrusting sponges. In this position their upper surfaces are exposed to predators and are equipped with acid-secreting glands. The gland openings are on the sides and in the front of the body.

In the same region *Aeolidia papillosa* feeds on sea anemones and other cnidarians, undeterred by the effects of the anemone's own stinging cells, the nematocysts. *Aeolidia* also has small saclike cavities present in the tips of its dorsal extensions, or cerata, that contain nematocysts like those found in sea anemones and other cnidarians. When *Aeolidia* feeds, the cnidarian food passes into the cerata, where the undischarged nematocysts are stored until a predator, such as a fish, bites the cerata. The nematocysts then flood out of the sac, much to the discomfort of the hungry fish! This ability is widespread in aeolids: *Glaucus atlanticus* can reuse the powerful nematocysts of surface-dwelling cnidarians like the Portuguese man-of-war.

Flabellinopsis iodinea, *an aeolid nudibranch, photographed in the seas off California. Its bright orange cerata are clearly visible.*

movements, give it the apt common name of the "Spanish dancer." The striking flashes of color that accompany these movements may serve as a warning to intending predators.

Drifting and Floating

Glaucus and *Glaucilla* (Aeolidiidae) spend their entire lives in the surface waters of the ocean preying on surface-dwelling organisms like by-the-wind sailor, *Velella velella*, and the Portuguese man-of-war, *Physalia physalia*. They are able to make themselves buoyant by taking in a bubble of air from above the surface of the water and holding it in the stomach as a float. They float upside down, so their camouflage is darker blue on the foot (the surface viewed from above the water's surface) and silvery on the back (the surface viewed from below the water's surface). Although they have a number of dorsal and lateral appendages—the cerata—they do not appear to supply the power for swimming, and the animals simply drift with the current. In other aeolids, such as *Cumanotus beaumonti* from northwestern Europe, beating of the cerata on the animal's back seems to provide the drive for swimming.

Reproduction

Almost as attractive as the adult nudibranchs themselves are their colored, ornate egg masses. Many species of nudibranch lay their eggs in a jelly spawn mass in which the eggs are embedded. In some cases millions of eggs can be laid over several spawnings in one season. The egg mass may be flat, ribbonlike, coiled, or threadlike. Most species are truly hermaphrodites, and some are capable of going through several generations in one year, while others produce just a single generation each year. Individuals of most species live only for about a year. The species that have several generations in one year are normally those that feed on seasonal food like hydroids.

Generally, the planktonic larvae emerge from the eggs and spend some time drifting in the surface waters, where they feed on minute food particles. Growth may be rapid in some

⊕ A pair of **Chromodoris** *species sea slugs mating in the seas off Indonesia. This is a case of hermaphroditic mating. The egg case is also being laid.*

cases, but overall the developmental phase takes from about five to 50 days. The larvae often have well-developed sensory systems so that when settlement and metamorphosis occur, the juveniles end up on the seabed on or close to their preferred food source.

⊖ *A species of* **Elysia**, *a sacoglossan from the Red Sea. This species feeds on plants and stores the chloroplasts, which continue to photosynthesize inside the animal's body.*

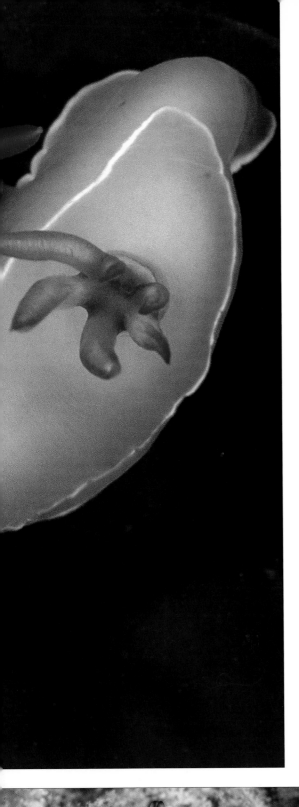

Sacoglossans

The Sacoglossa as an order probably displays more diversity than any other type of opisthobranch. In the main, sacoglossans are herbivorous animals, containing in their heads a specialized form of radula that is narrow and has just one row of teeth. Remarkably, when worn away by cutting into the cells of the seaweeds that form their diet, the teeth go back down the gut to be shed with fecal waste. The animals suck out the juice from the algal cells sliced open by the radula teeth, feeding on the nutrients they contain.

The diversity of sacoglossans (which are generally lacking in shells) is quite remarkable, since there are a few species that have single shells, and even a very few that have bivalve shells—a really astonishing situation! Although the majority feed on plants, there are a few specialists that feed on other organisms. *Stiliger vesiculosus,* from the Mediterranean, and *Olea hansineensis,* from northwestern Europe, feed on the egg masses of other opisthobranchs.

Elysia viridis has a narrow, sluglike body with a pair of parapodial flaps on either side and is usually colored green. It a has a slightly leafy appearance and is well suited to life creeping amid the fronds of green algae. Strangely, despite its parapodial lobes, it has never been seen to swim. *Elysia* has the ability to supplement its diet by using some of the contents of the plant cells on which it feeds in an unusual way. Green plants use chloroplasts—microscopic inclusions within their cells—to host photosynthesis (in which plants manufacture energy-giving substances like carbohydrate from mineral salts, carbon dioxide, and water). As *Elysia* feeds, it is able to retain some of these chloroplasts during the feeding process and send them to its own tissues. Once in place, the chloroplasts can photosynthesize inside the sacoglossan's body and supplement its energy supply, which may be of use when food is scarce. The huge bivalve mollusks of the genus *Tridacna*—the giant clams—do a similar thing. However, in *Tridacna* whole plant cells are retained for the purpose, not isolated chloroplasts as in *Elysia, and Tridacna* feeds on planktonic organisms.

Limapontia depressa is dark brown to black, sometimes covered in small paler spots, although there is a yellowish variety. It inhabits mud flats and salt marshes, where it can be found at most tide levels. It feeds on the fine filaments of green algae growing in shallow pools and may take refuge under the surface of the mud during adverse weather conditions like heavy rain or drought. Unlike many opisthobranchs, the head of *Limapontia depressa* lacks tentacles.

Perhaps the most bizarre of the sacoglossans is *Alderia modesta*, yet another salt-marsh inhabitant of California and European shores. This animal bears a number of club-shaped, hollow protrusions known as cerata on the back of its sluglike body. These cerata undergo rhythmic contractions that help move the blood around inside the blood spaces, known as sinuses, inside the animal. Because of this ability *Alderia* can manage without a heart—a unique situation within the mollusks. Like *Limapontia, Alderia modesta* also feeds on algae in the pools of mud flats.

Great pond snail (Lymnaea stagnalis)

Common names Freshwater snails, terrestrial snails, terrestrial slugs

Subclass Pulmonata

Class Gastropoda

Number of species About 17,000

Size 0.04 in (1 mm) to 7 in (17 cm)

Key features Lung formed from the mantle cavity; full torsion is usually reversed to some extent; shell present and body coiled, normally without operculum (freshwater and shore-dwelling snails); no shell and no obvious coiling (tropical slugs); shell present and body coiled (terrestrial snails) or reduced or absent, with body not obviously coiled (slugs); no operculum

Habits Aquatic (generally fresh water) and terrestrial; air breathing; terrestrial species found in damp or arid soils; often associated with vegetation and may hibernate in crevices in wood and stone; one group inhabits seashores and, like limpets, lives attached to rock surfaces

Breeding Hermaphrodites, but copulation, sometimes preceded by courtship, occurs; sperm transferred by special reproductive structures; eggs usually laid in egg masses on rocks, pond vegetation, or in soil; juveniles hatch from egg mass

Diet Herbivorous or carnivorous, using the well-developed radula

Habitat Freshwater lakes, ponds, rivers, and associated vegetation; widely distributed in terrestrial environments; limited distribution in seashore environments

Distribution Subtropical and tropical seashores and on almost all landmasses worldwide

↑ *The great pond snail,* Lymnaea stagnalis, *is found in ponds and lakes throughout Europe and in the Baltic Sea. It is a scavenger and eats mostly plants, but also dead plant and animal matter. Length about 2 inches (5 cm).*

MOLLUSKS AND ECHINODERMS

Snails and Slugs

Pulmonata

Snails and slugs are a common feature in gardens, where they can be pests on ornamental flowers and food crops. The unusual mating habits of some slugs are interesting to observe.

PULMONATES ARE GASTROPODS that have no gills and breathe air instead of water. The great majority live on land and include some of the most significant agricultural pests in the form of the terrestrial slugs and snails. The pulmonates also include a number of species that live in fresh water, the so-called freshwater snails, as well as some limpetlike species that live on the rocky shore, where their lifestyle resembles that of the limpets in the subclass Prosobranchia.

Forming a Lung

The key to living without gills lies in the evolution of a "lung," which is formed by closing off the front edge of the mantle cavity so that it becomes a chamber adapted for breathing. The moist walls of the cavity then become folded to increase their surface area. They also become rich with blood vessels to permit the exchange of oxygen and carbon dioxide between the blood and the air in the chamber. The entry and exit of air are achieved by a small opening or "breath hole" known as the pneumostome. This has the advantage in the land-dwelling forms of reducing the loss of water vapor during breathing.

In the freshwater and marine species the pneumostome can be closed while the animal is submerged to prevent the lung from becoming flooded. This has the drawback that when they are foraging in the water, the animals have to repeatedly climb back up to the surface to breathe.

↓ *A colored scanning electron micrograph showing at close range the surface of the radula of a snail. It is studded with rows of horny teeth, which are used to detach food particles from surfaces.*

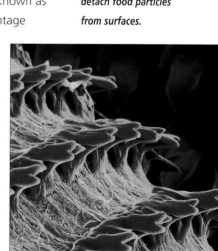

⟵ Helix aspersa, *the garden snail, was introduced to the United States in the 1850s from its native Europe as a source of food (escargot). It is now a serious pest species in California.*

The great majority of pulmonates, like their cousins in the subclass Prosobranchia, have a well-developed radula that is ideal for cutting into vegetation. In most cases the radula takes the form of a broad filelike structure with many hundreds of small unspecialized teeth.

Snails and slugs are unusual in the animal kingdom for having evolved an enzyme—cellulase—that digests cellulose. Most animals are unable to digest cellulose without the help of bacteria resident in the gut. Snails and slugs can manage without such help. As the cellulose moves along the gut, it is broken down, and the basic constituents are absorbed. The excretory pore and anus are positioned just inside the pneumostome (the opening to the mantle cavity), so snails often appear to be defecating from close to where they breathe!

Unlike the prosobranchs, pulmonates are hermaphrodites and have male and female organs that are active throughout their adult lives. The head carries well-developed sensory tentacles; in most land-dwelling types there are two pairs, the second, larger hind pair bearing eyes. The pulmonate body, like the prosobranch body, shows torsion. However, the nervous system has developed without being twisted, mainly because the connecting elements are relatively short.

Pulmonates are classified into three orders: Basommatophora (water snails), Systelommatophora (a small group of tropical snails and slugs), and Stylommatophora (terrestrial snails and slugs).

The Water Snails

The order Basommatophora contains all the pulmonates commonly known as water snails, plus a few others. Almost all of them are aquatic, and they can be generally distinguished from the prosobranch seasnails because they lack an operculum (a structure on the foot enabling the shell to be closed up), as well as by the fairly conspicuous pneumostome. Unlike

⟵ *A wandering snail,* Lymnaea peregra, *on pondweed in England. The snail has few habitat requirements and can occur at altitudes of 9,000 feet (2,800 m) in the European Alps.*

the other groups of pulmonates, they have only a single pair of tentacles, and the eyes are at the bases of them, not at the tips. Good examples are the pond snails, *Lymnaea,* and the ram's horn snails, *Planorbis*, which typically inhabit ponds, lakes, and rivers in Europe.

Conquering the Water

The water snails have almost certainly colonized fresh water not from the sea but from the land. They therefore represent terrestrial forms that have evolved back to live in water. Strangely, air breathing is maintained, and the animals have to return to the surface to breathe. However, there are some forms that have moved on from lung breathing to reinvent a gill—known as a secondary gill—that frees them from dependence on the water surface and means they can live at depth. *Planorbis corneus* is an example. Another way of coping with life under water is to keep a bubble of air in the lung and to rely on diffusion of oxygen into the bubble from the surrounding water.

While many of the water snails flourish in clean bodies of fresh water, there are some species, such as *Planorbis crista,* that can tolerate foul, polluted water. Such species may be aided by the red blood pigment hemoglobin in their blood, which allows efficient absorption of oxygen in dirty water with low oxygen levels.

Tropical seashores frequently abound with small pulmonate limpets of the genus *Siphonaria*. They look superficially very like small versions of the prosobranch limpets, but are much smaller. They too have almost certainly sprung from the terrestrial pulmonates, but they have readapted themselves to life in the sea, having reevolved a gill in place of the lung.

Water snails act as secondary hosts for the parasitic worm *Schistosoma* that causes the disease bilharzia, or schistosomiasis. It infects thousands of people in the world. Water snails also act as secondary hosts to parasites of sheep and cattle, weakening the health of domestic flocks, especially in poorer countries. One of the most effective ways of attacking the disease is to attack the host mollusk.

Terrestrial Snails

The garden snail is probably as familiar an animal as one can find outside the vertebrates. Snails can be found in mature city and country gardens alike, as long as the soil and vegetation are relatively undisturbed, and there is adequate calcium in the soil for shell building. Snails are also characteristic of open grasslands and even woodland. Good examples are *Helix pomatia*, the garden snail of northwestern Europe, *Helix romana*, the edible snail from the European mainland (much favored by the Romans), and *Cepaea nemoralis*, the banded snail from chalk grasslands.

Snails are highly adapted to life on land and can often overcome environmental difficulties by changing their behavior. For example, in temperatures exceeding 109°F (43°C) the South African snails *Helix lactaea* and *Helix desertorum* congregate in the shade under bushes. If it rains, they emerge to feed. During the dry season many snails may

⊕ *In Spain* Eobania vermiculata, *the dune snail, lays eggs in the sand after mating.*

burrow beneath the surface of the soil, where they find more acceptable temperatures at levels where they can hibernate. Hibernation, technically known as estivation, is one very successful means of avoiding environmental problems. The whole body slows down, the heartbeat is reduced, and the rate of respiration is slowed. A state of suspended animation ensues that may, in certain species, last for several years if the unfavorable conditions continue. A specimen of *H. desertorum,* whose shell had been fixed to a display plinth in a museum, was moved after four years to a more humid atmosphere. To everyone's astonishment, the snail emerged and crawled around!

Terrestrial snails are members of the order Stylommatophora, which groups together the equally familiar garden snails and garden slugs. It includes some 600 genera and many more species distributed in a variety of terrestrial habitats all over the world. There are few habitats that snails have not colonized. The one thing that they require is calcium in the soil. Very few actively seek habitats where calcium is scarce, such as acid heaths.

Reproduction in terrestrial snails shows various adaptations to life on land. The reproductive organs are

⊕ Edible snails, Helix pomatia, mating. A "love dart" has been placed in each partner's foot. The eggs that result are tiny, about 0.08 inches (2 mm) in size, and will be laid in an earth hole in spring.

⬆ Members of the order Stylommatophora often exhibit color camouflage. Most stylommatophores feed on plants and detritus, but a few feed on other snails.

complex. Individuals are hermaphrodites, meaning they have both male and female organs. As a prelude to mating a clearly defined courtship takes place. Intending partners are stimulated to mate by the firing of a love dart— the telum amoris—from the dart sac of one partner. It lodges in the skin of the other, exciting courtship behavior. Each partner can fire and receive a dart. Mating then follows and may last for several hours, during which each partner gives and receives a packet of sperm in a spermatophore. Fertilization occurs internally, and the eggs are then laid. In most species they are laid in a tough elasticated "shell" reinforced by calcium carbonate deposits. The protective coatings shield the developing embryos from predators; but they are permeable to water, so the eggs remain vulnerable to water loss, unlike the eggs of land vertebrates like reptiles. The large African snail, *Achatina fulica,* lays eggs the size of thrush's eggs protected by a thick limey covering.

Cepaea nemoralis has shells whose markings appear to alter according to habitat. It is suggested that evolution selects in favor of colors and patterns that aid camouflage and protection against predators, particularly thrushes. Research shows that there are

South Pacific Snails

Far away from continents, the South Pacific islands have unique collections of small, relatively inconspicuous snails belonging to the genus *Partula*. The environment on each island is slightly different, and in the absence of most natural predators the small snails evolved to become specialists, well adapted to their own circumstances. Eventually, different species of *Partula* became established on different islands, but these snails were not adapted to cope with the rapid environmental changes that were brought about by human activity.

Forty years ago a giant African land snail, *Achatina fulica*, was brought to some of the islands by farmers to be raised for food. This large immigrant snail soon escaped from the farms and established itself in the wild. Soon its populations got completely out of control, and it became a pest, devouring crops and other valuable plants. In order to control the giant African land snails, a second species of immigrant snail, this time the carnivore *Englandia rosea,* was brought to the islands to kill off the *Achatina*. However, instead of attacking the giant snails, it turned its attention to the native *Partula* snails. The results were devastating for *Partula*, which was no match for the predators. Population growth in *Partula* is not rapid, so they are particularly susceptible to predator pressure. In about 10 years many species were extinct.

By collecting surviving *Partula* snails and taking them from the islands to London Zoo, scientists have been able to raise new snails in captivity. This has been a successful exercise, and now many *Partula* snails, bred in the zoo, have been reintroduced to their native islands. Special *Partula* reserves have been created, where the snails can reestablish themselves free from competition and predators.

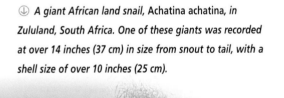

⊕ *A giant African land snail,* Achatina achatina, *in Zululand, South Africa. One of these giants was recorded at over 14 inches (37 cm) in size from snout to tail, with a shell size of over 10 inches (25 cm).*

advantages to different shell colors in different environments. In habitats where green plants provide the dominant background color, plain yellow-shelled snails appear to be the most abundant. An inspection of the thrushes' anvils (the killing grounds for the snails) showed that most of the victims had brown shells. This suggests that thrushes pick out brown-shelled snails more easily than yellow ones.

Surprising Slugs

In some respects the terrestrial slugs seem the least well adapted of animals to the type of life they lead. They are very obviously slippery and slimy, so

they have a lot of water in their bodies, yet outwardly they seem to lack any means of limiting water loss. For example, they have no impermeable outer covering, few have any signs of an external shell, and at first sight it would seem that they are vulnerable to predators like birds. However, terrestrial slugs have proved exceedingly successful. Many are herbivores; and some of them, like *Agrolimax reticulatus, Arion hortensis*, and *Milax budapestensis,* have achieved notoriety as agricultural pests. Potatoes, winter-sown wheat, sugarbeets, sprouts, and peas are crops that are particularly attacked. Slugs also transmit plant diseases like cabbage leaf spot and down mildew found in lima beans.

Animal Prey

Slugs, like snails and almost all gastropods, feed by means of a rasping radula. It is ideal for dealing with the wide range of herbivorous food that slugs consume, but it also allows for the conquest of animal prey. Some species of *Testacella*, for example, prey on earthworms. The radula is aided in this activity by the backward-pointing teeth on the odontophore—the cartilaginous pulleylike structure over which the radula slides back and forth. It may take several hours for the worm to be consumed, as it is slowly dragged in through the mouth and ingested bit by bit.

Reproduction

Reproduction in slugs generally follows the pattern seen in snails, but slug courtship behavior can be very elaborate. Some species court underground, and their courtship has never been seen. In *Arion* courtship occurs on the surface of the soil and begins with one animal pursuing the other, often eating its mucous trail. Selection of a partner seems to depend on how much mucus is present in the posterior caudal (tail) gland. The caudal gland only reaches full development in sexually mature adults, so the inspection by a potential partner will assess a partner's suitability. When one has been identified, the individuals circle around each other producing masses of mucus before eventually exchanging spermatophores. Circular courtship mucous trails can often be seen in the morning after night pairing.

The most amazing reproductive activity is the aerial courtship of slugs such as the Northern Hemisphere species *Limax maximus*. Pairing starts on a branch of a tree or on top of a wall. The couple cruise around in tight circles, stroking each other with their tentacles and secreting lots of mucus. Then they lower themselves on mucous ropes, entwining their bodies as they do so. The mucous ropes may reach nearly 20 inches (50 cm) in length. After pairing, one slug usually climbs back up the mucous rope, while the other descends to the ground or eats the mucus.

Slugs act as intermediate hosts to many other species of animal parasites. They include various protozoans, flatworms, roundworms, and insects. One serious parasite, the sheep lungworm, *Muellereus capillaries*, is carried by several slug species.

⤴ Great gray slugs, Limax maximus, *feeding on berries in England. The species performs the most unusual aerial courtship, in which the mating pair dangles from a rope of mucus.*

⤵ A pair of mating banana slugs, Ariolimax californicus, *in California performs the "combat dance," part of the slugs' mating ritual. The slugs inhabit redwood forest.*

Bivalves

Common name Bivalves **Class** Bivalvia

MAIN FAMILIES

Order Protobranchia: 1 family:	
Nuculidae	Nut shells
Order Taxodonta: 2 families:	
Glycimeridae	Dog cockles
Arcidae	Ark shells
Order Dysodonta: 1 family:	
Mytilidae	Mussels
Order Ostreiformes: 1 family:	
Ostreidae	Oysters
Order Pseudolamellibranchia: 5 families, including:	
Pectinidae	Scallops
Order Schizodonta: 5 families, including:	
Margaritiferidae	Freshwater pearl mussels
Unionidae	River mussels
Aetheriidae	Tropical freshwater mussels
Order Eulamellibranchia: 24 families, including:	
Lucinidae and Ercinidae	Lucines
Cardiidae	Cockles
Tridacnidae	Giant clams
Solenidae	Razor shells and razor clams
Chamoideae	Jewel boxes
Lutraridae	Otter shells
Veneridae	Venus and carpet shells

Number of species About 15,000

Size   0.08 in (2 mm) to 5.7 ft (1.8 m)

Key features Adult body compressed from side to side; shell consists of 2 valves hinged together by teeth and an elastic ligament; head poorly developed; no radula; eyes are not on the head, but possibly elsewhere, such as on tentacles; foot is finger shaped or hooklike; 1 pair of large gills used in conjunction with palps for filter feeding; well-developed mantle cavity whose hind edges are usually fused to form siphons for bringing in and expelling water; 1 pair of excretory organs (nephridia)

Habits   Adults aquatic bottom dwellers; locomotion is by the foot for burrowing or by flapping the shells for short-distance swimming; some attach to hard surfaces using hairlike byssus threads

Diet   Organic detritus and plankton collected by oral tentacles

Habitat   Marine—living on rocks, reefs, or burrowing in sediments; freshwater—living in or on the beds of ponds, lakes, or rivers

Distribution Worldwide

Bivalves are mollusks whose bodies are enclosed in two shells. They include the familiar mussels, oysters, cockles, and clams, as well as many other types. Their members all show similar basic anatomy and lack the wide range of body forms shown by some other mollusks, such as the snails and slugs.

All bivalves live in water, and most live in the sea. Unlike the terrestrial and aquatic snails and slugs (gastropods), which creep on a flattened solelike foot, or the fast-swimming cuttlefish, squids, and octopuses (cephalopods), many bivalves remain more or less stationary for their entire adult lives. Either they live fixed to rocks or dig in sediments like sand and mud. Only a very few, such as the scallops and file clams, can swim. Bivalves are a conspicuous element of the marine bottom-dwelling fauna. Although we may be more familiar with the dense mussel beds of the rocky shore or commercial oyster fisheries, such animals represent only a small minority of bivalves when compared with the populations of clams and trough shells on offshore sand banks.

The Bivalve Body

The bivalve body is complex and not very similar to the body plans of the gastropods or cephalopods. Essentially, the bivalve body consists of the main body, or visceral mass, which lies toward the top of the animal. It contains the gut, its associated glands, and the heart.

At the front end there is a reduced head that bears the mouth and usually carries a pair of sensory palps that often assist in gathering the food. The anus is situated at the rear of the visceral mass. On its course between the mouth and the anus the gut may make loops through the foot and pass close to the gonads, which are carried in the foot.

⬅ *Closeup of a file clam, Ctenoides ales (Limidae), in the seas off Sulawesi, Indonesia. The sensory tentacles at the edge of the mantle can be seen clearly.*

Passing over the top of the visceral mass and hanging down either side of it like two flaps is a sheet of tissue called the mantle. It forms the outer skin of the bivalve, and it is also responsible for secreting and maintaining the shell. The flaps of the mantle meet, left and right, at their edges so that they enclose a relatively large space that lies inside the mantle and inside the shells. This is the mantle cavity. A number of important structures hang down from the visceral mass into this cavity. They include the gills, usually a double pair—one left and one right. In between the gills lies a muscular foot. Elements of the gut are contained here, along with the gonads and blood spaces.

The edges of the mantle are often equipped with sensory tentacles and light receptors. Some groups like the scallops even have well-developed eyes. Water needs to enter and leave the mantle cavity so that the gills get a supply of clean seawater and so that waste material can be swept away. The passage of water in and out would be easy if the animals all lived on the seabed. However, many bivalves live a burrowing life under sands and

gravels. Burrowing forms have developed siphons, which are tubular extensions of the mantle. There are two—one bringing water in, known as the inhalant siphon, and one carrying water out, known as the exhalant siphon. Sometimes these siphons are very short or almost

⬇ *Body plan of a bivalve. It consists of the mantle, often with one or two siphons, the visceral mass, and a small foot. It lacks a developed head. Usually the siphons can be seen extending from the shell.*

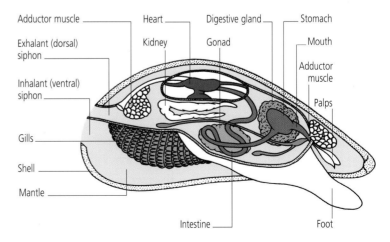

Adductor muscle — Heart — Digestive gland — Stomach
Exhalant (dorsal) siphon — Kidney — Gonad — Mouth
Inhalant (ventral) siphon — Adductor muscle
Gills — Palps
Shell —
Mantle —
Intestine — Foot

nonexistent, as in the mussels (Mytilidae), since the animals do not burrow. Some are limited in length and permit shallow burrowing so that only part of the animal is below the sand's surface, as in the cockles (Cardiidae). Others are much longer, as in the clams and razor shells (Solenidae), to enable the animals to dig well below the surface. Apart from delivering oxygenated water for respiration and carrying away excretory materials and sperm and eggs, the siphons collect and carry food to the animal's mouth.

Opening and Closing

One of the great features of bivalve shells is the way they fit together exactly and open and close so perfectly. Three

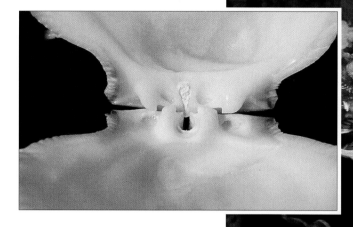
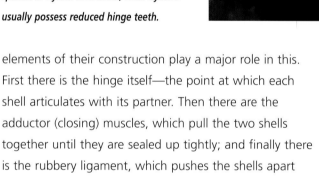

① → Right: Closeup of a Pacific oyster showing the mantle, which secretes and maintains the animal's shell. Above: Closeup of a spiny oyster, Spondylus species, showing the hinge teeth. This species of oyster is unusual, since oysters usually possess reduced hinge teeth.

Byssus—Bivalve Mooring Lines

A visit to a seashore almost anywhere in the world will reveal that many intertidal bivalves are attached to other shells, rocks, or pebbles by tough threads known as byssus. Byssus threads are formed by bivalves living on the surface of the seabed or on rocky or pebbly shores, rather than those that burrow. These threads are formed from protein that has undergone a special hardening process called tanning. When forming a thread, the bivalve presses its foot against a rock or shell. A secretion runs along a special groove on the rear of the foot down to the tip where it touches the rock or pebble that will serve as the anchor point. The secretion hardens when it makes contact with the seawater. The foot is then pulled back inside the shell. More threads are formed in the same way until the bivalve is firmly anchored by a mass of byssus filaments. If the bivalve subsequently needs to move, the byssus can be detached from the foot. Mussels use byssus threads to attach themselves, while other bivalves, such as oysters, may actually be cemented to a surface.

Byssus threads of a mussel. The threads are made of a strong, water-resistant protein glue. Research is being conducted, which may mean the glue is eventually used to fix broken human bones and teeth.

elements of their construction play a major role in this. First there is the hinge itself—the point at which each shell articulates with its partner. Then there are the adductor (closing) muscles, which pull the two shells together until they are sealed up tightly; and finally there is the rubbery ligament, which pushes the shells apart when the adductor muscles relax. The form and structure of the hinge are important in classifying bivalves.

The hinge is made up of a series of ridges and teeth facing each other and arranged underneath and on either side of the ligament. Each tooth fits into an opposing socket, but the two shells and their teeth are always just kept apart by a thin layer of living mantle tissue. The simplest arrangement of teeth is found in the order Taxodonta, where there are many similar interlocking teeth, as in *Glycymeris*, the dog cockle. This is known as taxodont condition. By contrast, some bivalves possess a number of central (cardinal) teeth, with lateral teeth on either side (known as heterodont condition). There are various intermediary conditions between these two extremes.

the mouth. *Nucula* gives an impression of how early bivalves existed in Paleozoic seas.

Ark Shells and Relatives

The ark shells (Arcidae) are widely distributed in the seas of the world. The long, flat top of the shell recalls the hull of a sailing boat. An example is *Arca tetragona,* the Noah's ark shell from the northeastern Atlantic and Mediterranean, which lives in rocky crevices firmly attached by strong byssus filaments.

In the same family as the ark shells are members of the genus *Andara*, such as the bloody cockle of West Africa. These unusual mollusks have red hemoglobin as their blood pigment, hence the common name. Mollusks normally carry hemocyanin, a green, copper-based pigment, to enhance the oxygen-carrying properties of the blood. Hemoglobin is used by forms that live in oxygen-deficient water such as some parts of the deep sea. The bloody cockles burrow in muddy sediments and have been food items for local communities for thousands of years.

Characteristic of coarser sediments, where rapid currents sweep away the fine silty particles from the seabed, are the dog cockles (Glycimeridae). They have thick, heavy, almost round shells. Although they lack siphons, they are able to exploit the water trickling through the sediment and draw a supply into the mantle cavity, which brings in oxygen and food particles.

⊝ *A fossil of the bivalve* **Plagiostoma giganteum** *from the* **lower Jurassic period (195 to 172 million years ago), found in Britain.**

Early Bivalves

Fossil evidence shows that during the Paleozoic era (began 65 million years ago), the early bivalves were probably all fairly similar in appearance and in habits. They somewhat resembled the present-day nut shells in the family Nuculidae that live in a variety of sediments from coarse gravels to fine sands and muds.

The two shells of these rather primitive bivalves hinge together in the taxodont fashion. In these bivalves the gills are primarily concerned with obtaining oxygen. On either side of the gills are structures called palp lamellae, which can be extended outside of the shells in order to grope for food. They correspond to the labial palps of other bivalves, which channel food into the mouth after it has been sieved out from the water running over the gills.

Lacking extendable siphons, nut shells such as *Nucula* cannot burrow deeply under the surface of the sediment because, unlike more advanced bivalves, they have no way of piping in fresh seawater into the mantle cavity from a distance. By remaining near the surface, the mantle cavity can keep in direct contact with seawater. Cilia on the palp lamellae convey the food particles into the mantle cavity, where they are passed to

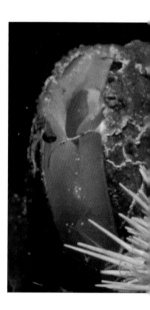

Brown mussel
(Perna perna)

Common names Marine mussels, edible
mussels, fan mussels, date mussels

Family Mytilidae

Order Dysodonta

Class Bivalvia

Number of species About 250

Size Up to about 18 in (46 cm) (fan mussels), but
many less than 4.5 in (12 cm)

Key features Adult body enclosed in 2 equal, almost
triangular-shaped shells with hinge near the
pointed end; shells sometimes ornamented
with spines, scales, or hairs; hinge more or
less without teeth; mantle opens on the
underside, and its left and right edges are not
fused together on the ventral side; inhalant
and exhalant siphons not very well developed

Habits Generally live attached to hard surfaces using
the byssus filaments spun from a special
gland on the foot; some live in soft sediments
with byssus attaching them to a buried stone
or pebble (fan mussels); others bore into
rocks (date mussels); some live in mud
wrapped in byssus filaments (mangrove
mussels)

Breeding Sexes separate or hermaphrodites; sperm and
eggs released into the water via exhalant
water current; external fertilizaton takes place
in seawater, and a planktonic larva results

Diet Adults feed on suspended microorganisms
and particles of detritus; free-swimming
larvae feed on phytoplankton

Habitat Widely distributed in marine environments,
mainly in shallow water

Distribution Most of the world's seas and oceans

⊕ *The brown mussel,* Perna perna, *occurs naturally in
tropical and subtropical regions, specifically on the Atlantic
coasts of Africa and South America. On both continents it is
cultivated for human consumption. Maximum length 4.8
inches (12 cm).*

MOLLUSKS AND ECHINODERMS

Mussels

Dysodonta

*A colony of mussels clustered on rocks along the
shoreline is a familiar seaside sight. However, the
mussels are not a permanent feature and often move
onto different areas as they mature and grow.*

THE MUSSELS ARE PERHAPS THE most common
bivalves on rocky shores and rocky seabeds
worldwide. Owing to their habit of attaching to
smooth, hard surfaces with their byssus threads,
they are able to grow on man-made structures
like piers, pilings, and ships' hulls, and so have
become widely distributed. The California
mussel, *Mytilus californianus*, may be found
living in its native California alongside the
smaller, smoother-shelled *Mytilus edulis* from
northern Europe. Ships have carried different
species of mussel all around the world.

Mussel Use

The ability of mussels to accept man-made
structures for attachment means that the
commercially significant species like *Mytilus
edulis* can be farmed effectively using artificial
structures. It also means that mussels can be
employed as naturally growing structures to
enforce coastal defenses, where they can be
encouraged to grow over and solidify soft
sediments that could easily be eroded. Less
happily, though, it also means that mussels can
become fouling organisms with economic
implications for power plants, desalination
plants, and shipping.

Famous Food

Mussels are, of course, famous as seafood. The
Mediterranean *Mytilus galloprovincialis* is
renowned as food in southern Europe. In some
parts of the world they are collected wild from
rocky grounds, while elsewhere a variety of
culture methods have been developed. They
may be grown on ropes suspended from craft
or on wooden stakes driven into the seabed
and interwoven with sticks to form hurdlelike

⊕ *Horse mussels are
found on the northern
shores of Europe and the
United States. Here in the
Atlantic Ocean a horse
mussel is seen among sea
urchins and a sea star.*

structures. Some species, such as *Perna canaliculus*, the green-lipped mussel from New Zealand, are believed to contain some substances beneficial to humans suffering from diseases such as arthritis and are harvested commercially for this purpose.

Not all species inhabit the seashore. Some, like the European horse mussel, *Modiolus modiolus*, live in shallow water. Its relative *Pinna* actually burrows partly in the sediment.

Many people who visit exposed coasts notice the appearance of well-developed clusters of small mussels on the middle shore. Such small mussels are collected all together

when there is a successful "spat fall"—the moment when the planktonic mussel larvae undergo metamorphosis and seek out a suitable place to settle. The youngsters attach to the rocks by their byssus threads spun from the byssus gland on the foot.

These mussels are ideally suited to life where the sea can be rough and breakers crash on the shore. Since their shells are tapering and streamlined in shape, they can easily withstand powerful waves breaking over them. Where there is a rich supply of phytoplankton in the water circulating over the beach, the mussels grow rapidly. However, when the animals reach a certain size, they offer more resistance to the waves and after heavy weather are often dislodged by wave action, which can break the byssus filaments. This is not necessarily a fatal situation, since the dislodged mussels can be rolled around in the water and transported to other areas by currents, where they can reestablish themselves in better conditions. So mussels grow, disappear, move, and reappear again as part of the natural cycle of seashore populations. Their ability to close their shells and retain water inside when the tide is out serves them well for life between the tidemarks.

⬇ *Common mussels,* Mytilus edulis, *in Scotland gathered on rocks at low tide. Mussels can be found from the barnacle belt down to the kelp zones.*

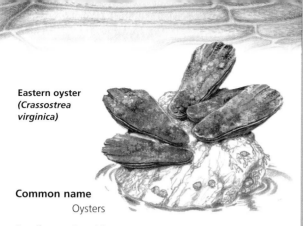

Eastern oyster
(*Crassostrea
virginica*)

Common name
Oysters

Family Ostreidae

Order Ostreiformes

Class Bivalvia

Number of species About 40

Size Up to 8 in (20 cm), occasionally larger

Key features Adult body enclosed in 2 unequal shells, which move together by a hinge with reduced teeth; mantle opens all around the shell, and its left and right edges are not fused together; the inhalant and exhalant openings are weakly marked

Habits Nonburrowing marine bivalves generally living attached to hard surfaces such as other shells, rocks, and corals

Breeding Hermaphrodites—begin as male and change to female, then changing back to male again a number of times over seasons; sperm and eggs released into water via the exhalant water current, where external fertilization takes place; no courtship or mating behavior; planktonic larva results, which feeds in the plankton until settlement and metamorphosis; no maternal care

Diet Adults feed on suspended microorganisms and particles of detritus; free-swimming larvae feed on phytoplankton

Habitat Widely distributed in shallow marine environments, lagoons, estuaries, rocky shores, and reefs

Distribution Most of the world's seas and oceans except polar regions

↑ *Crassostrea virginica*, **the eastern oyster, is roughly pear shaped, but members of the species vary in size and shape. The outside of the shell is dirty gray or brownish in color, and the inside is white except for the muscle scar, which is deep purple. It is found in the Atlantic Ocean from the Gulf of St. Lawrence to the Gulf of Mexico and the West Indies. Length up to 8 inches (20 cm).**

Oysters

Ostreiformes

Oysters are probably familiar to most people for one of two reasons: They may have a piece of jewelry containing a beautiful pearl, or they may have seen the expensive seafood on a restaurant menu.

THE OSTREIFORMES INCLUDE the well-known oysters and several groups of less familiar species. The oysters are of great significance, supporting economically important fisheries in various parts of the world.

Oysters (family Ostreidae) have been cultivated for centuries in both tropical and temperate seas. There is demand for their pearls as well as their flesh. Oysters prefer sheltered shallow habitats such as estuaries and lagoons, and can survive in water of fluctuating salinity; but they need some hard substrate such as rocks or pebbles on which to settle. The European oyster, *Ostrea edulis*, has been conserved and fished commercially from oyster beds in many countries for centuries. *Ostrea lurida* occurs in California. *Crassostrea virginica* occurs in the northeastern United States, where it is now widely raised from recently settled oyster larvae, known as cultured spat. They are collected artificially on plates or tiles and "planted" out in the oyster beds, where a good supply of planktonic food is available for the animals to grow to commercially usable sizes.

Cultured Pearls

Pearl oysters are cultivated in Japan and the Arabian Gulf, but their natural distribution is much wider. The genus *Pinctada* is perhaps the best known, and its shells are sometimes displayed in jewelers' shops along with a pearl! A pearl is produced by the oyster (and other bivalve types) in response to an irritant such as a grain of sand or a parasite occurring between the mantle and the shell. While pearls can form naturally, and as such are rare and very expensive, they can be raised artificially, or "cultured." Various techniques, for example,

⊖ *A Japanese oyster is opened to reveal a glistening pearl. A pearl is made by an oyster responding to an irritant inside its shell.*

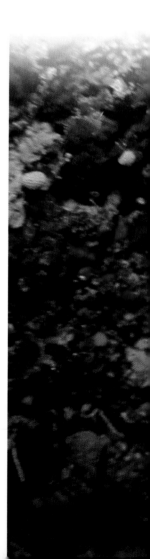

the lower parts of rocky shores. They are known as rock oysters. Their rough shells provide an environment rich in crevices and irregularities that is exploited by many other animals, notably ragworms and small crustaceans.

Oysters have a number of predators, particularly starfish and gastropods. Some whelks are well adapted to drilling through the rather flaky oyster shells and sucking out the meat. Starfish are able to clamber on top of the victim, pull its shells slightly apart with their tube feet, and insert their stomach through the narrow gap to digest the contents of the shell.

introducing irritants made from freshwater mussel shells, are used to interfere with the mantle and the shell-secreting process, resulting in the formation of a pearl.

Small oysters of little commercial significance occur in many parts of the tropics, where they can form a conspicuous zone on

⊕ *These oysters in the Gulf of California favor rocky, shallow waters. The layered nature of their shells can be seen.*

⊕ Lophia folium, *attached to a rock beneath the sea in the Philippines.*

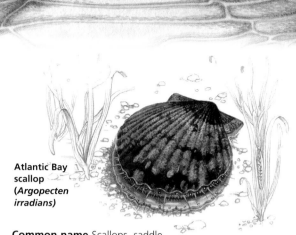

Atlantic Bay
scallop
(*Argopecten
irradians*)

Common name Scallops, saddle
oysters, wing oysters, file shells, fan mussels

Order Pseudolamellibranchiata

Class Bivalvia

Number of species About 60

Size Up to about 6 in (15 cm)

Key features Adult body enclosed in 2 unequal shells,
which move together by a hinge with
reduced teeth; mantle edges not fused
together and open all around the margins of
the shell; positions of the inhalant and
exhalant apertures weakly marked; the foot
may secrete byssus filaments; in some species
the juveniles are attached to weeds and rocks
but break free as they age

Habits Nonburrowing; usually living free as adults;
juveniles may be attached to hard surfaces or
weeds by byssus threads; some species can
swim by flapping their shells

Breeding May be hermaphrodites, being male first,
then female, but sexes separate at any one
time; sperm and eggs released into water via
exhalant water current, where external
fertilization takes place; no courtship or
mating behavior; larva lives among plankton
until settlement and metamorphosis; no
parental care

Diet Adults feed on suspended microorganisms
and particles of detritus; free-swimming
larvae feed on phytoplankton

Habitat Widely distributed in shallow marine
environments

Distribution Most of the world's seas and oceans, usually
in relatively shallow water

ⓐ *The edible Atlantic Bay scallop,* Argopecten irradians, *is
found in Atlantic waters in beds of eelgrass. Its ribbed shell is
gray to reddish-brown in color. Length 1.5–4 inches
(3.8–10 cm).*

Scallops and Allies
Pseudolamellibranchiata

*Scallops, like their mussel and oyster
relations, are perhaps more commonly
thought of as seafood than living creatures.
They have rather less sedentary lives than
their counterparts and can even swim.*

UNLIKE THE OYSTERS, scallops (family Pectinidae)
are not usually farmed, since the adults of most
species need to swim freely.

Swimming Scallops

Adult scallops swim by flapping their shells.
When swimming, the lips of the mantle of one
shell are inflated to overlap with those of the
other, forming a concertinalike connection
between the two valves. Water is drawn in
between the lips when the shells open but
cannot escape from there when they close.
Instead, jets of water are squirted out through
gaps at the top of the shell on either side of the
hinge. These jets propel the animal forward in a
characteristic jerky fashion. Swimming is in
short bursts and occurs particularly in response
to attacks by starfish and disturbances by

ⓓ *Jet swimming by the
scallop* Pecten maximus
*as it escapes from a
starfish (bottom right). It
flaps the two valves of
its shell, expelling jets of
water from its mantle
cavity.*

humans. Jetting up from the seabed may carry the scallops up into a current, which increases the distances they can move.

Fertilized scallop eggs hatch into microscopic drifting planktonic larvae that metamorphose into juveniles on the seabed. These juveniles frequently attach to the substratum by byssus filaments similar to those used by mussels. As they grow, most species break free and begin to swim.

Large species of scallop are traditionally the most sought after for food and are dredged with special fishing gear. As stocks diminish, other smaller species have been pursued.

Related Groups

Saddle oysters—family Anomiidae—are generally small and round in shape, and have a hole in the right shell or valve so that the byssus threads can pass through from the foot to attach to the rocks underneath. The foot muscle is so powerful it contracts the byssus threads and tightens the animal up to the rocks, and has taken over the responsibility for keeping the shells closed.

The wing oysters— family Pteriidae—live in warmer waters like those of the Mediterranean and have unusually shaped shells.

The fan mussels—family Pinnidae—include species that grow to a considerable size, and one North Atlantic form, *Pinna fragilis*, may reach 12 inches (30 cm) in length and be nearly half that in width. After their larval phase they usually establish themselves in soft sediments like sands and muds. Byssus filaments run from the foot through a gap between the shells to attach to a submerged stone or rock. Species such as *Pinna nobilis*, from the Mediterranean Sea, used to be harvested by fishermen. Its highly prized golden byssus threads were used to make fine gloves.

File shells (family Limidae) are another group that contains swimming as well as attached members. The shells are ridged and oval in shape. When these animals settle on the seabed, they construct "nests" of shell debris and pebbles lined with byssus filaments. Several individuals may join in the nesting process. Other species live attached to the substrate by their byssus and do not swim. They include the large *Lima excavata* found in the deep Norwegian fjords.

⊕ **Chlamys hastata** *in the seas off British Columbia, Canada. The inflated lips of the mantle effectively seal the edge of the shell and allow water to be pumped out through the "jet holes" either side of the hinge.*

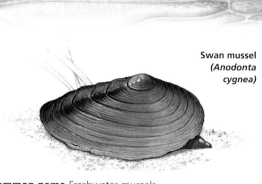

Swan mussel
(Anodonta cygnea)

Common name Freshwater mussels

Order Schizodonta

Class Bivalvia

Number of species About 1,000

Size Up to 10 in (25 cm)

Key features Adult body enclosed in 2 equal shells hinged together by a few teeth; the mantle opens on the underside, and its left and right edges are not fused together at the back; there are inhalant and exhalant openings; no well-developed siphons, except in *Dreisenia*

Habits Generally shallow burrowers

Breeding Sexes usually separate, but some hermaphrodites occur; sperm and eggs released into the water via exhalant water current; external fertilization takes place in the water, or eggs retained in the female's body and fertilized by sperm drawn in by her inhalant water stream; no courtship or mating behavior; in a few cases planktonic larvae may result; often developing embryos retained in female's body; sometimes developing embryos released when a suitable fish host passes so that the shelled larvae (glochidia) can become attached to its fins for distribution; otherwise no care of young

Diet Adults feed on suspended microorganisms and particles of detritus; free-swimming larvae (when they occur) feed on phytoplankton

Habitat Widely distributed in freshwater environments, rivers, canals, ponds, and lakes, sometimes among vegetation

Distribution Most of the world's continents

⊕ Anodonta cygnea, *the swan mussel, is a common freshwater mussel. It originates in Europe, and its preferred habitat is the silty bottoms of rivers, where it lies half buried beneath the sediment. Length up to 9 inches (23 cm).*

Freshwater Mussels

Schizodonta

The diverse freshwater mussels are found all around the world. Some species have developed mutually beneficial relationships with freshwater fish, and some produce pearls, making them highly sought after.

FRESHWATER MUSSELS PROBABLY evolved from marine ancestors. Today, marine and freshwater species can be seen coexisting in brackish water habitats. The name Schizodonta refers to the hinge teeth of their shells (*schizo* means "split" and *donta* means "teeth"), which are divided so that they diverge away from the pointed umbo (the top of the shell).

To look at, freshwater mussels are typical bivalves. Their bodies are enclosed within two shells joined by a hinge and ligament, just like their marine relatives. They have many other structural features in common with them, such as the gills, gut, and foot. They differ in their distribution and their physiological adaptations to life in brackish or fresh water.

The freshwater mussels are generally grouped into two families, the Unionidae and the Dreisseniidae. In the former there are no byssus filaments (threads by which the animals attach themselves to rocks or reefs), and the siphons are variously developed (the exhalant one may be short or even missing). The female broods the young in her gills and releases them as juveniles or as parasitic glochidia larvae. In contrast, the Dreisseniidae live on hard surfaces, so the byssus filaments are developed, and the two siphons are prominent. Their larvae resemble the larvae of marine bivalves.

⊕ *A female southern rainbow mussel,* Villosa vibex, *seen here in Mississippi, flares her egg-laden gills to tempt a fish closer. A suitable fish will be used as host for the mussel's glochidia larvae to attach to and develop.*

Burrowing with One Foot

Freshwater mussels usually live in gravel, mud, and sand on the beds of rivers and lakes. Normally part of the body lies buried in the sediment, and they maintain their position in it

Bringing Up the Kids

Reproduction in many freshwater mussels is considerably different than in their marine counterparts. In the Dreisseniidae it follows the same pattern as in marine species (sperm and eggs are released into the sea, where they are fertilized); but in the Unionidae the eggs hatch and develop inside the mother, and the young emerge as miniature adults, as in *Pisidium.* Alternatively, as in *Anodonta* and *Villosa*, they develop into a larva known as a glochidium. Glochidia larvae develop on the parent's gills, where the eggs are deposited at spawning time and then fertilized. When the mother detects a suitable host fish, she expels them from the mantle cavity. They resemble minute mussels with the two characteristic hooks, one on each of their paired shells. They use the hooks to attach themselves to the fins of the passing fish. In this way they are dispersed around the freshwater environment for a period of about two weeks, living as parasites on the tissues of the fish. After this period they drop off and complete their development into adult mussels on the floor of the stream or lake.

Glochidia exhibit an interesting relationship with the freshwater bitterling fish (so called because of its bitter taste). Female bitterlings lay their eggs through a long tubular ovipositor and deposit them two at a time in the mantle cavity of the mussel, where they develop into fry. After they have hatched, the fry escape from the mussel and lead a free life outside. The favor is often returned because bitterlings and other freshwater fish species may act as a host for some of the freshwater mussel larvae.

by digging with the well-developed foot. When fully extended outside the shells, the tip of the foot broadens out to form an "anchor" in the sediment. Special muscles inside the foot not only keep the mussel in the substratum but enable it to plow laboriously through the sediments in a jerky movement.

Sphaerium rivicola, the river orb mussel, can climb as well as burrow. It secretes a sticky substance from a gland on its foot, which helps it attach to objects such as stems. *Anodonta cygnea,* the swan mussel, favors muddy freshwater beds, while *A. anatine*, the duck mussel, prefers sand. *Unio pictorum*, the painter's mussel, has a depression in front of the umbo. Its large shells were once used as painters' pallets. *Dreissenia*, the zebra mussel,

⊕ **The vibrant color of the** Sphaerium **species orb mussel is in stark contrast to the stones and pebbles around it.**

was widespread in Tertiary times (65 to 5 million years ago) but later died out over much of its range. Recently it has spread to many parts of the world from the Caspian Sea in Russia, helped by shipping traffic. It is considered a pest because it fouls underwater structures and blocks industrial inlet pipes by means of its byssus filaments.

Bivalve mollusks such as oysters and mussels are well known for the way in which they respond to irritants from foreign bodies or parasites inside the shell. A coating of nacre—the pearly innermost layer of the bivalve shell—is deposited around the intrusion; as it is secreted, a pearl grows. *Margaritifera auricularia* and its close relative *M. margaritifera* are known for their ability to form pearls, which although less lustrous than the traditional oyster pearls, are still very desirable. The search for pearls has led to a serious reduction in populations of these species.

Common names Lucines, astartes, hatchet shells, cockles, giant clams, venus shells, carpet shells, razor shells, soft-shelled clams, jewel box shells, wedge shells, piddocks

Order   Eulamellibranchia

Class   Bivalvia

Number of Species About 4,000

Size   0.04 in (1 mm) to 4.3 ft (1.3 m)

Key features Adult body enclosed in 2 equal or nearly equal shells hinged together by a few large hinge teeth separated from distinct long side teeth by a clear space; head poorly developed; mantle edges fused together in the lower back, forming distinct inhalant and exhalant water openings, which are sometimes extended out as tubular siphons; many highly adapted to life burrowing in sediment; deep burrowers have long siphons

Habits   Bottom-dwelling burrowing animals; almost all species are marine; found at all depths in seas and oceans

Breeding   Hermaphrodites, with sexes changing from males to females with age and sometimes changing back to male again to repeat the cycle; sperm and eggs released into the seawater via the exhalant water current and siphon; fertilization occurs in seawater; no courtship or mating behavior; planktonic suspension-feeding larva; no care of young

Diet   Adults feed on suspended or deposited microorganisms and particles of detritus; larvae feed on phytoplankton

Habitat   Widely distributed on the seabed and between the tidemarks

Distribution All the world's seas and oceans at most depths

⤊ *The sand gaper,* Mya arenaria, *is found in European waters, the North Atlantic, and the eastern Pacific. It is harvested commercially in the United States for research and culinary use. Length about 6 inches (15 cm).*

Cockles, Clams, and Razor Shells

Eulamellibranchia

The cockles, clams, and razor shells are a large, widespread group of burrowing bivalves. Some of them have even developed sophisticated techniques for boring into solid rock.

THE ORDER EULAMELLIBRANCHIA COVERS A diversity of animals, which will be described in groups. First, there are the shallow burrowers (astartes, lucines, and their relatives). All these animals lack siphons of any length, and apart from the lucines, none of them is able to burrow deeply.

The lucines have overcome the lack of siphons with a remarkable foot that doubles as a probe. All the animals in this group show various patterns of hinge teeth and shell shape that have enabled them to exploit just about every type of sediment.

The shell of astartes is simple in shape, rounded, with equal valves and no siphons. The European *Astarte borealis* has solid shells and reaches about 1.8 inches (4.5 cm) in length. Its shells are covered by a thick brown outer layer

⬆ Donax deltoides, also known as the pipi, showing its foot and siphons. The foot (on the left) and the inhalant and exhalant siphons can be clearly seen.

⬅ The common cockle, Cardium edule, with its shells gaping open. This cockle is commonly found buried in mud and sand in estuaries and on expansive beaches.

animals all have the typical inhalant and exhalant openings on the posterior edge of the shell, but it is the exceptional adaptations of the foot that allow the animal to burrow deeply.

The foot is long and thin, and has a swollen end that shows a pronounced "heel" when inflated. When buried in the sand, the heel serves as a lever, helping push the animal through the sediment, and can take it to depths where the inhalant and exhalant openings cannot communicate with the surface. In this situation the foot pushes out as a long, slim probe. As it lengthens and contracts, it excavates a mucus-lined tube in the sand. The mucus is secreted by a gland at its bulbous tip and binds the sand particles together so that the tube stays open when the foot has withdrawn. A mucous tube is formed between the animal and the surface of the sediment. It actually continues a short distance along on the surface. Therefore fresh seawater bearing suspended food particles and oxygen can be drawn down into the mantle cavity even in the absence of a siphon. The animal makes a posterior exhalant tube for water to travel back up to the surface. These remarkable animals can therefore inhabit substrates where food and oxygen are in short supply. They are often found in sea-grass beds among Caribbean coral reefs.

(the periostracum). These animals appear to be quite sluggish and burrow only slowly. Their relatives worldwide are similar in overall appearance, but they vary in size. A small California species, *Cardita carpenteri*, is only a few millimeters long and lives on granite rocks or boulders attached by just one thread (known as a byssus thread). In contrast, *Cardita suborbicularis*, a big, flattened, triangular-shaped shell, lives in crevices of rocks and reefs attached by powerful byssus threads.

Lucines or Hatchet Shells (Lucinidae)

Perhaps the most interesting of this group are the lucines, or hatchet shells. They are found in many parts of the world. They all have little color and are characterized by forward-pointing umbones (the upper limits of each shell). They are also unusual because their inhalant water pathway is situated at the front. (Most bivalves have posterior inhalant and exhalant siphons.) The smallest lucines are a millimeter or so long, and the largest reach 1 inch (2.5 cm). These

Coin Shells

Although an anterior inhalant pathway is unusual in bivalves, the coin shells make up another group with this arrangement. In the coin shells, however, it is a real inhalant siphon leading to the front of the shell. These animals live on rock surfaces, usually in crevices or attached to the outsides of other animals. For example, the outside of the shell of *Kellia laperousii* from California can be covered by extensions of the mantle, and their inhalant siphon is so long that the animals can live in

63

deep cavities and crevices among the rocks. The foot is large and can produce anchoring byssus threads, but it can also be used as a creeping organ to move around, rather like gastropods.

Lasaea rubra occupies an unusual position high up on the rocky shore of northwestern Europe, where it lives among barnacles and lichens. It manages to exist even though it is submerged only for a short period, therefore limiting the time available for feeding. Another strange example is *Galeomma turtoni*, from the same region, where the two shells are arranged so wide open that when viewed from above, they look like the roof of a building. The considerable space made available beneath the shells is taken up by a wide extension of the mantle tissue, which means that the shells appear overfilled with flesh. The animal can also move around actively on its foot and in some ways behaves more like a seasnail than a bivalve. It can climb rocks and rests by attaching itself with byssus threads.

Close Relationships

Montacuta ferruginosa is a small bivalve from European waters reaching only a few millimeters in length, which lives attached to the burrowing sea urchin, *Echinocardium caudatum*. Living in association with other organisms is not an unusual strategy among

⬆ *Two creeping cockles,* Galeomma turtoni, *beneath a rock in the Mediterranean Sea.*

SEE ALSO Snails and Slugs **30:44**

⊙ In the western Pacific Ocean a scuba diver swims over a giant Tridacna clam. The vivid colors come from the minute plants (zooxanthellae) that live on the clams.

marine animals. Young shells attach themselves to the spines on the undersurface of the urchins, but older individuals live freely in the burrow of the urchin. Other relatives live attached to brittle stars and to sea cucumbers, and one species in California waters lives attached to the legs of sand crabs. They all seem to feed on detritus from the environment.

Cockles (Cardiidae)

Their familiar plump shape, ribbed shells, and wide distribution on sandy shores worldwide make cockles among the best-known bivalves. Their ready availability and succulent, tasty flesh have made the cockles very significant in commercial terms, and cockle fisheries are found in many countries. Some species grow to enormous sizes—the giant cockle of East Africa grows nearly as large as the coconuts that fall onto the beaches they inhabit. In the Gulf of California *Cardium elatum*, the great cockle, whose shells reach 6 inches (15 cm) across, can sometimes be found washed up on the shore.

The cockle body plan is fairly typical. The strongly ribbed shells are rounded, making the animal almost spherical. When the shells open to their fullest extent, the two umbones strike against each other. The siphons are short and have frilly sensory ornaments. The siphons are equipped with eyes so that they can detect predators such as birds and starfish approaching over the surface of the sand. The foot is well developed and, apart from its use in burrowing, can be used in some species to make jumping movements, enabling the animals to escape from predators. The prickly cockle, *Cardium echinata* from the North Atlantic, whose outer shell ribs are ornamented with thorns, can jump nearly 10 inches (25 cm) to escape from approaching starfish.

Although we think of cockles as classical shellfish from sandy-bottomed, temperate

The Giant Clam

These strange animals include the largest bivalves known to exist. Giant clams are found exclusively in tropical seas and are normally associated with coral reefs. One species, *Tridacna crocea*, actually burrows into coral rock. Others sit amid pebbles, rubble, or live corals and may become partially overgrown by them. Many types attach by byssus threads, at least when they are juveniles.

The largest species is *Tridacna gigas*, which can reach over 40 inches (100 cm) in length. The two massive, thick, ribbed shells protect their soft body, and because of their thin shape and the ribbing on the outside there is more than a passing resemblance between these shells and the temperate water cockles. In living specimens the gape of the shells, apparently on the upward side of the body, reveals frilly, bright, and often vividly colored flesh. In reality these animals are living upside down, so the gape of the shells is really on the underside. The siphons themselves are short but conspicuous. The flesh is brightly colored because it contains millions of colorful minute plants (zooxanthellae) that live in a symbiotic relationship within the clam. The clam provides the symbionts with its metabolic waste materials, such as nitrates and phosphates, and in return the plants produce starch and sugars by photosynthesis. The clam can then feed on these substances. The clams sieve seawater for suspended food particles like so many bivalves, but they also live on the photosynthetic products of the zooxanthellae. That explains why giant clams can live in such numbers in the apparently nutrient-poor waters of coral reefs.

Giant clams are very slow growing; and since they do not burrow, but live attached to rocks and corals by byssus threads, they are often conspicuous and easy to collect. Consequently, really large giant clams are now rare in their natural habitats, and strict conservation measures have been applied by some countries. The international trade in giant clam shells is also strictly limited.

Rock Drilling

Not all bivalves inhabit soft sediments—a number of species live attached to other shells, rocks, and corals. There are even a number of specialized bivalve mollusks that can actually bore mechanically or chemically into hard substances to make a suitable lodging place.

Mechanical boring is achieved by the animal rubbing and rotating its rough shells systematically against the rock, creating boreholes (or tubes). On the rocky shores of the North Atlantic and the northern Pacific it is common to find specimens of the red nose, *Hiatella arctica*, nestling in nooks and crevices at various levels of the tide. Elsewhere individuals may be found in boreholes. It is their sizable, pinkish-red siphons protruding through the entrance to their retreats that have given rise to their common name. Disturbing the animals or causing vibrations in the rocks will make them retract their siphons and squirt out a jet of water. In the Mediterranean Sea the date mussel, *Lithophaga lithophaga*, is a borer, and its bullet-shaped shells are ideally suited to its lifestyle. The animal retains its byssus filaments when boring, which hold it in position in its tube. In California the pea-pod shells, *Botula*, which are close relatives of the date mussel, bore mechanically into shales and mudstones.

Fungiacava is a mussel that bores using chemical methods. It has a close relationship with a stony coral, *Fungia*. The animal's delicate shells are enclosed in mantle tissue, and its inhalant siphon leads directly into the gastric cavity of the coral polyp. The bivalve uses secreted chemicals to dissolve its way through the skeleton of the coral in which it lives. The flask shells, such as *Gastrochaena dubia*, are also chemical drillers. They bore into limestone and sandstone, making a flask-shaped hole that tapers toward the opening. They secrete calcareous linings to the borehole that grow outward as tubes to support and protect the siphons. Another example is *Lithophaga*, which attaches itself to the walls of the tube with byssus threads and moves to and fro, forcing the front end of the shells against the head of the borehole. Secretions from the animal's mantle tissue soften the rock, which turns into a paste that is then scraped away by the shells.

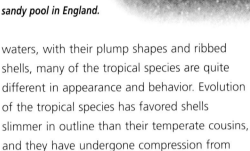

⊙ *The siphons of the prickly cockle,* **Acanthocardia echinata,** *can be seen clearly beneath the water of this sandy pool in England.*

waters, with their plump shapes and ribbed shells, many of the tropical species are quite different in appearance and behavior. Evolution of the tropical species has favored shells slimmer in outline than their temperate cousins, and they have undergone compression from front to back.

Cockles like these inhabit surface waters on coral reefs, where they lie with their foot pointing down into crevices, while their siphons open upward. The shells are exposed to light and are visible from above. They have incorporated minute, single-celled plants into their tissues. The plants are symbionts (organisms that live together) of the cockles. Because the cockle shells are thin and translucent, unlike those of their temperate neighbors, the strong sunlight in coral reef regions can reach the plants in the shells. These "captive" plants can photosynthesize and generate oxygen and plant sugars, which are then made available to the host animal in its

⊙ **Tridacna crocea,** *a boring clam from Australia and the Indo-Pacific region, is not only the most colorful of all giant clam species, it is also the smallest, with a shell size of up to 5 inches (13 cm).*

shell. In return, the bivalve provides waste materials, carbon dioxide, nitrates, and phosphates, which are the raw materials for the photosynthetic process of the plant cells.

Sitting on the Sand

Arctica islandica is a large, plump bivalve. Its shells are strong, heavy, and thick, and are typically covered with a black or brown horny periostracum. This species lives on sand and mud from the extreme lower shore to well out on the continental shelf (the shallow underwater plain bordering a continent). It is found on the eastern seaboard of North America and the coasts of northwestern Europe as far north as the Arctic. Its siphons are very short, so it cannot burrow far into the sediment, since it has no way of drawing water down below the sand. It sits in the sand or mud in a vertical position with its inhalant and exhalant openings just reaching the surface. It draws in a stream of water, which it sieves for plankton. Its strong hatchet-shaped foot is used to pull itself along through the sediment.

Glossus humanus is quite similar to *Arctica islandica*. However, in *G. humanus* the umbones do not curve inward as in most bivalves. Instead, they coil, giving it a slight snail-like shape when viewed from the side. The combined shape and size of the two shells when they close together has been said to resemble a human heart. The first scientific name for this species was *Cardium humanus*.

Glossus humanus inhabits the substratum on the continental shelf and is found in the North Atlantic from the Arctic Circle to Morocco. It does not have such a powerful foot as *Arctica islandica*, so it can only move through soft mud. The siphons are very short, making it a shallow burrower. While *A. islandica* has a strong rubbery ligament that pushes its two valves open against heavy sand, *G. humanus* has only a weak ligament, just about capable of forcing the shells apart in soft mud.

Jewel box shells are absent from the North Atlantic and are found on coral reefs and rocky zones in the Indo-west Pacific. They also occur

in the Mediterranean. They have coiling similar to *G. humanus,* but one shell is cemented to the rocky substratum. The lower shell is usually deeply cupped, while the upper shell forms a flat lid. These shells are also very strong and have a distinct boxlike appearance.

Venus or Carpet Shells (Veneridae)

The venus shells, sometimes known as the carpet shells, are widely distributed throughout the world in a variety of habitats. There are many species in several closely related genera. They occur in shallow water and on the seashore, often in great numbers, and their solid, robust shells are frequently found washed up. They are shallow burrowers, living in sediments. *Venus* and *Dosinia* have shells that are roughly circular in outline and are distinguished by a heart-shaped depression called the lunule close to the point near the hinge of the shells. The shells of *Venerupis* are more oval, with no lunule, and are often ornamented by concentric ridges. They may be pigmented and patterned.

The venus shells include small bivalves of just a few millimeters to medium-sized shells of about 5 inches (12 cm) in length. They inhabit a range of substrate types from fine sands to coarse gravels. There are a few species that actually live among pebbles and, in the case of *Petricola*, rocky crevices, attached by byssus threads. All the venus and carpet shells are plankton feeders, using their short siphons to move water in and out of the mantle cavity, where the food material is sieved out by the gills. The siphons bear a slight resemblance to those of the cockles; but although they have tentacles surrounding the openings that help strain the water entering the siphons, their siphons lack eyes.

Various species of venus and carpet shells are used as food in different parts of the world

⬆ *The coral clam,* Pedum spondyloidum, *lodges itself in cracks among colonies of live corals. The beautiful blue mantle is dotted with bright red spots, which are the light- and pressure-sensitive cells that signal the animal to close its shells when disturbed.*

⬇ *The pullet carpet shell,* Venerupis senegalensis, *is a common species in wave-protected areas such as sheltered inlets. Here it is seen on a muddy shore in England.*

and are highly prized in a number of Mediterranean countries.

Another relative is the hard-shelled clam, *Mercenaria mercenaria*. An important commercial species, the hard-shelled clam is a native of northeastern America, where it lives in mud among stones and pebbles from the water's edge down to several feet in depth. It is found from Nova Scotia, Canada, in the north to the Yucatán Peninsula in Central America and is harvested for food over much of this range. It was accidentally introduced into northwestern European waters in the middle of the 19th century, possibly via the galleys of transatlantic liners. Since then there have been various successful efforts to cultivate it commercially both in Britain and in France.

Razor Shells (Solenidae)

In contrast with many other bivalve species, the razor shells include animals that burrow deeply into the substratum. Deep burrowing brings with it a number of benefits, notably safety from the majority of predators, constant levels of temperature and salinity, and a reduced risk of drying out at low tide. Deep burrowing can be achieved either by developing long siphons that can reach up to the sediment surface from below or by evolving a long, smooth, streamlined shell shape. Such a shape enables the animal to move easily in the sand when burrowing and up and down in its burrow when it is established.

Razor shells get their name from their similarity in appearance to the old-fashioned straight razor. *Ensis siliqua* and *Solen marginatus* have evolved a long, streamlined shape. They are widely distributed on the lower shore and in shallow waters in the North Atlantic and in the Mediterranean. The related *Siliqua patula*, known as the razor clam, is found on open sandy beaches in Washington State. All these animals are burrowers. In their burrows they are protected, but outside they are relatively weak and vulnerable, and need to dig rapidly to escape the hazards of life on the sand's surface.

The hinge and the ligament are positioned at the extreme front end of the animals. The animals have become long front to back and narrow top to bottom. *Siliqua patula* is not as elongated as *Ensis siliqua* and *Solen marginatus*, and the shells are less narrow. The foot has become bent forward so that it can be protruded at the front of the shells for burrowing. The gut and the gills are at the rear of the shells, and the short siphons also emerge from the rear.

Commercial Uses

Residents of the Shetland Islands in the far north of Britain and elsewhere in northern Europe have traditionally fished for razor shells such as *Ensis siliqua* for food. In North America, in the states of Washington and Alaska, the Pacific razor clam, *Siliqua patula*, has been dug commercially for many years, where it is one of the most sought-after West Coast shellfish. Tourists also collect it for food, and not surprisingly, the stocks are being overexploited. To help control the supply levels, clam digging is limited to specific times of the day within a fixed season of the year, and only shells over 3 inches (8 cm) can be taken. Recently there have been outbreaks in razor clams of a naturally occurring marine toxin known as domoic acid. The toxin causes shellfish poisoning in humans. The symptoms can be quite severe, affecting the gut, the nervous system, and the heart. Coma and even death have been reported.

Tellins or Wedge Shells (Donacidae)

Another group of deep burrowers are the tellins, or wedge shells. They have long siphons to reach to the surface. Although the lucine shells are able to exploit the rich organic deposits that occur where the water meets the sediment, the wedge shells are even more successful. That is mainly because of the development of long separate siphons and a

⬆ *Above: The washed-up valve of the razor shell,* Ensis siliqua, *is long, fragile, smooth, and whitish in color. Inset: the siphons can be seen clearly on this living European specimen.*

⬇ *Thousands of* Donax gouldii *bean clams seen on a California beach. In the late 19th century vast numbers of bean clams were harvested to make soups and chowders.*

large, active compressed foot. The siphons are highly muscular and can be moved around. The inner diameter of the siphons is quite narrow, and they generate strong inhalant and exhalant streams of water. The ciliated gills provide the important pumping action needed to drive the stream so that the inhalant siphon collects large quantities of settled particles of detritus from the surface of the sand. It does so just as a vacuum cleaner collects dust.

Under the microscope animals living in aquaria can be seen with the detritus pouring down the siphon and into the mantle cavity, where it is filtered and sorted by the gills. *Abra, Angulus, Macoma, Scrobicularia*, and *Tellina* all provide examples of this successful burrowing and detrital feeding lifestyle.

Donax vittatus, the banded wedge shell from northwestern Europe and the Mediterranean, is a relative of the tellins. Like its relatives, it has beautifully colored, quite long shells. Unlike *Tellina, Donax* inhabits exposed surf-washed beaches, not the sort of places where small organic detrital particles accumulate in great quantities, since the surf washes them away. It is a shallow burrower and depends on its powerful hook-shaped foot to retain its position below the sediment. Despite its burrowing habit, it is often exposed by the surf, and individuals can sometimes be seen tossed up in the waves, only to reburrow when they land on the sand. For its food supply it depends on the wave action to release food

Clam Harvesting

Clams have been highly valued food products in the United States for hundreds of years. A thriving clam industry was established in Maine by the 1860s, and it also provided local fishermen with fresh "shucked-out" clams for use as bait. "Steamed-out" clams were preserved in salt and stored in barrels for winter food and for sale as bait to fishermen working offshore. By 1875 steamed clams, still in their shells, became popular at social occasions such as clambakes and shore dinners throughout the various New England states.

In 1884 a law was passed allowing coastal towns to set a season for harvesting clams. The authorities were also then allowed to set license fees permitting the fishermen to collect clams. Just after the turn of the century shipping or transportation of clams outside the state of Maine was prohibited for the period June 1 to September 15 unless they had been harvested, canned, packed, or barreled outside of the closed season.

In 1905 experiments to propagate clams artificially at Popham Beach, Maine, were funded by the state authorities. The authorities recognized shortly afterward that the success of the clam industry affected more people directly or indirectly than any other form of fishing. From that time the preservation of the clam industry was an important issue. In 1935 a law was passed requiring all collected clams to be 2 inches (5 cm) in length. The law was repealed in 1949 but reinstated in 1984, strongly supported by the industry because the clam harvests of the early 1980s had shown a dramatic decline. Intense efforts to conserve and manage the clam flats were made to prevent the collapse of the industry. These efforts are beginning to succeed, and recent clam harvests have shown encouraging rises. The demand for clams remains high, and careful control over harvesting and marketing is still required to prevent overexploitation.

Burrowing in Razor Shells

Burrowing is achieved by a succession of rapid movements. The two shells are pulled together, compressing the body and increasing the blood pressure. That makes the animal's foot extend from the shell. The foot then makes probing movements into the sand. The tip of the foot is shaped either like a forward-facing "u" or a swollen hammer end. These shapes act as anchors in the sand.

Water is squirted from the mantle cavity out around the hole where the foot leaves the body. The water jets loosen the sand and help the long, narrow foot and the anchor penetrate the sand. Next, the foot muscles contract and pull the animal into the substratum. The shell adductor muscles then relax, and the shells open slightly. That holds the animal in position while the cycle is repeated, the foot burrowing farther before a second contraction of the foot muscles draws the animal deeper into the sand, and so on. These steps are repeated until the animal is well below the surface of the sediment.

The siphons are short and with fringes of tentacles at the end. Having excavated its tubelike burrow in the sand, the animal can rise to near the top of the burrow to pump in water for normal activities such as feeding and respiration. However, it can plunge down deeply by foot retraction when danger threatens. The foot achieves these movements by gripping against the sandy walls of the burrows.

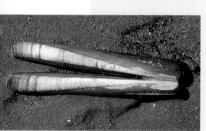

The razor shell Ensis siliqua *is common from Norway to the Atlantic coast of Spain.*

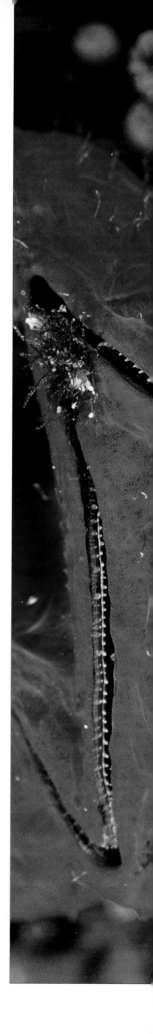

particles trapped between the sand or gravel. By being thrown up in the waves itself, it can move back and forth with the tide, so it is relatively mobile.

Clams (Myidae)

The deep-burrowing shell *Mya arenaria*, the sand gaper from the North Atlantic region, can be found burrowing in muddy deposits on the lower shore. Characteristically it has oval shells that are not quite equal in shape, and its thick, united siphons cannot be withdrawn completely inside the shells. Interestingly, it is capable of living in environments lacking in oxygen, such as those found in estuarine muds where accumulations of sulfide bacteria occur. It is therefore found in places not favored by other bivalve species. *Mya arenaria* has also been accidentally introduced into the eastern Pacific and now occurs on the coasts of California. The species is much prized in the United States, where it is also known as the soft-shelled clam.

The closely related blunt gaper, *Mya truncata*, occurs throughout the northeastern Pacific and North Atlantic. The large siphons protrude through a gap when the shells are closed.

Otter Shells

Somewhat similar to the gapers or soft-shelled clams are the otter shells of the genus *Lutraria*. Like *Mya, Lutraria* has long siphons for reaching up to the sand's surface from deep in the sediment. Their long siphons are also encased in a horny tissue that supports and protects them. The otter shells are relatives of the abundant and more shallow burrowing trough shells, *Mactra* and *Spisula*. The presence of a horny protection around the siphons of *Mactra* and *Spisula* reveals their relationship to their deeper-burrowing relatives.

Common in the shallow water of the northern Pacific is *Panope generosa*, which is probably the largest of all the burrowing bivalves. The common name for this shell is the

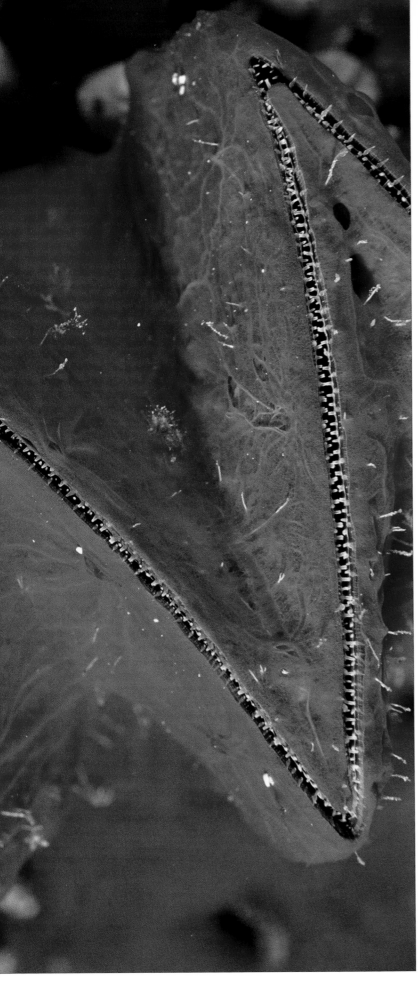

↷ Lutraria lutraria, *the common otter shell. Otter shells live in similar habitats to clams or gapers.*

geoduck, which is probably derived from the Native American Indian word for "dig deep." It inhabits soft mud or soft sand and may reach a length of 35 inches (90 cm) overall. However, since it is edible, natural populations in British Columbia and Washington State have been greatly reduced by clam diggers.

Piddocks (Pholadidae)

A conspicuous group of boring bivalves is the piddocks, sometimes known as the pholads. Generally, they are common in temperate seas. Three common species in northwestern Europe are the common piddock, *Pholas dactylas*, the white piddock, *Barnea candida*, and the little piddock, *Barnea parva*. In addition there is the oval piddock, *Zirphaea crispata*. *Barnea* occurs on the middle and lower shores, and the other species can be found from the lower shore to about 30 feet (10 m) down.

Shipworms (Teredinidae)

In times when commercial ships and naval vessels had wooden hulls, the efficient burrowing behavior of shipworms caused great damage to ships. The borings are lined with a calcareous secretion, and the shells themselves have become efficient wood-cutting tools. They are abundant all over the world, but they are particularly well represented in the tropics.

↶ Lopha cristagalli, *the zigzag razor clam, photographed in Malaysia. Closeup showing detail. The design of the Sydney Opera House in Australia was based on the zigzagging lines of this bivalve.*

Cephalopods

The cephalopods are the most sophisticated mollusks. They are efficient predators with highly developed sense organs, brains, and locomotive systems. They have been present in the oceans and seas since Cambrian times, 500 million years ago. The fossil record shows that there have been at least 10,000 species of cephalopod, but the real number is certainly higher. The supremacy of cephalopods as swift marine predators was threatened and then replaced by the evolution of fish. Also, unlike so many other types of mollusk, they have never conquered fresh water or land, but today we find them in all oceanic realms from the shallow inshore habitats of the continents to the open oceans and the deepest seas.

Different Types of Cephalopod

The precise classification of cephalopods is complex and still being debated. The nautiluses are an ancient group of which only six species occur today and are limited in their distribution to the southwestern Pacific. They have a number of features that mark them out as different from the other living cephalopods. The Vampyromorpha is another exceptional group, with living representatives that resemble fossils. *Vampyroteuthis,* which many people regard as the only representative of the order, has 10 tentacles, but two are minute and can be withdrawn into small chambers set in the skinlike web that links the other eight tentacles. These small tentacles probably act as sensory structures.

The squids are the most diverse and numerous of the cephalopod species alive today. They include the largest and most powerful of all known invertebrate predators, the giant squids. Their shelly skeletons have been reduced to a fragile internal structure known as the "pen" because of its resemblance to a feather. By contrast, the cuttlefish have quite massive internal cuttlebones. The

---

Common name Cephalopods **Class** Cephalopoda

MAIN FAMILIES

Subclass Nautiloidea: 3 families, including:

Nautilidae	Nautiluses

Subclass Coleoidea: 3 orders:
Order Decapoda: 14 families, including:

Sepiidae	Cuttlefish
Loliginidae	Squids

Order Vampyromorpha: 1 family, 1 species *Vampyroteuthis infernalis*

Order Octopoda: 3 families, including:

Octopodidae	Octopuses
Argonauta	Argonauts

Number of species About 900

Size 2 in (5 cm) to 66 ft (20 m)

Key features Head very well developed, carries complex eyes and 8 or more prehensile tentacles, usually bearing suckers; radula well developed; jaws beaklike; spiral, chambered shell, characteristic of nautiluses, is usually lost in other members of the group; body cavity housing the digestive organs is well developed; circulatory system, paired gonads, and 1 or 2 pairs of kidneys present; mantle cavity contains the gills and a muscular funnel to direct jets of water for rapid movement

Habits Sophisticated predatory animals; may show schooling behavior (squids) and solitary lifestyles, except during breeding seasons (octopuses); capable of learning

Diet Generally carnivorous, feeding on fish, other squids (squids), or invertebrate prey, especially crustaceans (octopuses); may stalk prey using excellent eyesight; camouflage patterns hide the predatory cephalopod from its prey

Habitat Pelagic, sometimes over sand (squids) and bottom dwelling, usually among rocks, wrecks, and reefs (octopuses); many species adapted for life at great depth

Distribution All the world's seas and oceans, at all depths

 SEE ALSO Gastropods **30**:18; Bivalves **30**:50; Nautiluses **30**:74; Cuttlefish and Squids **30**:76; Octopuses **30**:84

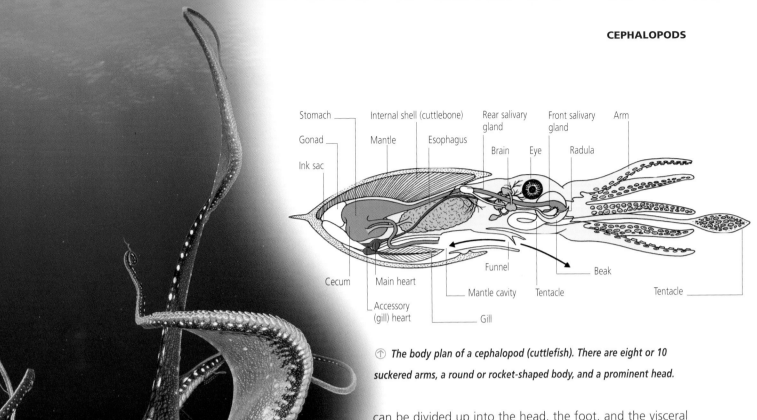

⊕ *The body plan of a cephalopod (cuttlefish). There are eight or 10 suckered arms, a round or rocket-shaped body, and a prominent head.*

can be divided up into the head, the foot, and the visceral mass, just like the other mollusk types. The head lies in the middle of the body. Situated to the back of the head is the large visceral mass, which is long and rocket shaped in the squids, coiled in the nautiluses, oval or rounded in the cuttlefish, and bulbous in the octopuses. It is enclosed by the muscular covering of the mantle (except in the nautiluses). In emergencies water can be squirted out of the mantle through the funnel to provide jet propulsion for escape. The foot is split up into arms or tentacles—10 in the squids and cuttlefish, and eight in the octopuses. The shell is less of a defensive structure than in the gastropods and bivalves. With the exception of the argonauts, the octopuses lack any form of shell.

While the nautiluses, squids, and argonauts spend much of their time (in many cases all of it) swimming, the cuttlefish and octopuses are primarily bottom-dwelling animals. The method of swimming varies from group to group; in cuttlefish the fins are important, while in octopuses the animals creep over the seabed or, like the squids, use jet propulsion for escaping in emergencies.

Cephalopods appear to exhibit emotions, changing their coloration patterns in response to environmental stimuli. Their sensitivity, together with the ability to execute complex behavioral activities controlled by the well-developed brain, which enables them to learn, places these animals at the pinnacle of invertebrate evolution.

⊖ *A day octopus,*
Octopus cyanea, on
a reef off Hawaii.
Octopuses and their
relatives are among the
most sophisticated creatures
in the seas and oceans.

octopuses are the most familiar of the cephalopods, and about 150 species are found worldwide, varying in size from about 2 inches (5 cm) to 30 feet (9 m).

Links to Other Mollusks

The word cephalopod means "head-footed," but merely looking at a squid or octopus does not easily explain how the various parts of the body are related to those of a snail or bivalve. Essentially, however, the cephalopod body

![Pearly nautilus (Nautilus pompilus)]

**Pearly nautilus
(Nautilus pompilus)**

Common name Nautiluses

Order   Tetrabranchia

Subclass   Nautiloidea

Class   Cephalopoda

Number of species About 6

Size   Shell diameter up to about 10 in (25 cm)

Key features Conspicuous coiled, external shell divided
into many chambers; outer surface of shell
usually beautifully patterned, internal surface
mother-of-pearl; adult body housed in the
largest, newest chamber; older chambers
help regulate buoyancy; head bears 80–90
suckerless tentacles protected by a hood; in
males 4 tentacles are adapted to form the
"mating arms" (the spadix); mantle cavity
and siphon used in "jet propulsion"; mantle
cavity contains 4 gills; eyes not as well
developed as in squids and octopuses, and
lack cornea and lens, functioning more like a
pinhole camera; brain, statocyst, and nervous
system also less well developed

Habits   Adults are midwater predatory marine
animals; found at various depths from
shallow water down to 2,300 ft (700 m)

Breeding   Sexes separate; mating achieved by the male
transferring a packet of sperm into the
female's mantle cavity using a group of
modified arms; eggs laid on seabed;
planktonic larval phase is present

Diet   Carnivorous, relying on senses to detect
mobile prey, which often includes crustaceans

Habitat   Tropical seas, from surface to midwater or
near the bottom

Distribution Limited to certain parts of the southwestern
Pacific Ocean

⤴ *The nautilus is the last of a vanishing line of cephalopods
once abundant approximately 400 million years ago. Nautilus
pompilus is known as the pearly nautilus. Shell diameter up
to 10 inches (25 cm).*

Nautiluses

Tetrabranchia

*With their coiled external shell nautiluses
are an exception among living
cephalopods. However, they are an
important link with the past, having
about 3,000 known fossil species.*

THE NAUTILUSES, REPRESENTED by just a handful of
living species, live on or near the seabed in the
southwestern Pacific Ocean. Their most
noticeable feature is the coiled, chambered shell
made of calcium carbonate. Its attractive outer
surface is brownish-red with white markings,
but the inside is lined with mother-of-pearl.

The shell is divided into a number of
internal chambers that reflect the way in which
the animal and the shell itself grow. The
juvenile postlarval nautilus secretes a small
cuplike shell. As the animal grows, so does the
shell, and the newest shell part becomes wider,
allowing the growing animal to move forward
and occupy it. The developing nautilus then
seals off the part it first occupied, making a thin
concave partition known as a septa, which is
perforated by a small hole. The hole allows a
tubular structure called the siphuncle to run
from the original chamber at the end of the
shell to the newest one occupied by the
animal's body. *Nautilus pompilus,* which reaches
about 10 inches (25 cm) across, may have as
many as 36 chambers in its shell.

Buoyancy Control

Animals that swim in the oceans
need to control their buoyancy in
order to remain at specific
depths. Nautiluses, with their
chambered shell, have the ideal
equipment for regulating their
buoyancy and therefore their
vertical position in the sea. The
siphuncle secretes gas into the
shell chambers and regulates the
amount of gas present. The

⤵ *An empty shell of
Nautilus pompilus, the
pearly nautilus. The
cross-section clearly
shows the inner shell
divisions.*

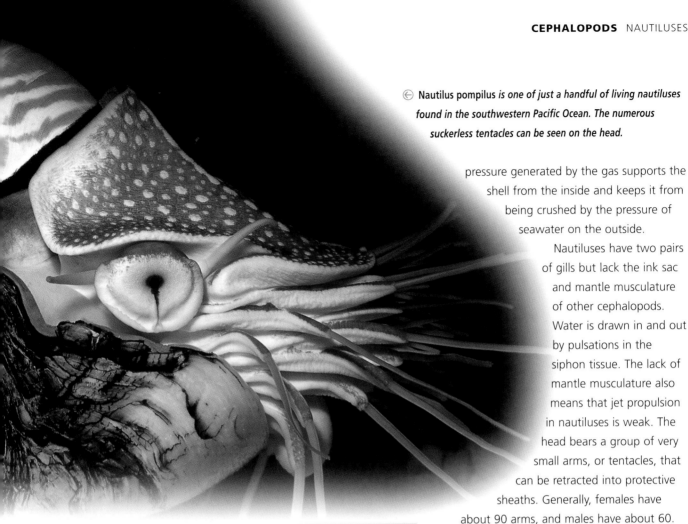

⊖ Nautilus pompilus *is one of just a handful of living nautiluses found in the southwestern Pacific Ocean. The numerous suckerless tentacles can be seen on the head.*

pressure generated by the gas supports the shell from the inside and keeps it from being crushed by the pressure of seawater on the outside.

Nautiluses have two pairs of gills but lack the ink sac and mantle musculature of other cephalopods. Water is drawn in and out by pulsations in the siphon tissue. The lack of mantle musculature also means that jet propulsion in nautiluses is weak. The head bears a group of very small arms, or tentacles, that can be retracted into protective sheaths. Generally, females have about 90 arms, and males have about 60.

The Vampyromorpha

Related to the nautiluses are the Vampyromorpha, a very small order of cephalopods with just one species. It is *Vampyroteuthis infernalis*, a rarely seen deep-sea species that occurs in subtropical and tropical regions. It is regarded by some people as a living fossil because it displays a mixture of squidlike and octopuslike features. The bases of the eight large tentacles are joined together by a thick web of skin, so that only the tips of the tentacles are free. The body is a very dark purple color, which may be because they are exclusively deep-sea organisms, living between 2,000 and 11,500 feet (600 and 3,500 m) deep.

The male transfers bundles of sperm known as spermatophores—probably with the help of his mantle funnel—to special pockets in front of each of the female's eyes. Once fertilized, the eggs are released and float free in the deep sea until they hatch.

The strange-looking Vampyroteuthis infernalis—*its name means the vampire squid from hell!*

Modified Tentacles

Nautiluses feed mainly on bottom-dwelling crustaceans, using their tentacles to grab their victims. For reproduction purposes four of the smaller tentacles in the male are modified to form a cone-shaped structure known as the spadix. The spadix transfers packets of sperm to the female's body. After fertilization the eggs are laid one at a time. They are the largest eggs known among the cephalopods, reaching nearly 1.6 inches (4 cm) long.

Nautiluses are remarkable relics from former times. Their main interest lies in their evolutionary significance and their fossil connections. They are, however, of some economic significance, since in the Philippines fishermen use them as bait. The shells also attract attention and are used as ornaments, drinking cups, and vases.

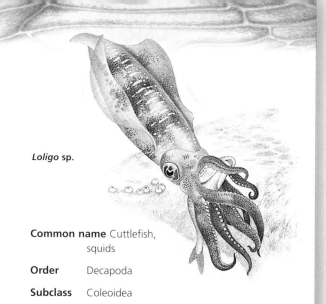

Loligo sp.

Common name Cuttlefish, squids

Order Decapoda

Subclass Coleoidea

Class Cephalopoda

Number of species About 400

Size Length (excluding tentacles) from about 1.2 inches (3 cm) to 65 ft (20 m)

Key features Adult body short and flattened (cuttlefish) or long and torpedo shaped (squids), both with side fins; external shell lacking, but represented internally by a thick calcareous "cuttlebone" (cuttlefish) or a thin membranous horny "pen" (squid); 10 arms, 8 are similar in form, suckered, and shorter (1 modified in males for mating), 2 are longer; mantle cavity and siphon used in "jet propulsion"; cavity contains 2 gills; well-developed eyes with cornea and lens; brain and nervous system present; well-developed statocyst for balance and chromatophores for color change and camouflage

Habits Many adults are midwater- or surface-swimming predatory marine animals; some squids live in very deep water

Breeding Sexes separate; courtship and mating occur; male transfers sperm into female's mantle cavity using arm with specially modified suckers; planktonic larval phase is present

Diet Carnivores; well-developed hunting behavior using camouflage; prey subdued by toxic saliva injected using beaklike jaws

Habitat Most marine environments; more common in shallow coastal and pelagic oceanic habitats

Distribution All the world's seas and oceans at all depths

⊕ *A Loligo species squid holds a captured fish in its jaw. Loligo paralyzes its prey with venom produced by its salivary glands. This squid is found in the warmer waters off the West Coast of North America. Length up to 8 inches (20 cm).*

Cuttlefish and Squids

Decapoda

Although the reputation of giant squids as man-eating monsters is greatly exaggerated, both the cuttlefish and the squids are formidable hunters. They are well adapted for life in the unpredictable oceans.

MOST CUTTLEFISH ARE EASILY RECOGNIZABLE by their oval-shaped body bearing two narrow frilly fins along the left and right edges. Cuttlefish give the impression of being slightly compressed from top to bottom, and the pigmentation of the upper surface is normally darker than that of the underside, although they have an amazing capacity to change their appearance.

The body is relatively large and bears the conspicuous siphon that opens in a central position on the underside immediately next to the relatively small head. The head is dominated by two prominent eyes. It also bears four pairs of arms and one pair of longer tentacles that are kept in pouches near the eyes when not in use. Both the arms and the tentacles have suckers, but on the tentacles the suckers are only on the tips. When the cuttlefish is swimming, the eight arms are normally held together, giving the body a conical tip.

Skeletal Support

The shape of the cuttlefish's body is defined by the large cuttlebone, or internal skeleton, that lies immediately below the skin. The cuttlebone is calcareous and porous, and has many small chambers inside. It is secreted by glands in the mantle and gives the animal solidity and rigidity. At the same time, it is very light. The minute chambers contain gas, which aids buoyancy. The cuttlebone has a horny edge and usually ends in a small, pointed rostrum. Taxonomists have used the structure of the cuttlebone to identify different species of cuttlefish—some species may be completely indistinguishable apart from the cuttlebone details.

⊕ *A cuttlefish,* Sepia pharaonis, *swims just above the seabed in the Andaman Sea, in Southeast Asia. These cuttlefish are fast growing: They mate and spawn at 110 days, and their life span is just 240 days.*

 SEE ALSO Octopuses **30**:84

Waves of Color

Cuttlefish can undergo rapid changes of color as a result of stimuli from the environment. These color changes are brought about by specialized cells in the animal's skin, called chromatophores. They are controlled by the nervous system, and they lie in three layers. Near the surface they are bright yellow, in the middle they are red-orange, and deeper down they are very dark, varying from black to reddish-brown according to species.

Chromatophores can expand to spread the color effect, or they can contract to concentrate the color into a minute spot. By overlapping the colors and varying their intensity, a cuttlefish can produce a range of color effects. They are good enough to mimic background, such as the color and texture of sand. Cuttlefish can rapidly change their appearance, almost as if experiencing emotions. At rest they show small waves of color continually passing over the skin, giving a stripy effect—the so-called "zebra pattern." First comes a wave of dark brown and then one of whitish-gray. The stripes are not all the same size, but they seem to occupy the same positions on the skin, which presumably relate to the positions of the chromatophores.

Stripy camouflage is useful when the animal is swimming through weed beds or among sea grasses.

Color-changing behavior can also be seen during courtship and mating, but just being in an aquarium and being offered food or being disturbed can cause the cuttlefish to produce rapid, complex changes in appearance. In aquaria where there are a variety of different colored rocks and pebbles, small cuttlefish have been observed to match their basic colors precisely to those of the objects over which they are swimming—light gray for corals, green for weeds, brown for sand, and so on. In completely black tanks with no light the animal becomes black, but can develop white markings if part of its body lies over a white marker. The cuttlefish is a genuine master of camouflage, which aids its hunting ability and protects it from predators.

Reproductive behavior in cuttlefish is quite elaborate. In the breeding season, which is

⊙ **Sepia apama,** *the giant Australian cuttlefish, is the largest cuttlefish species in the world. Individuals in excess of 11 pounds (5 kg) are not uncommon. Above, it shows its ability to camouflage itself against the rocks in Jervis Bay, Australia.*

The Stealthy Hunter

The cuttlefish is an efficient predator. Young cuttlefish begin hunting soon after birth. *Sepia officinalis* hunts in daylight for small crustaceans such as the common shrimp, *Crangon crangon,* and for small fish like whiting. Shrimps of the genus *Crangon* cover themselves with a thin layer of sand to act as camouflage. Eyesight is therefore important to cuttlefish in hunting. They patrol up and down, blowing water out from their siphon as they go. Sooner or later the process unmasks a shrimp, but the shrimp will throw more sand onto its upper surface to cover itself again. The cuttlefish sees this activity and pounces.

Tropical cuttlefish have been seen hunting in clumps of sargassum weed, where they change their overall body color to match the brownish color of the floating plants. However, the tips of their tentacles remain a different color, and small, inquisitive fish that approach too close—no doubt on the lookout for food—are grabbed as prey themselves! Cuttlefish have also been seen stalking crabs, which can be quite formidable prey for a soft-bodied mollusk. After maneuvering around the crab to find the best position, the cuttlefish strikes from behind, using its tentacles. A quick bite from the beak pierces a weak part of the crab's skeleton and allows the toxic saliva to penetrate the crab's body. This subdues the crab so it can be handled and consumed more easily.

Stealth and surprise are important elements in the success of cuttlefish hunting. In many of its predatory movements the pair of tentacles acts like tongs, and the fins and siphon are carefully coordinated to control the animal's movements. The eyes are very important, and the ability of the cuttlefish to change color rapidly may help with camouflage and to confuse the prey.

Many years ago the Victorian naturalist P. H. Gosse noted an individual little cuttle, *Sepiola atlantica,* feeding as a cannibal, attacking and consuming other little cuttles. There are also accounts of humans being bitten when handling little cuttles caught in shrimp nets. However, it is uncertain whether or not cuttlefish routinely bite to defend themselves.

Top: The well-developed eyes of Sepia officinalis *help make it an efficient hunter. Below: The giant cuttlefish,* Sepia latimanus, *devours a fish in the seas off Indonesia. The tail end can just be seen between its tightly closed tentacles.*

generally in the spring and summer, female *Sepia* swim near or at the surface at night and show bright luminescence. The light is produced by luminescent bacteria in the skin, and it encourages the male cuttles to swim toward the females. When they are sexually excited, the males display striped markings, showing the pattern more strongly than the females. These markings are sometimes referred to as the "love dress."

Some male *Sepia* will fight each other in order to win a particular female. When the male is accepted, the pair swims close together. There is some characteristic play with the arms before they clasp each other, and the spermatophores are transferred from male to female. The fourth arm of the male cuttlefish is specialized for the transfer of spermatophores from his siphon opening to the female's sperm receptacle—a narrow gutter on the inner membrane around her mouth. This specialized arm, known as the hectocotylized arm, differs from the other arms in *Sepia* because it has very few suckers near its base.

Berrylike Eggs

The female transfers the eggs via her siphon to the sperm receptacle, where they are fertilized. She secretes a rubbery substance to make a capsule in which each fertilized egg is sealed for protection. Cuttlefish eggs look like small black berries, normally tinted with ink. Most females lay between 100 and 300 eggs, but not all in the same place. The male may accompany the female during the egg-laying process. The eggs are normally laid with a pliable, rubbery stalk. Using her large fourth arm, the female winds the stalk around some suitable support, such as a marine plant, dead submerged wood, or a fisherman's basket. The young cuttlefish are about 0.5 inches (12 mm) long when they emerge from the eggs. They can swim and eject ink from the moment they hatch.

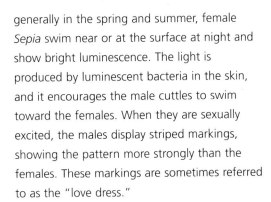

⊖ *In the Indian Ocean a male* Sepia *species cuttlefish approaches a female during courtship. He strokes her with his tentacles in an attempt to persuade her to mate.*

Amazing Squids

Few marine animals conjure up more mysterious and strange ideas than the squids. In popular seafaring tales the deep-sea monsters frequently turn out to be bizarre squids of enormous and terrifying proportions. In his book *20,000 Leagues under the Sea* Jules Verne describes a battle between the submarine *Nautilus* and a giant squid. The story was made famous in the Walt Disney movie of the same name, and Hollywood constructed a model of a squid weighing 2 tons (1.8 tonnes), which needed 14 men to operate it during the filming. The model weighed far more than any real giant squid that has ever been landed.

The squid body is usually cigar shaped. At the rear are either paired side fins or one terminal fin. The head is small relative to the overall size of the animal. It bears prominent eyes on the side and a siphon on the underside, as in the cuttlefish. At the front are eight arms and two tentacles. In some species the arms are united by a web of skin, while in others they are free. The tentacles are shot out rapidly to seize prey and are then withdrawn when the arms take over, subduing the catch.

The arms surround the mouth, which bears the powerful beaklike jaws. The animals range in size from very small—as in *Sandalops pathopsis*, which is about 0.8 inches (2 cm) long—to huge, like the giant squid, *Architeuthis princeps*. This enormous animal may reach 65 feet (20 m) in length and have tentacles up to 55 feet (17 m) long.

⊕ *An X-ray of* Spirula spirula *(also known as the ram's horn squid) shows the internal coiled shell that most other related species have discarded during evolution.*

The Spirula

Spirula is a close relative of the cuttlefish, represented by just one species, *Spirula spirula*. To accommodate it, a special family (the Spirulidae) has been created within the suborder Sepiodea. *Spirula spirula* is a small animal, measuring about 1.6 inches (4 cm) long. It inhabits most tropical and subtropical seas. It is a deep-water cephalopod, living at depths between 650 and 3,000 feet (200–1,000 m), where the water temperature is between 50 and 68°F (10 and 20°C). Because of this *Spirula* is rarely observed, but the characteristic shells that are washed up on seashores in all parts of the world are evidence that the species is widely distributed.

Spirula has a cylindrical body shape. The hind end bears two small terminal fins that assist in swimming, together with jets of water expelled from the siphon by contractions of the mantle, as in cuttlefish. *Spirula* swims in a vertical position, and most of its movements are up and down, unlike the majority of other animals, which move back and forth. Between the hind fins is a round luminescent structure that emits light for long periods of time. *Spirula* can adjust the intensity of the light from full strength to "off" by a diaphragmlike structure. The source of the light is probably the many luminescent bacteria that live in this structure. The tiny coiled shell—rarely more than 0.8 inches (2 cm) in diameter—lies inside the body at the very rear. The animal secretes gas into the shell for buoyancy control. After the animal dies, the gas trapped inside the shell brings it to the surface, and it is washed up on the shore. The head of *Spirula* bears eight arms and two tentacles, a pair of eyes, and a conspicuous siphon. It can withdraw its head inside the mantle cavity to protect itself from some of its smaller enemies.

⊕ *The iridescent dumpling squid,* Euprymna tasmanica *from Australia, is a shy night feeder that usually buries itself in the sand during the day. This individual is in a defensive pose, ready to pounce.*

Inside the skin of the mantle that surrounds the body is a thin shell. It is a narrow, featherlike structure made up of a horny material and is referred to as the pen. It ranges in size from less than 0.4 inches (10 mm) in small species to nearly 5 feet (1.5 m) in giant squid. In some species such as *Chiroteuthis vermicularis* and in immature forms of *Chiroteuthis veranyi* the pen may extend beyond the body, forming a sort of tail.

Creatures of the Deep

About 350 species of squids have been identified from the world's oceans, living in all habitats at all depths. Species that inhabit the deep have special adaptations, and the most distinctive ones in squids are their luminescent organs. Most squids, even the coastal forms, live at depth in the daytime and rise to the surface at night, probably moving upward with the daily cycle of zooplankton and small fish on which they depend for food.

Not much is known about the age span of squids. Smaller species are thought to live for four years or so, and giant squids probably live much longer.

Suckered Tentacles

Squids feed on a variety of other animals. Species such as *Cranchia scabra* that feed on small, delicate food have small, weak suckers on their arms to handle it. Species that feed on powerful, active, slippery fish need special adaptations to handle such prey. The relative size and length of the arms and tentacles vary among the different families. The common northern European squid, *Loligo vulgaris*, has eight comparatively short arms—all similar—as well as two longer tentacles. *Chiroteuthis* has two arms of medium length and six of various sizes as well as two very long tentacles. In *Histoteuthis* a web of skin joins six of the arms.

The suckers are usually connected to the tentacles and arms by short, muscular stalks. In most species the suckers on the tentacles are situated on the underside and only toward the tips, which are expanded to accommodate

⟲ *Squid tentacles with their strong suckers can keep a firm hold on their prey. Once attached, they are difficult for the victim to remove. Here a squid hangs onto the handle of a small brush.*

Giant Squids

There are many seafaring stories about giant squids. The word *kraken* is sometimes used to refer to large squids. It is derived from a Norwegian dialect spoken by people whose seafaring folklore is rich in stories about sea monsters. Other terms include the French *poulpe colossal*. But what is the truth about giant squids?

Many stories tell of animals of monstrous proportions. In reality, more reliable estimates suggest that these animals reach much more modest sizes. The well-known *Architeuthis* is frequently stranded in northern European and New Zealand waters. Its overall length is about 60 feet (18 m), with a mantle length of 17 feet (5.2 m). Such animals weigh about 1,100 pounds (500 kg). While all the legends suggest that giant squids must be among the most ferocious and powerful animals dwelling in the oceans, investigations of their anatomy show that this is not entirely the case. The mantle structures that hold the siphon in place during rapid jet propulsion in the smaller forms of squid and in cuttlefish are not well developed in giant squids. The neurons used to coordinate escape activity are also less well developed in giant squids, and their fins are small in relation to the overall size of the body. They are therefore not rapid swimmers, and may lurk near the seabed at depths of about 650 to 1,000 feet (200–300 m), feeding on smaller, inactive prey.

The Mexican giant Humboldt squid, Dosidicus gigas, has 1,200 suckers, each one lined with 20 to 26 razor-sharp teeth.

However, these relatively sluggish animals can be involved in vigorous activity. Their main predators are sperm whales, but sharks may also prey on them from time to time. Sperm whales have been captured with giant squids in their stomachs and with wounds in their skin an inch deep made by the squid's hooked suckers. It appears, therefore, that gargantuan struggles take place at great depths between the giant squids and their even more enormous predators.

In the Walt Disney movie 20,000 Leagues under the Sea a giant squid with 40-foot tentacles attacks helpless submariners.

them. However, in a few species, such as *Cranchia scabra*, the suckers are distributed all along the tentacles. The size and form of the suckers themselves also vary. In giant squids they can exceed 2 inches (5 cm) in diameter, but in *Inioteuthis* they are minute—around 0.004 inches (0.1 mm)! Again, the variation reflects the different types of food captured.

Some suckers are unarmed, meaning that they are made of skin and muscle. When the base of the sucker cup is raised by muscular activity, a vacuum is created, enabling the sucker to "stick" to its victim. This occurs in squids such as *Loligo*. Other species have rims to their suckers with up to 50 small thornlike teeth that help the sucker maintain grip on slippery flesh.

The most astonishing and fearsome adaptations are in species such as *Abralia*, *Galiteuthis*, and *Onychoteuthis*, in which some of the tentacle suckers have evolved into retractile, sheathed claws rather like the claws of cats. When catching prey, they are extended rapidly out of their sheaths and buried in the struggling victim's flesh. Just to make the tentacles even more deadly, at their bases there are pop studs, like the poppers on clothing. The studs of one tentacle click into the corresponding holes on the other, enabling the two tentacles to be linked and to apply joint pressure on the struggling prey.

Jet Streams

An important element in the survival of cephalopods is the rapid escape response. In essence it consists of sealing the edge of the mantle on the underside of the animal so that the water contained in the mantle cavity can be ejected only through the siphon opening. Two adaptations help this happen. The first is the strengthening of the mantle wall by cartilage stiffeners on the underside. The cartilage is extended into shapes like pop studs in the cuttlefish and into ridges in the squids. When the mantle wall muscles contract, these structures fit into their opposite corresponding structures, making an efficient seal and ensuring that all the water leaves only via the siphon—creating a "jet stream" for rapid propulsion. The second adaptation is the development of giant axons (nerve cells) in the nervous system that can conduct impulses rapidly from the brain to the muscles of the mantle. They are then distributed quickly and equally to all the muscles of the mantle by devices known as the stellate ganglia.

To Catch a Squid

Squid are fished commercially and for sport. There are graphic tales of angling for the Humboldt squid, *Ommastrephes gigas*, in the Pacific Ocean off South America. Squids rise to the surface at night in search of prey and are attracted to boats with light. The animals make

⊕ The short-finned squid, Illex illecebrosus, *is found in the Atlantic Ocean along the eastern coast of North America, where it is fished commercially. It has well-developed senses and a large brain.*

⊖ The California market squid, Loligo opalescens, *is found on the West Coast of North America from California to southeastern Alaska. Market squid can reach a total length of 12 inches (30 cm), including arms and feeding tentacles, and they are an important commerical species.*

trails of light in the water as they jet to and fro. Large hooks attached to a very strong fishing line baited with pieces of fish may lead to the capture of one of these monster squids, which can reach over 11 feet (3.5 m) in length. The squids squirt out ink and put up a great fight when hooked. In some cases their cannibalistic brethren bite huge chunks out of those individuals unlucky enough to get hooked.

Commercial fishermen concentrate mainly on species of *Loligo*. In the past the traditional way of catching squids was to row a small boat around at night. The boat carried a strong gas or kerosene lamp, which attracted shoals of squids to the surface. They were caught in a purse seine net strung out between two more small boats. (A purse seine net forms a bag-shaped trap that can be closed as it is brought to the surface to keep the catch from escaping.) Off the Pacific coast of North and South America the *lampara* (a bag net with side wings) has taken the place of the purse seine. In a number of regions it is used to great effect, catching as many as 24 tons (20 tonnes) of squid in a single haul.

Another well-known method for catching squids is called jigging. The jig consists of a small squid-shaped piece of metal fitted with a circle of unbarbed hooks. The jig is lowered from a boat to just below the surface when the squids are present in large numbers. As they rush to attack it, they are swept up in a hand net. When they are less abundant, the jigger can be twitched up and down. Any curious squid that gets too close becomes impaled on the hooks and can be landed or netted. Japan probably leads the world for commercial squid catches—cephalopods play an important part in the total fishing trade of Japan.

Common name Octopuses

Order Octopoda

Subclass Coleoidea

Class Cephalopoda

Number of species About 200

Size Arm span from less than 2 in (5 cm) to 33 ft (10 m)

Key features Adult body usually round and relatively short; shell usually lacking, but occasionally present or may exist as a reduced internal structure; no lateral fins; 8 arms, all similar in form and linked by a web of skin for part of their length; suckers arranged in 1 or 2 rows; mantle cavity and siphon used in "jet propulsion"; mantle cavity contains 2 gills; well-developed eyes; brain and nervous system present; well-developed statocyst for balance and chromatophores for color change and camouflage

Habits Almost all adults are bottom-dwelling, predatory marine animals; many are solitary; behaviors complex, including use of ink to distract predators

Breeding Sexes separate; male transfers sperm into female's mantle cavity using arm with specially modified suckers; female often guards her eggs; planktonic larval phase present in many species

Diet Powerful carnivores; prey includes crustaceans, fish, and sometimes other octopuses; toxic saliva injected by well-developed beaklike jaws to subdue prey

Habitat Widely distributed in most marine environments, more common in shallow coastal habitats

Distribution All the world's seas and oceans

① *Hapalochlaena lunulata, one of several species called the blue-ringed octopus, is found in the Indo-west Pacific and Indian Oceans. It is extremely toxic and can inflict a fatal bite. Arm span up to 8 inches (20 cm).*

Pacific blue-ringed octopus (*Hapalochlaena lunulata*)

Octopuses

Octopoda

Along with squids and cuttlefish, octopuses are the most intelligent invertebrate animals. However, despite their complex brains, octopuses are solitary animals, living alone in their underwater lairs.

ALTHOUGH OCTOPUSES ARE THE best known of all cephalopods, in reality very few people have seen one alive at close quarters, let alone felt the astonishing, all-embracing grip of its muscled arms and suckers.

Misunderstood Creatures

As well as describing an animal, the phrase "octopus" is frequently used to denote someone or something that extends and insinuates itself in every direction, grasping more and more. That idea no doubt comes from the way the animal behaves, and it gives octopuses a negative image. Many people find the odd-shaped eyes, warty skin, and pulsating body strange. Extraordinary seafaring tales of giant cephalopods have added to the misunderstanding. These tales have contributed to the octopus's bad reputation, leading to names like "devil fish." This is a great pity, since octopuses are among the most interesting and most intelligent of animals.

About 150 to 200 species of octopus are recognized throughout the world. They inhabit waters from the tropics to the Arctic and Antarctic. Generally they are restricted to shallower habitats, and they are not normally found in the extreme depths of the ocean. That is because they lack the special adaptations needed to cope with life in the highly pressurized deep-sea environment. There are a few exceptions to this. One deep-living species is *Cirrothauma murrayi,* a blind, almost jellylike octopus whose tissues have a watery texture like those of jellyfish and other deep-sea organisms. It is thought that the high water content of its gelatinous tissues keeps the flesh from being compressed, since water itself

① *The Maori octopus,* Octopus maorum, *is the largest octopus found in waters around Australia and New Zealand, with a mantle length of 12 inches (30 cm). The average individual weighs about 13 pounds (5 kg).*

SEE ALSO Jellyfish 21:50; Cuttlefish and Squids 30:76

cannot be compressed. The few other deep-sea octopuses that exist also look strange—they are frequently black, and the skin webs that unite their arms reach almost to the very tips of the arms themselves.

Octopuses show a considerable variation in size, with arm spans ranging from less than 2 inches (5 cm) in the very small *Octopus arborescens* to nearly 33 feet (10 m) in the case of the northeastern Pacific species *Octopus hongkongensis*. However, it should be mentioned that the body of *Octopus hongkongensis* is less than 2 feet (0.6 m) long and that most of its size is accounted for by the extremely long and gradually tapering arms, which are very thin at the tips.

The main structures of the octopuses are similar to those of the squids and cuttlefish. The skin of the mantle covers the visceral mass or "body," which is often warty. The body is more flexible than that of the cuttlefish or squids because it lacks a hard skeleton, and it narrows just before it joins the head to form a pronounced "neck."

The underside of the body bears the siphon by which the mantle cavity opens to the exterior. It provides the exhalant route (by which water is breathed out) from the mantle cavity. Water is drawn in through the free openings at the "neck" when the walls of the mantle dilate. In some species there are small internal rods or plates that are the relics of the shell carried by their ancestors. In others they are missing entirely, but in one group—the six species of argonauts—there is a beautiful, delicate external shell, which has made this form of octopus famous.

The head has a pair of prominent eyes. The head bears the eight strong arms. Typically

⬆ *A lesser octopus,* **Eledone cirrhosa,** *is found on rocky lower shores. This one was photographed off the coast of Devon, England.*

these arms are linked together by a web of skin, and they carry one or two rows of suckers. The number of rows of suckers, the extent of the web linking the arms, and the relative length of the arms vary according to species. In many cases the arms are all the same length, but in some there may be a few arms that are considerably longer than the rest.

Complex Brains

Octopus, squid, and cuttlefish brains are the most complex found in any invertebrate (animals without a backbone). Like the brains of vertebrates (animals with backbones), they are enclosed in a skeletal box, or brain case, for protection. However, in octopuses, squids, and

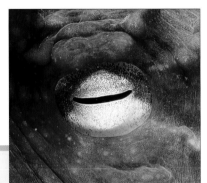

⬇ *Closeup of the eye of a giant octopus. Octopus eyes have many features in common with a human eye, including well-developed eyelids.*

cuttlefish the brain case is made from cartilage and is very different from the bony vertebrate skull. The brain is organized into 14 main areas, or lobes. Each set of lobes has a specific responsibility. For example, one set controls the siphon and the jet-swimming escape response, another deals with memory matters, another with the jaws and feeding, while yet another—the largest—deals with vision.

Octopuses appear to learn by their experience of sight and touch. In order to do so, their skin is richly supplied with sensory structures. Near each of the eyes octopuses have a small papilla, or projection, which seems to act as an organ of taste or smell. In addition to the prominent eyes light receptors may be scattered over the surface of the skin, greatly enhancing the animal's awareness of fluctuations in light intensity, such as shadows falling on the body. Experiments have shown that the outer surface of octopuses is sensitive to taste and smell all over, but the arms and suckers seem especially sensitive. Consequently, these animals continually perceive information about the environment around them, and they can respond to the slightest changes in physical conditions. In an experiment an octopus was taught to discriminate between a crab that had a white square painted on its shell and one that did not. The crab with the white painted square delivered an electric shock when the octopus touched it. The octopus soon learned that touching a crab with a white painted square meant that it would get a shock, while touching an unpainted crab did not have the same effect.

Octopus Eyes

Octopuses, being mollusks, are not closely related to vertebrates such as fish, amphibians, reptiles, birds, and mammals. Nevertheless, it is amazing that the eye of an octopus bears so many similarities to the eye of a mammal, such as a human, when there is no common ancestry. Both octopus and human eyes have a transparent outer layer, the cornea, behind which are small spaces filled with fluid. Another common feature is an iris diaphragm that can open and close to control the amount of light going through. In addition there is a lens whose shape is controlled by muscles, and which is held in place by ligaments. Behind that is more fluid and a special lining of photoreceptor cells—the retina.

The retina is responsible for receiving light formed into images by the lens, then converting it to electrical impulses and sending it to the brain for interpretation. The eyes of both octopuses and humans are surrounded by tough fibrous membranes to keep them in shape and to prevent optic distortion. Finally, most octopuses—unlike their squid relatives, but like humans—have well-developed eyelids.

The eyes of cuttlefish and squids follow the same pattern, but those of the nautiluses are simpler, perhaps reflecting their evolutionary position as more primitive cephalopods. The nautilus eye lacks a lens and functions more like a "pinhole" camera with a very small opening.

Squid eyes display some of the strangest adaptations in the whole of the animal kingdom. Some deep-sea squid such as *Toxeuma belone* and *Bathothauma lyromma* carry their eyes on stalks and have their own light organs attached to the eyeballs so that they can illuminate their field of vision in the perpetual darkness of the deep sea. It is almost as if they had small headlights with which to find their way!

Homebuilding and Hazards

A great number of octopus species live near the shore in quite shallow water, and they are easily observed by snorkelers and scuba divers. They are not very social and tend to live alone, even in the breeding season. Individuals construct a

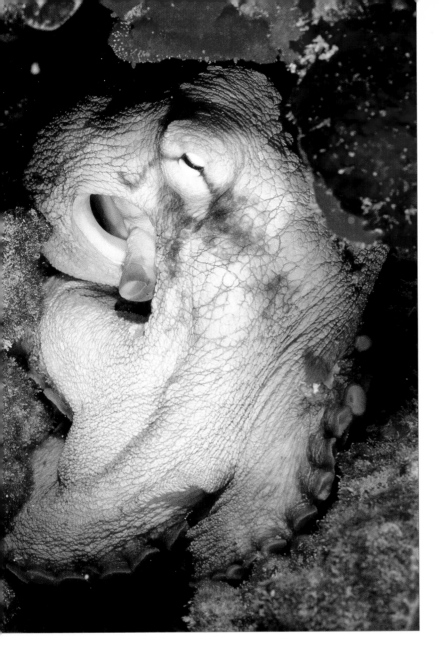

effectively by lowering a line of clay pots attached to a long rope. Floats on the surface mark the line so it can be easily retrieved. Some octopuses take up residence in the pots, believing they have found a safe new home; but the pots are soon hauled to the surface, and the unlucky octopuses are sold as food.

There are many accounts of pottery—especially wine jars, known as amphorae—from Greek and Roman shipwrecks being used as homes by octopuses. This habit has led to one of the strangest uses of animals by humans. About 200 years ago a ship with a cargo of valuable porcelain bowls was wrecked in Japan. For a hundred years nothing was done about salvaging the wreck. But then fishermen, remembering that octopuses like living in pottery containers, hit on a good way of retrieving the cargo. An octopus was attached to a cord and lowered to the wreck. Sure enough, the animal crept into a bowl and clung there with its suckers. The fishermen hauled up the cord, the octopus, and the bowl. This was repeated many times with great success.

Reproduction in Octopuses

In octopuses reproductive behavior is straightforward, and breeding animals make no obvious display. The male and female come within arm's length of each other. In the male octopus the fourth arm from the right is adapted for spermatophore transfer.

Mating begins with the male stroking the female with this specialized arm. The arm is then inserted into the female's mantle cavity so that the spermatophores can be delivered to the entrance of her oviducts. When the spermatophores enter the oviducts, they burst

den or lair in which to live. It can be in a recess in the rocks, a cavity in a reef, or inside a pile of large stones. The position of the entrance to an octopus's den can often be spotted by the piles of stones and empty shells left outside. They also give evidence of past dining habits. Sometimes large stones are heaped over the entrance, blocking it off as a security measure.

Den construction takes place mainly at night and especially after feeding. Some species even burrow in mud if there is no alternative. In the Mediterranean Sea the common octopus, *Octopus vulgaris*, has been observed living happily inside a discarded tin can! The habit of colonizing discarded objects has been the undoing of some octopuses. In North Africa, especially in Tunisia, octopuses are fished very

An octopus in its lair off the British Virgin Islands.

The mimic octopus was recently discovered in Indonesia and has no scientific name yet. It has the unusual ability to change its body shape to resemble other marine animals as a means of defense. Here it is mimicking a starfish.

and release sperm, which are used to fertilize the eggs as the female begins to lay them. The eggs appear like small grapes when they are laid, and they are attached to strings festooned from the roof of the female's den or lair.

The egg-laying process goes on for some time in many species and may last for up to a week, during which 150,000 or more eggs may be produced. The male withdraws after the spermatophores have been delivered. The female remains with the eggs, guarding them as they develop and squirting jets of water around them to ensure adequate oxygenation.

The mother probably dies after her eggs hatch, since during the guarding process she is unlikely to feed. The juveniles hatch out as minute octopods with eight suckered arms and a developing mantle cavity. When they reach about 0.1 inches (3 mm) in length, they rise to the surface and join the

Below: Two males extend sperm-tipped arms to a female two-spotted octopus, Octopus bimaculoides, *in a mating action. (The female is tucked away in a crevice). Inset: Octopus hatchlings emerge from eggs.*

community of plankton, where they live for about a month. As members of the plankton, the minute octopuses will be swept along by surface currents and may be distributed far away from their place of birth. At about the end of the month they fall from the plankton and land on the seabed, where they start life as young bottom-dwelling predators. Individuals grow rapidly and become sexually mature at around three to four years of age.

Poisonous Practices

In the seas around Australia and islands of the Pacific two species of small octopus, both known as blue-ringed octopuses, have achieved notoriety because of their powerful venom. The

larger of the two is *Hapalochlaena lunulata*, which grows up to 8 inches (20 cm) across its arm span. *Hapalochlaena maculosa* is a little smaller, about the size of a tennis ball (with its arms drawn up inside the body). These animals inhabit shallow coastal waters and are sometimes seen by beachcombers, snorkelers, and scuba divers. *Hapalochlaena lunulata* is found in the warmer waters of the Great Barrier Reef and the coasts of Queensland, while *Hapalochlaena maculosa* occurs in cooler waters off the southern states of New South Wales, Victoria, and South Australia. Since they are well camouflaged, they are very often overlooked. Typically the latter are yellow-brown in color, and the characteristic circular blue markings become conspicuous when the animals are frightened or ready to attack.

Inside the head are two salivary glands that secrete venom in the saliva. It is used to poison and subdue their prey, which consists of animals such as crabs and shrimps, but it is also used for defense. It can be squirted into the water around the animals and introduced into the bloodstream of humans via a bite from the beaklike jaws. The bite itself is painless, but the effects include nausea, hazy vision, loss of sight, and respiratory collapse, which can even cause death. Victims may not be able to speak or swallow following a bite, and paralysis may set in within a few minutes. There is no antidote, but patients can survive if they are given artificial respiration and heart massage. The active element of the venom is tetrodotoxin, which is also found in puffer fish.

Because the octopus is small, it cannot bite through thick skin, but it is effective where the skin is thin, such as on the back of the hand. Fortunately, there have been few recorded cases of fatalities as the result of an octopus bite.

Octopuses in a Shell

The argonauts are possibly the most remarkable of all the cephalopods. Because they form and live in a coiled shell, they bear more than a passing resemblance to the nautiluses, but the structure of the shell and the animal inside it are different. Argonauts are well known for their ability to navigate around the warm seas of the world supported and protected by their very beautiful paper-thin shells. They have been familiar to seafarers for over 2,000 years. Six species are recognized, including *Argonauta argo*. The delicate texture of its shell has given it the common name of paper nautilus.

The most remarkable thing about these animals is the difference in size between males and females. Including the length of her arms, the female can be 12 inches (30 cm) long, 20 times as long as a male! Normally most of the female body is hidden from view within the fluted shell. She can occasionally leave its protection but must return; and if separated from her shell, she cannot make a new one. However, she can repair damage to the shell, and sometimes holes are mended by cementing in fragments taken from near the edge or lip of the shell.

The growth and maintenance of the shell are the responsibility of the first pair of arms. They have broad, leaflike membranous tips. The membranous areas have skin glands that secrete calcium carbonate, which forms the distinctive white, fluted shell material. By holding the two arms together, rather like hands held in prayer, the argonaut secretes a thin layer of jellylike material that hardens when it comes into contact with seawater. The secreted portion of shell can then be cemented into place as required.

As in other cephalopods, the funnel on the lower side of the body of the argonauts is important in locomotion. It protrudes from the shell like a nozzle and is the main propulsive organ, working by jetting water out of the mantle cavity.

The discovery of the male argonaut in 1853 was a milestone in understanding cephalopod reproduction. In the male the sperm duct extends into the third arm on the left-hand side. How the diminutive male copulates with a female 20 times his size is not entirely clear. There are accounts of males being found inside the shell of females; but more interestingly, detached hectocotyli (the male's specialized reproductive arm) are sometimes found on the female's body. It is possible that the arm may break free from the male and may be capable of surviving and moving independently in seawater, and finding its own way to the female. It has also been suggested that the males themselves may be parasites of the females for at least part of their life span.

Argonauta nodosa is able to change color to match its background, just like octopuses. It is also able to shoot ink.

SPINY-SKINNED ANIMALS

Animals with spiny skins belong to a distinct group known as the phylum Echinodermata. Echinoderms have existed on earth for a long time—the earliest ones were present in the seas 500 million years ago during the Cambrian period. Many species are now known only as fossils, but about 6,000 species survive on earth today. They are found in all the seas and oceans of the world, but not in fresh water or on land (except as fossils). There are five types of present-day echinoderms, the best known of which are the starfish. The other members of the group are the sea lilies and feather stars, the brittle stars and0. basket stars, the sea urchins, and the sea cucumbers.

What Is an Echinoderm?

Adult echinoderms live on or in the seabed. They are quite unlike most other animals such as worms, fish, and mammals, which all have distinct front and rear ends as well as left and right sides. Echinoderms have no head, and their bodies are either star shaped, globular, or cucumber shaped. Generally there is no left or right side, and in some cases it is not easy to tell which is the top and which is the bottom of the animal. In nearly every case the mouth is in the middle and is often situated on the underside of the animal. The anus is usually opposite it, on the upper side. Animals that are round, meaning those that are headless and have no left or right side, are known as radially symmetrical. Other examples include sea anemones, jellyfish, and corals. The starfish and their relatives follow this pattern, but in a special way. Their body is marked by five conspicuous lines (radii) running out from the mouth. This form of five-sided symmetry is known as pentameric symmetry, or pentamerism.

Apart from their unusual shape, echinoderms have special shelly skeletons made up of calcareous (chalky) plates known as ossicles. Each plate is a crystal of calcium carbonate perforated by many fine holes, giving it a spongy appearance. In most echinoderms the plates are loosely connected so that the animal appears flexible. In the sea urchins, however, the plates interlock like pieces of a jigsaw puzzle so that the animal appears quite rigid. Technically, the skeletons of these animals lie inside the body, even though they do not appear to. That is because a thin layer of skin covers the plates. The whole of the body wall, skin, skeleton, and lining is referred to as the "test." The test of most echinoderms bears chalky ornaments, including spines, that have special functions, such as defense and food gathering.

Managing without a Head

A well-developed head at the front of the body, in which the major sensory organs are close to the brain, is a typical feature of most animals. It enables them to move efficiently, to locate food sources, and to find a mate. Remarkably, the echinoderms manage without such an arrangement. There is no concentration of nervous tissue to form a brain. Instead, each radius (segment) of the pentameric body is equipped with a radial nerve cord, all connected via a nerve that runs around the gut—the circum esophageal nerve ring. The radial nerve cord controls the muscles of the particular part of the animal through which it runs. It also receives information from stimuli such as touch, chemicals, and light that strike the surface of the animal. Some echinoderms—for example, starfish and sea urchins—have movable structures (such as spines) on the outside of the test. They are controlled by diffuse nerves leading outward from the radial nerve cords to the skin. Despite the lack of a head, this type of nervous system enables echinoderms to receive stimuli and to coordinate their responses so that they can move purposefully over the seabed.

Masses of Feet

Echinoderms have tube feet (sometimes by the hundreds) arranged in five double rows, called ambulacra. In the starfish they are on the underside of the body. Most starfish, as well as sea urchins and sea cucumbers, have

Subphylum Crinozoa, 1 living class
Class: Crinoidea—Sea lilies and feather stars
1 order, about 9 families, about 625 species

Subphylum Asterozoa, 2 classes
Class: Asteroidea—Starfish or seastars
6 orders, about 20 families, about 1,500 species
Class: Ophiuroidea—Basket stars and brittle stars
3 orders, about 15 families, about 2,000 species

Subphylum Echinozoa, 2 classes
Class: Echinoidea—Sea urchins, sand dollars, and heart urchins
9 orders, about 22 families, about 950 species
Class: Holothuroidea—Sea cucumbers
6 orders, about 11 families, about 1,150 species

⊕ The sturdy defensive spines on the body of the horned seastar, Protoreaster nodosus *from the Indo-Pacific, do indeed resemble "horns."*

Starfish

Anus — Gonads
Intestine — Hepatic ceca
— Spines
Stomach — Ampulla
— Tube feet
— Radial nerve cord
Gonads
Ampulla
Nerve ring
Mouth — Radial canal

⊖ *A typical starfish. Each radius carries rows of tube feet and is linked to the nervous system by a radial nerve cord.*

suckers on the ends of their tube feet. The suckers help grip the substratum and aid walking. They do not occur in the feather stars or the brittle stars, which rely on bending the arms of their bodies for movement.

The tube feet are the visible part of a unique system found in the echinoderms—the water vascular system. It has no parallel anywhere else in the animal kingdom. Each tube foot is elastic and can be lengthened or extended by filling up with fluid from inside the body. Muscles running up and down the tube-foot shaft can make the tube foot contract and shorten by emptying the fluid back into the body. The muscles also make the tube foot bend, allowing it to take "steps." In most echinoderms, apart from the sea lilies and feather stars, each tube foot connects with a flexible bulb, or ampulla, that appears to store water vascular fluid for the tube

Sea cucumber

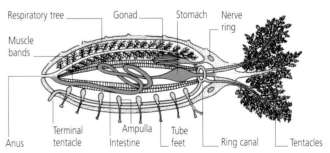

Respiratory tree — Gonad — Stomach — Nerve ring
Muscle bands
Anus — Terminal tentacle — Intestine — Ampulla — Tube feet — Ring canal — Tentacles

Sea urchin

⊕ ⊖ *Above: The elongated sea cucumber lies on its side, giving it a "top" and a "bottom." Organs for respiration are on the top. Right: The sea urchin is rounded, and its organs are more symmetrical.*

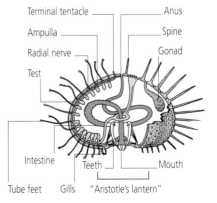

Terminal tentacle — Anus
Ampulla — Spine
Radial nerve — Gonad
Test
Intestine — Teeth — Mouth
Tube feet — Gills — "Aristotle's lantern"

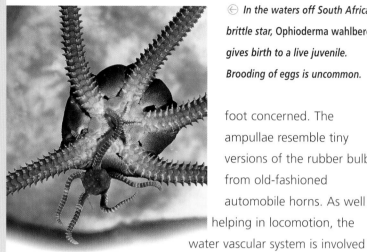

⊕ In the waters off South Africa a brittle star, Ophioderma wahlbergi, gives birth to a live juvenile. Brooding of eggs is uncommon.

foot concerned. The ampullae resemble tiny versions of the rubber bulbs from old-fashioned automobile horns. As well as helping in locomotion, the water vascular system is involved with respiration and food collection.

Reproduction in Echinoderms

Most young echinoderms hatch from a floating egg. The eggs are usually released directly into the sea when the ripe females spawn. Once in the seawater, they are fertilized by sperm released simultaneously by spawning males. The fertilized egg usually develops into a drifting microscopic animal that is swept around by currents. The young animal, known as a larva, looks very different from its parents and has no control over where the currents take it. During this part of its life it lives in the community of organisms known as plankton (from the Greek word meaning "drifting.")

When the larva is sufficiently developed, it ends its drifting stage and settles on the seabed. At the same time, it changes from the larval body form to that of a miniature adult. This process is known as metamorphosis and is seen in all types of animal that have larvae.

A few echinoderms brood their young either on their skin or in special pouches and do not have planktonic larvae. The juvenile develops on the parent's body until it is mature enough to lead an independent existence.

Feeding Feet

Tube feet play an important part in the feeding strategies of most echinoderms, but methods of catching food vary from group to group. In the sea lilies and feather stars the mouth and anus are situated on the upper side of the face and body respectively, away from the seabed. They

⊕ A sea cucumber species, Neothyonidium magnum, seen here in the Philippines, feeds by "licking" one tentacle at a time.

use their tube feet, which occur in great numbers on their branching arms, to filter the seawater and collect small particles of suspended food. The particles move down the arms to the mouth via special food grooves.

Starfish hunt their prey using their sense of smell. They can hold the prey with their suckered tube feet and can even pull apart the shells of clams in this way. They frequently turn their stomach inside out over their prey or insert it directly into the gaping shells of bivalves such as clams or oysters. Digestion occurs inside the stomach and digestive ceca, and the resulting products are absorbed and distributed to the rest of the body. The mouth, on the underside, is well positioned for this type of feeding.

Brittle stars are scavengers and particle feeders. Moving across the seabed by levering themselves with

When Is a Shell Not a Shell?

Many land- and water-dwelling animals have hard outer coverings. The shells belonging to sea snails and bivalves are hard and are made from calcium carbonate. They support and protect the animals' soft bodies. Birds' eggs are also covered with protective chalky shells. Shells are not always made of chalky substances, however. Some tiny sea-dwelling animals have shells made from glasslike material known as silica.

Crabs and lobsters carry their shells on the outside. The protective layer of the echinoderms, however, lies just below the surface of the skin. It is made up of calcareous plates set in living tissue, which maintains and nurtures the calcium carbonate. When an echinoderm dies, the test decomposes, and the skeletal plates fall apart. When a snail or a clam dies, however, its hard shell survives for a long time.

their flexible arms, they use their tube feet to pass food to their mouths. There is no anus, and waste material is passed out through the mouth.

Jaws and Spines

Most round sea urchins browse on plant and animal growths on the rocks of the seabed. Protruding from their mouth is a five-toothed chewing organ (known as Aristotle's lantern) that acts as a set of jaws. The test is covered with movable spines that are used for locomotion and defense. They also detect incoming touch stimuli. Multitudes of minute pincerlike organs (pedicellariae) help keep the surface of the test clean. The suckered tube feet can be extended considerable distances from the body to assist with posture, often resembling the guy ropes on a tent. They are also important in locomotion.

The tube feet of sand dollars and heart urchins as well as the shape of the test and the spines are modified

for burrowing. They get their food from rotting plant and animal tissue lying in the sand and gravel where they live.

In sea cucumbers the chalky parts of the skeleton are often considerably reduced, giving the animals a softer texture. Tube feet are arranged around the mouth to gather food either by filtering seawater or by sweeping in organic matter from the surface of the sand. Sea cucumbers usually move with one end leading, as do the sand dollars and heart urchins. In some species there are no tube feet other than those around the mouth, and the animal crawls along in a wormlike fashion.

⊖ *A feather star feeds on a reef in Papua New Guinea. Gripping onto the rocks with its clawlike cirri, it sieves suspended food material from the currents.*

**Rosy feather star
(Antedon bifida)**

Common name Sea lilies, feather stars

Order Articulata

Class Crinoidea

Subphylum Crinozoa

Phylum Echinodermata

Number of species About 625

Size From 0.1 in (3 mm) to 3 ft (1 m)

Key features Adult body cup shaped; upper side bears featherlike arms in multiples of 5; underside of cup attached to substrata by flexible jointed stalk (sea lilies) or has jointed, clawlike cirri in groups of 5 (feather stars); color varied, often black, brown, or red; featherlike arms have side branches (pinnules); tube feet in clusters of 3 on arms and pinnules and in rows on either side of a food groove; head and brain absent

Habits Adults bottom-dwelling marine animals; sea lilies attached to hard base by a flexible stalk; feather stars free living but grip rocks and stones with cirri; sea lilies can swim for short periods by coordinated arm bending

Breeding No mating; sperm and eggs released into seawater; fertilization occurs outside the body; eggs hatch into microscopic planktonic larvae that metamorphose and settle on the substratum attached by a stalk; sea lilies retain stalk into adult life, feather stars break free from attachment as they develop

Diet Filter feeders, feeding on plankton and suspended organic particles

Habitat Exclusively marine, living on rocks, reefs, or deep-sea substratum

Distribution All the world's seas and oceans at all depths

⤉ *Feather stars prefer to live above the seabed, often congregating on vertical rock faces and sometimes perching on other animals. The rosy feather star,* Antedon bifida, *is found in northwestern Europe. Size about 6 inches (15 cm).*

MOLLUSKS AND ECHINODERMS

Sea Lilies and Feather Stars

Articulata

Sea lilies are mysterious deep-sea animals. They have rarely been caught alive and are not often seen. Divers in tropical waters are more likely to see their cousins, the feather stars, clinging to coral reefs.

THE CLASS CRINOIDEA, to which the sea lilies and feather stars belong, is the only class in the subphylum Crinozoa that still has living representatives. Five other groups are known today only from fossils dating back to the Cambrian period 570 to 500 million years ago.

Life in the early seas was hazardous for soft-bodied animals, and few, if any, organisms survived without heavy protective armor, shells, or other defense mechanisms.

Dual-Purpose Organs

Living inside their protected, armored bodies and attached to a base, early echinoderms needed gills or tentacles to obtain oxygen from the water moving over them, as well as to remove carbon dioxide and other waste materials from the body tissues. It seems likely that the tube feet evolved initially as respiratory organs, which could be extended and retracted like tentacles through openings in the calcified

The tube feet are not really feet at all. They have no locomotive function, since they point away from the walking surface. They are arranged in two rows in groups of three along the upper surfaces of the arms and the pinnules. Between each row is a food groove that leads from the tips of the pinnules to the mouth located in the center of the upper surface of the cup. The anus is situated near the mouth, but to one side.

Mucus Strings

The tube feet are complex and are divided into three branches. They have no suckers; but they are covered in cilia (hairs), and they secrete mucus. When a particle of food touches them, it is flicked into the groove, where it is bound up in a string of mucus. The groove is lined with beating cilia that move the mucus strings containing the food along toward the mouth.

This is a successful conveyor-belt system for transferring food from the water column to the gut, and it is not surprising that other animals exploit it. A very peculiar, microscopic wormlike invertebrate belonging to a group known as the Myzostomaria is an uninvited guest. The myzostomes perch on the sides of the crinoid's arms. A favorite place is near the mouth, where there is a lot of food passing by. From there they can suck the food out of the grooves with their small tubular mouthparts. An easy life!

Because the crinoid's food is in particle form, no jaws or chewing structures are necessary. The gut descends into the body from the mouth, makes a loop through the spacious body cavity, and returns to the anus. Food waste is released onto the upper surface of the cup and swept away by currents of water driven by the animal's beating cilia.

⬆ The feather star, Oxycomanthus bennetti, has quite large thick arms and is a favorite home for some species of tiny shrimps. This feather star was photographed in Fiji.

⬅ This fossilized crinoid is from rocks of the Carboniferous period (334 to 280 million years ago). The stalk, usually attached to the body, has been broken off.

body wall (known as the test). When these "feet" became grouped in patterns around the mouth, they took on an additional role of food gathering by sieving suspended particles of food from the passing water.

The crinoid body plan consists of a cuplike body. The walls of the cup form the flexible test, with plates of calcium carbonate secreted within them (known as ossicles). The ossicles are knitted together with threads of connective tissue. The five-sided symmetry is shown by the arms, which are arranged in five pairs (or in some species in multiples of five) around the edge of the upper surface of the cup. The arms bear side branches known as pinnules.

The tube feet also provide a good exchange surface for respiratory gases. The tube feet are supplied with fluid from a branch of the animal's water vascular system, known as the radial water vascular canal, which runs along each arm under the skin. The water vascular canals are joined to each other by a ring canal. The arrangement of the water vascular system is similar to the arrangement of the nervous system—in each arm there is also a radial nerve cord that controls the tube feet and is linked to all the other radial nerve cords by a nerve ring, which encircles the esophagus.

Lifelines

The key difference between the sea lilies and the feather stars lies in the structures on the underside of the body cup. The feather stars are free-living as adults; and although they attach to the substratum as juveniles, the attachment breaks as the animals develop and become mobile. In order to hold onto rocks and weeds, they develop grasping structures on the underside of the cup, known as cirri. The cirri are arranged in fives or multiples of five and are supported internally by a series of calcareous plates connected by "joints" to make them flexible. The cirri end in a clawlike joint used for gripping onto rocks and shells. The claws allow the animal to position itself so that it can face into currents and sieve suspended food material from the water.

Locomotion in the feather stars consists of creeping over the substratum by bending the arms or occasionally swimming using a beating movement of the arms. Feather star movements are graceful and beautiful to watch. Free-living feather stars (or cormatulids, as they are sometimes known) usually range in size from 2 inches (5 cm) to 6 inches (15 cm) high.

Sea lilies lack cirri. Instead, the base of the cup connects with a well-developed stalk, which is made up of jointed segments. The stalk is usually longer than the rest of the animal and holds the body and arms well away from the substratum so that they can reach up into the water currents. Some stalked crinoids are very large, reaching well over 3 feet (1 m) high, while others are very small, not much more than a fraction of an inch tall.

External Reproduction

The reproductive organs in sea lilies and feather stars are carried on the underside of the pinnules—unlike all other echinoderms, whose reproductive organs are inside the central body cavity. Sperm and eggs are released into the seawater, and fertilization occurs there without mating taking place. A drifting planktonic larva forms from the developing embryo.

By the time it is fully developed, the larva (called a pentacrinule larva) has settled and is attached to a hard base. It has arms and suspension-feeding tube feet. It has the typical stalk attachment of the adult sea lily, and for species in that group the attachment is retained throughout life. Feather stars break free.

It is likely that crinoids are preyed on by a variety of omnivorous bottom-dwelling fish and other invertebrate species, but very little is known of their predators. Individuals with broken or missing arms are often found, probably as a result of being attacked by other animals. Apart from their microscopic prey, the crinoids are not able to defend themselves from or attack other animals.

⊙ *The orange sea lily,* Nemaster rubiginosa, *is the most common sea lily on many Caribbean reefs. It is bright orange and usually curled on the tips. This one is extending its arms to feed on a lettuce leaf coral in Honduras.*

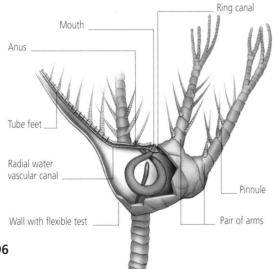

Mouth

Anus

Tube feet

Radial water vascular canal

Wall with flexible test

Ring canal

Pinnule

Pair of arms

⊙ *Cross-section of a typical crinoid body, showing the main feeding and respiratory systems.*

⊙ *This tropical feather star from the Arabian Sea is perched on a colony of branching coral. Its arms are held over the body, probably because it has been disturbed.*

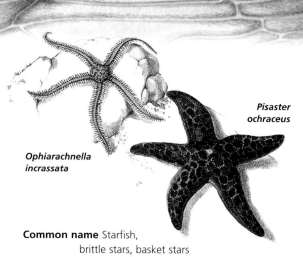

Ophiarachnella incrassata

Pisaster ochraceus

Common name Starfish, brittle stars, basket stars

Class Asteroidea (starfish), Ophiuroidea (brittle stars and basket stars)

Subphylum Asterozoa

Phylum Echinodermata

Number of species About 1,500 (Asteroidea) and 2,000 (Ophiuroidea)

Size From 0.2 inches (4 mm) to 5 ft (1.5 m)

Key features Adult body star shaped; central body has 5 (occasionally more) arms; color varied, sometimes patterned; head and brain absent; no conspicuous sensory organs; flexible calcareous skeleton set in body wall; body surface covered in skin, sometimes decorated with spines; tube feet on underside of each arm, locomotion by tube feet (starfish) or arm movements (brittle stars and basket stars)

Habits Marine; adults live on seabed on rocks, reefs, and sand; normally lie with mouth against substratum; some burrow in sediments; movement in starfish generally by slow crawling using tube feet; brittle stars and basket stars move by flexing their arms

Breeding Courtship and mating absent; sexes usually separate; adults release sperm and eggs into seawater, where fertilization occurs; fertilized egg develops into microscopic larva that drifts in plankton; juveniles settle on seabed following metamorphosis

Diet Starfish are carnivores or detritus feeders; brittle stars feed on carrion, minute animals, detritus, or suspended food; basket stars are plankton and detritus feeders

Habitat Exclusively marine bottom dwellers

Distribution All the world's seas and oceans

ⓣ *Ophiarachnella incrassata is a brittle star found on the Great Barrier Reef of Australia. Diameter 12 inches (30 cm). Pisaster ochraceus is found on rocky shores from Alaska to Baja California. Diameter 10 inches (25 cm).*

Starfish, Brittle Stars, and Basket Stars
Asterozoa

The image of a starfish clinging unobtrusively to a rock in a rock pool belies the real nature of these animals. They are fearsome predators, often pinning down and externally digesting their unfortunate prey.

STARFISH ARE AMONG THE MOST familiar of marine animals—they are often seen during trips to the beach or visits to the aquarium. Brittle stars and basket stars are less well known, possibly because many species are smaller and less conspicuous than starfish.

Most adult starfish show the five-sided echinoderm body plan very clearly. The mouth is central on the underside. From the edge of the mouth two rows of tube feet radiate out toward the tip of each arm.

What's the Difference?
The subphylum Asterozoa contains two types of echinoderm, the starfish (in the class Asteroidea) and the brittle stars and basket stars (in the class Ophiuroidea). As in all echinoderms, their bodies are supported and protected by the chalky plates of the protective layer known as the "test." The test usually has spines and other ornaments on the surface to increase the amount of protection.

It is fairly easy to tell the difference between a starfish and a brittle star. In starfish the central body merges into each of the arms, and the gut and reproductive organs are housed in the central body as well as inside the arms. In brittle stars there is normally a sharp division between the body, which is disklike, and the arms, which are flexible and snakelike (the word Ophiuroidea comes from the Greek *ophites,* meaning "snake.")

The gut and reproductive organs of brittle stars are contained entirely inside the body disk. None of these animals has branching arms, except one type of brittle star—the basket stars—in which the arms branch many times.

ⓓ *A common brittle star, Ophiotrix fragilis. The elevated arms are sieving the water column for suspended food particles.*

Killer Starfish

Most starfish are carnivores, but a few species live as scavengers or collect rotting particles that fall to the seabed. Despite the apparent lack of well-developed eyes and smelling organs, the animals can detect suitable prey at considerable distances and navigate toward it. They respond to the waterborne scent of potential food as it passes over them and then follow the scent to its source. The scent comes from chemicals that leak from their prey.

Scientists have been able to demonstrate how starfish can navigate using scent. They put the animals into "y"-shaped mazes and introduced a scent into one arm of the "y." The starfish followed the scent and moved into the arm where the source was. Reversing the scent source did not fool the starfish.

⊝ *A starfish among tunicates off the Palau Islands in the western Pacific.*

The exact style of feeding varies between the different groups or families of starfish. Starfish have no jaws, so they cannot break up their food before it is swallowed. Food is either swallowed whole or digested outside the body. In general, starfish that feed on mobile animals smaller than themselves swallow their prey whole. Sometimes it is possible to make out the shapes of recently swallowed victims lying inside the bodies of starfish such as *Astropecten*.

Turning the Stomach

Asterias and many of its relatives use a different method that is suitable for larger items or for prey attached to rocks: They turn part of their stomach inside out through the mouth and push it between the shells of bivalves such as oysters, mussels, and clams. The stomach comes out in the form of thin membranous sheets that contain digestive and absorbent tissues. Next the starfish clambers on top of its victim. Using groups of tube feet in turn, it pulls on the shells until the muscles inside that hold them shut weaken a little, and they gape apart. The starfish can fit its stomach between even a minute gap in the bivalve shells. The victim's tissues are then digested right there, often inside its own shell!

Surprisingly, some starfish are also able to capture fish in spite of being much slower-moving than their victims. Among the spiny ornaments on the outside of many starfish species are minute forcepslike grooming organs

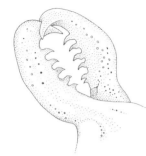

⬆ *Most starfish carry small grooming organs between their spines, consisting of two or more jaws called pedicellariae. They are specialized for dealing with intruders, but may help in feeding. They have an impressive grip for their size!*

⬇ *Below: A starfish on its back showing its tube feet. Inset: A starfish in New England prepares to open and feed on a mussel. The animal will evert its stomach and digest its prey externally.*

called pedicellariae. In one American species, *Stylasterias forreri*, these pedicellariae are large and curved. They can catch hold of the frilly fins of small rockpool fish such as sculpins when they settle close by or even when they land on top of the starfish. When the fish tries to swim away, it is trapped, and the starfish climbs on top of it, pins it against the rocks, and slowly digests it. It is hardly surprising that starfish have achieved a reputation as pests, particularly in oyster and mussel farms.

Varied Lifestyles

Starfish and brittle stars inhabit all types of seabed. The most commonly observed species live among rocks and reefs, sometimes hiding in crevices or among corals in the daytime, and coming out at night to hunt for food. Others burrow in shell gravel or sand and move around under the sediment in search of prey. Some brittle stars are adapted to live many inches beneath the sand. An example is *Amphiura brachiata* from the North Atlantic. Its long arms can be 15 times as long as the diameter of its body, so most of the animal can be well below the surface of the sand provided a couple of arms are communicating with the surface. The

tube feet on these arms move back and forth sweeping currents of seawater along one arm, down to the animal in the sand, and back along another arm up to the surface again. Deep in its burrow, the brittle star gets a fresh supply of oxygenated seawater, while waste materials are swept away with the returning current. It feeds on detritus and small organisms sent down to the mouth.

A few brittle stars live on the outside of other organisms such as sea fans and sponges. They are not truly parasitic, since they do not draw sustenance from the creatures on which

Broken Bodies

The name brittle star suggests that these animals are fragile and that pieces break off them easily, but starfish can also break up or divide. Fission, the phenomenon in which a starfish or brittle star can divide into two or more parts, only happens in certain species. It is sometimes described as a form of asexual reproduction. However, it rarely produces more than two new individuals, and it requires some of the central body to be present to form part of each "daughter." There are descriptions of starfish actually pulling themselves apart, with their tube feet walking in opposite directions. An example is the small, multiarmed New Zealand starfish *Allostichaster*. It is not uncommon to find individuals in which the arms on one half of the body are larger (being from the original "parent") than those of the other half (being regenerated and new). The West Indian brittle star, *Ophiocomella ophiactoides*, can tear itself apart across the body disk, and each part can regenerate the missing structures.

A starfish arm regenerating. Some starfish can regrow an entire body from just a small part of an arm.

Some starfish, for example, species of *Linckia*, can regrow new bodies from just a small part of one arm and do not need part of the parent's central body to do so. The ability to regrow lost parts allows the formation of two or more new animals from parts of one old one. It is useful in cases of injury, but as a means of reproduction it is not as efficient as sexual reproduction because relatively few offspring are produced. Brittle stars are particularly good at repairing damage to their arms. It is not uncommon to see individuals with one or more arms that are obviously regrowing lost pieces.

Only a few predators feed on starfish and brittle stars, including other starfish. A good example is *Crossaster papposus*, a sun star that feeds on *Asterias rubens*, the common starfish of northwestern Europe. A small *C. papposus* will attack an *A. rubens* many times larger than itself. Other predators include bottom-feeding fish and seabirds.

One group of brittle stars—the basket stars—grows to a much greater size and may stretch to 3 feet (1 m) or more when they are fully expanded. Unusually, they have branching arms and in many respects bear a superficial resemblance to the crinoids, or sea lilies, rather than to brittle stars. This is particularly the case when they are standing on a rocky outcrop or the edge of a reef, sieving the water column for suspended food particles. They form their body into a curved shape, a bit like a basket, and face into the prevailing current. Basket stars exploit larger suspended particles than most other suspension-feeding echinoderms. When hiding in a crevice, their arms are intertwined and folded up.

they live. Brittle stars feed in a variety of ways. Many are scavengers and carrion feeders, hunting out small dead or dying organisms. Others run water over their bodies and use their tube feet to create a mesh with which they can filter out suspended food particles from the water. Some are specially adapted to use their tube feet to collect suitable particles that have landed as sediment on the seabed.

→ *Basket stars in the genus* Gorgonocephalus *have twisted, branching arms.* Gorgonocephalus *is a reference to the twisted Gorgon's knot of Greek mythology.*

The Crown-of-Thorns Conundrum

The infamous crown-of-thorns starfish, *Acanthaster planci*, is a large starfish found in the Indo-west Pacific, where reef-building corals grow. The crown-of-thorns is a specialized feeder, eating the soft tissues of coral polyps. It feeds by turning its stomach inside out through its mouth (known as everting its stomach). At night it climbs onto a coral colony, wraps its everted stomach over the coral polyps, and digests them on the spot. When it has finished its meal, it pulls the stomach membranes back into its body and then moves back into a crevice, where it shelters in the daytime.

The crown-of-thorns has been causing concern to scientists and conservation experts since 1963. In some parts of the Indo-west Pacific coral feeding by the crown-of-thorns has created a serious pressure on reefs, especially when the starfish is present in great numbers. It was the occurrence of great swarms of the species (referred to as plagues) on the Great Barrier Reef of Australia that brought it notoriety in the 1960s and 1970s. It was suggested that the plagues were a direct result of human interference with the marine environment. (It was thought that natural predators of the starfish were being collected as souvenirs.) However, sudden population explosions of animals are not unusual. In fact, many marine invertebrates such as starfish and mussels have the sort of life cycle—producing millions of eggs each year—in which a population explosion can occur if the conditions for the survival of the young are favorable.

Until 1950 the crown-of-thorns was regarded as a rare animal. Only one specimen was collected during the famous Great Barrier Reef Expedition of 1928 and 1929. Since the late 1950s scuba diving has greatly increased in popularity. At the same time, the perceived population of the crown-of-thorns has increased. Perhaps it never was so rare, but relatively few people had seen it.

However, the idea that humans have disturbed the reef environment and therefore affected the crown-of-thorns has never really gone away. There is now evidence that commercial fishing has removed natural predators of the starfish. Some of the most sought-after commercial fish in Australia, such as the emperor fish, are ones that feed on bottom-dwelling invertebrates such as the crown-of-thorns.

Increasingly, coral reefs all over the world are under threat from environmental changes resulting from pollution, sea-level changes due to global warming, overfishing, and damage caused by tourists. Any additional pressure on corals, many species of which take years to grow, is a cause for concern.

Right: A brightly colored crown-of-thorns starfish in the Andaman Sea, Southeast Asia. Left: Closeup of the tube feet of the crown-of-thorns. The animals' feeding habits are putting pressure on threatened coral reef habitats.

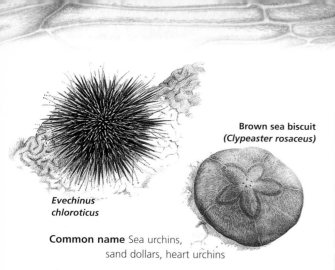

**Brown sea biscuit
(Clypeaster rosaceus)**

*Evechinus
chloroticus*

Common name Sea urchins,
sand dollars, heart urchins

Class Echinoidea

Subphylum Echinozoa

Phylum Echinodermata

Number of species About 950

Size 0.1 in (3 mm) to 7 in (17 cm)

Key features Adult body round, disklike, or heart
shaped, showing 5-sided symmetry; colors
varied, often black, green, gray, or brown;
head and brain lacking; 5 paired rows of tube
feet bearing suckers at tips; calcareous
skeleton set in body wall (the test); test is
usually rigid and bears mobile spines and
minute grooming organs (pedicellariae) that
may be venomous; many species have
chewing organ (Aristotle's lantern) and teeth;
long gut opens via mouth on underside and
via anus on upper side of body

Habits Adults bottom-dwelling marine animals;
usually lie with mouth downward; move
using tube feet; spines used for defense and
for burrowing in some forms

Breeding No mating behavior; sperm and eggs released
into seawater; fertilization occurs outside the
body; microscopic larvae generally planktonic;
a few species brood their embryos

Diet Algae, sea grasses, encrusting invertebrate
animals, and organic detritus

Habitat Exclusively marine, living on rocks and reefs
or burrowing in sediment

Distribution All the world's seas and oceans at all depth

⊕ *Evechinus chloroticus is a regular (rounded) sea urchin
with a mass of bristling spines and is found in rocky pools in
New Zealand. Diameter 4 inches (10 cm).* Clypeaster rosaceus,
the brown sea biscuit, *is very common around reefs in
southern Florida, where it burrows just underneath the sand.
Diameter 4.5 inches (11 cm).*

Sea Urchins
Echinoidea

*A stab from one of the spines of a sea
urchin can be very painful—the sharp barbs
of* Diadema *can even penetrate a rubber
diving suit. The related sand dollars
and heart urchins have shorter, less
fearsome-looking spines.*

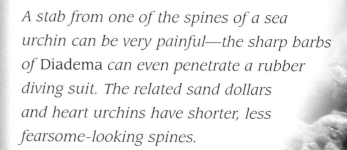

SEA URCHINS ARE PROBABLY LESS FAMILIAR than their
cousins the starfish because relatively few of
them live between the tidemarks. However, in
some parts of the world, such as the
Mediterranean Sea, sea urchins frequently make
their presence felt when bathers accidentally
step on them, and the sharp spines become
embedded in their feet. Many snorkelers and
scuba divers have unpleasant memories of
encounters with the black, long-spined sea
urchins that inhabit the rocks and reefs of
tropical waters—their barbed spines are capable
of penetrating rubber suits and can cause great
discomfort if they puncture the skin. Other
types of sea urchin inhabit the rocky seabed
and burrow into sands and gravel, but they are
usually seen only by fishermen and scientists.

There are several types of sea urchin, and
their classification is quite complex. In simple
terms adult sea urchins can either be round
(when they are known as regular echinoids) or
oval or heart shaped (when they are known as
irregular echinoids). The regular echinoids
include *Cidaris* and *Arbacia,* while the irregular
echinoids are represented by the flat sand
dollars and the heart-shaped urchins.

Spiny Armaments

The most characteristic features of the sea
urchins are their movable spines. These
structures are important for defense and
posture. In some urchins, such as *Cidaris,* there
are two distinct types of spines—the larger
club- or pencil-like spines (known as primaries)
and the much smaller bladelike spines
(secondaries) that surround and protect the

⤊ Echinus esculentus *is the common sea urchin of northwestern European coasts. It is famed for its tests (shells), which are used as ornaments.*

⤊ *The slate pencil sea urchin (*Heterocentrotus *species) is found in the coral reefs of Hawaii. It has three types of spines: long triangular ones for defense, shorter ones for clinging to the reef, and flat, armorlike ones that encase and protect the body.*

bases of the primaries. Secondary spines also line the rows of tube feet. *Cidaris* and its relatives live on rocky and stony grounds from shallow to very deep water.

In most other species of sea urchins there is no obvious division of the spines into large primaries and small secondaries. Instead, there is a gradient from one to the other, as in *Diadema*—an urchin that is widely distributed in shallow waters in the tropics, particularly on coral reefs. The long black spines of these animals can be formidable defense weapons. *Diadema* responds rapidly to changes in light intensity, such as shadows, and can point its spines in the direction of approaching attackers. To add to their effectiveness, the spines are covered in fine barbs and are capable of stinging. Near their tips the barbs point backward, allowing easy penetration of a victim's flesh, but lower down they reverse. That makes them break off inside the victim.

Diadema also uses its spines to assist in posture, particularly helping it stand on irregular

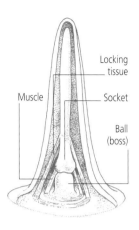

⤒ *A ball-and-socket joint attaches the spine of the echinoid to its test. The indented socket fits over the raised "boss," or ball, and is secured with a ring of muscle and a ring of locking tissue.*

⤓ *Echinothrix calamaris, the banded sea urchin, occurs in the Red Sea, the Indian Ocean, the western Pacific, and off Hawaii. The smaller spines are venomous, and contact with them causes burning pain in the wound.*

surfaces. The spines also aid movement, acting as levers and working in conjunction with the tube feet to push the animal along the seabed.

Shallow rocky bottoms provide homes for a variety of other regular urchins, such as *Arbacia*, *Echinus*, and *Paracentrotus*. As in all echinoderms, there is no head, and these regular, round-shaped animals are able to move in all directions equally well. They show a range of spine sizes. The spines are mechanically defensive, working like thorns or prickles; but unlike those of *Diadema* and its relatives, they do not sting. They also help the animal stand and wedge itself into crevices, and they move food particles over the surface of the animal toward the mouth.

Each spine is attached to the test by a ball-and-socket joint. The socket is carried at the end of the spine, and the ball (or "boss" as it is known) is carried on the test.

A band of muscle lies around the joint; when the muscle contracts on one side, it pulls the spine in that direction. Contracting the muscle on the opposite side has the opposite effect. Inside the muscle is a band of locking tissue that has remarkable properties. The tissue cannot contract, but the animal can control the extent to which it can be stretched when the spine moves. An urchin can therefore point its spine using the joint muscles and then lock it by making the locking tissue hard to stretch.

Renewable Teeth

Regular sea urchins live on the seabed and feed on encrusting plants and animals, including seaweeds, barnacles, and moss animals. They have five teeth, which form part of a complex structure of bony ossicles and muscles known as Aristotle's lantern. The teeth can be moved

Protective Appendages

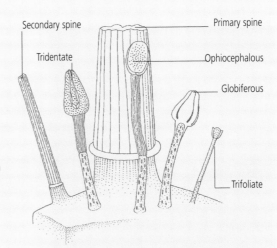

Lying between the spines on the surface of the sea urchin (known as the test) are thousands of remarkable small organs called pedicellariae. They are so small that they are difficult to see with the naked eye, but they can be found clearly with a hand lens. There may be up to four types on any one urchin, but they all have certain features in common. Pedicellariae are mounted on flexible stalks, which move on a joint that resembles a miniature version of the sea urchin's spine joint. The stalk supports a set of jaws, usually three, which form the pedicellariae head. Some pedicellariae are pointed and have finger-shaped (tridentate) jaws, others are blunt and spoon shaped (ophiocephalous), and one type (globiferous) bears venom glands and can inject the venom into other organisms.

These three different types of pedicellariae open and close their jaws in response to touch and chemical stimuli. The globiferous (venomous) pedicellariae respond in particular to chemicals released by predators and can inject venom into the skin of an attacker, causing it to withdraw. When that happens, the pedicellaria breaks off and continues to inject its venom into the intruder. A minute fourth type, known as a trifoliate pedicellaria, has a grooming function: Its jaws move spontaneously and "mouth over" the delicate skin of the animal, picking up particles of silt and organic debris from the animal's surface.

Four different types of pedicellariae lie between the spines of most echinoids. The jaws open at the touch of an intruding organism and snap shut, trapping it.

in and out, and they can bite against each other or gape apart. They are pointed and protude from the mouth on the underside of the test, where the mouth is set in the center of a flexible membrane. The teeth are ideally placed to scrape against the rocky seabed; and since they are made from specially toughened calcium carbonate, they can scrape over the rocks to remove food. The teeth grow continuously, so as they wear away, they are replaced. The food material they scrape off is sent into the esophagus and then up into the long gut that is coiled around the interior of the test. The food is digested in the gut, and the products of digestion are absorbed. After digestion the waste materials are defecated from the anus on the top of the test.

Ecologically Friendly

Regular sea urchins are important in marine communities, since they control the development of encrusting algae and animals. This is particularly true on coral reefs, where their grazing activities limit the growth of the marine plants (and therefore the areas of shade they produce). In this way they help create the sunlit spaces needed by the reef-building corals for their development.

Remarkably, there are descriptions of some urchins that fight among themselves to secure living space on rocks and reefs. They belong to

⬇ *A pair of sea urchins,* Holopneustes inflatus, *feed on kelp in Tasmania. The tests (shells) of these urchins are commonly washed onto southern Australian shores.*

↑ *This sea urchin from California is trying to disguise itself beneath an abalone shell. Regular echinoids often camouflage themselves with pieces of shell, gravel, or algae—with varying degrees of success.*

a widely distributed genus—*Echinometra*—that is commonly found in coral reef areas. Although it is technically a regular echinoid, its test is oval instead of round. Individuals bite each other with their teeth when defending their living space.

Sand Dollars

Unlike the regular echinoids, the irregular ones lack a perfectly circular body. They usually move with the same edge leading all the time, effectively giving them a front end.

The sand dollars are flat, disklike sea urchins. There is no head, but the distinct front end can be identified by the arrangement of the rows of tube feet. They are located mainly on the upper surface and can be seen as petal-like markings, often with contrasting colors. One "petal" points ahead and forms the leading row of tube feet, and two more "petals" lie behind on either side. The rear edge of the animal lies between these hindmost left and right "petals."

Close examination of the outside of a sand dollar such as *Clypeaster* or *Mellita* reveals that the spines are all short and similar in shape and size. They give the animal's surface an almost furlike texture. The spines play a role in protecting the test as well as in burrowing and in moving grains of sand and gravel over the test surface.

Some sand dollars have unusual slotlike openings or notches in the test. It is believed that these openings help the animal move more easily through the sand. That is because some sediment particles can go right through the openings from the lower to the upper side, while others move around the edges of the test. However, sand dollars do not burrow

deeply. They remain close to the surface of the sediment, often with part of the rim of the test exposed to view. Sand dollars have a reduced chewing organ (Aristotle's lantern) situated inside the mouth on the underside of the body. It enables them to browse on and crush particles of organic matter to feed on as they go through the sediment.

Heart Urchins

Heart urchins are more globular in shape than sand dollars, and their common name gives a clue to their shape. In some genera, for example, *Spatangus*, the heart shape is very obvious. Heart urchins are highly evolved for a life of burrowing in sediments, and their spines are beautifully adapted for this purpose, with different shapes and sizes of spines at different points on the test.

Unlike the sand dollars, the heart urchins can burrow down well below the surface of the sediment. In order to obtain a supply of clean oxygenated seawater, they maintain a vertical burrow up through the sand to the surface. As in the sand dollars, their tube feet are arranged in five double rows and resemble petals, but those near the mouth are often extensible.

The widely distributed sea potato, *Echinocardium*, is a heart urchin that shows some of the most effective adaptations to

⬇ **Echinocardium caudatum** *is a European sea potato. This individual, photographed in England, is exposed on the surface of the sand below which it normally lives.*

burrowing life found in the animal kingdom. Several factors have allowed it to be particularly successful under the sand. First, *Echinocardium* has highly modified spines of different shapes and sizes, situated in different positions on the test. The bladelike, curved shape of some spines is good at shifting sand, while the shorter, less-flat ones help maintain the burrow wall. Second, it has highly modified tube feet arranged in five petal-like double rows. Finally, some of the tube feet lack developed suckers, but they secrete quantities of mucus and are used for moving sand particles. Others, such as those positioned around the mouth, have elaborate tips like a chimney sweep's brush and can be extended a very long way.

As the animal moves along under the sand, it communicates with the surface by creating and maintaining a series of vertical tubes or galleries. The long tube feet move up and down the galleries and assist in the circulation of fresh seawater. By keeping itself under the sediment, *Echinocardium* is relatively safe from predators and can feed safely by ingesting the sand in which it lives. The sand is scooped in by the shield-shaped mouth on the underside of the animal's front end. Any organic material in the sediment is digested as food, and the waste material goes out of the anus at the rear end and is buried behind the urchin as it moves along.

One of the great unanswered questions about sea urchins is how animals such as *Echinocardium* navigate under the sand. A study of sea potatoes has shown that the larvae settle offshore on the seabed and that the young urchins all move shoreward, pointing in the same direction. How this precise orientation is achieved is unknown.

⬇ *On a California coast a group of sand dollars feeds on particles of detritus, which they collect using their spines and tube feet.*

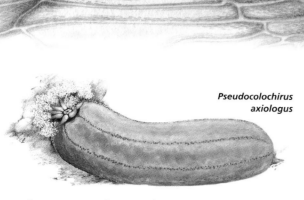

Pseudocolochirus
axiologus

Common name Sea cucumbers

Class Holothuroidea

Subphylum Echinozoa

Phylum Echinodermata

Number of species About 1,150

Size 0.1 in (3 mm) to 5 ft (1.5 m)

Key features Adult body cylindrical or cucumber or
sausage shaped, occasionally very elongated
or slightly flattened; colors varied, often black
or brown, sometimes patterned; 5-sided
symmetry evident in the number of rows of
tube feet on the body; no distinct head;
anterior mouth surrounded by a ring of
specialized, retractable, branched feeding
tube feet (oral tentacles); no brain; tube feet
used for moving usually bear suckers at tips;
calcareous skeleton weakly developed, set in
body wall, which is usually soft and flexible
and lacks ornaments apart from warts; no
jaws; long gut opens via anterior mouth and
posterior anus

Habits Adults bottom-dwelling marine animals;
animal lies on its side; locomotion by tube
feet or wavelike contractions; some forms live
in crevices or burrows

Breeding No mating; sperm and eggs released into
seawater; fertilization occurs outside the
body; eggs develop into microscopic
planktonic larvae

Diet Detritus and plankton collected by deposit- or
suspension-feeding oral tentacles

Habitat Exclusively marine, living on rocks and reefs
or burrowing in sediment

Distribution All the world's seas and oceans at all depths

⤒ *The sea cucumber* Pseudocolochirus axiologus *comes
from the warm waters of the Pacific Ocean. Length 8–10
inches (20–25 cm).*

Sea Cucumbers

Holothuroidea

*Sea cucumbers are considered gourmet food in Asia.
Pharmaceutical companies have also discovered the
anti-inflammatory and anticoagulant properties
of toxins produced by these animals.*

SEA CUCUMBERS ARE BELIEVED to be closely related
to the sea urchins, and both groups belong to
the subphylum Echinozoa. Sea cucumbers are
surprisingly diverse, and all species show a
particular form of five-sided symmetry
(pentamerism). They are basically cucumber
shaped, but have the five characteristic radii
(rows of tube feet) leading away from the
mouth. As in all other echinoderms, the
skeleton is set in the body wall to form the test,
but in sea cucumbers it is of varying thickness
and flexibility. Inside the test there is a body
cavity that houses the intestines, reproductive
organs, and other internal structures.

The relationship between sea cucumbers
and sea urchins is easier to understand if one
imagines that a sea cucumber is rather like a
regular urchin that has grown tall and
cucumberlike and then toppled over onto its
side. At the same time, it has lost its rigid
skeleton and become flexible. These cucumber-
or sausage-shaped animals generally lie
sideways on the seabed, with the mouth at the
front and the anus at the back.

Lopsided Feet

The five-sided symmetry can be seen in the five
double rows of tube feet running along the
body from the mouth toward the anus, just as
in sea urchins. However, because the animals lie
on their side, only three of these rows can
make contact with the seabed. The lower tube
feet are therefore better developed than the
upper ones and function particularly in
locomotion. The upper tube feet do not have a
locomotory role, but instead aid in respiration

⤓ *The amberfish,*
Thelenota anax, *feeds on
the seabed in the Indo-
Pacific Ocean. The upper
surface of this large, flat
cucumber is covered in
rounded tubercles. Warty
growths form an
unbroken line along the
side of its body.*

and in camouflage by holding small items such as sand grains, weeds, and shells against the skin of the upper surface. The nervous system and the vascular system of sea cucumbers are arranged similarly to those of sea urchins, and there is no brain or cluster of sensory organs like those found on the heads of other types of animal.

Sea cucumbers live mainly on the seabed. Many are creeping forms that move over the surface of the sand or gravel using the lower three rows of tube feet. A good example is *Holothuria*. As it creeps along, its oral tentacles sweep the seabed surface for food particles, which are sent into the downward-facing mouth. In *Psolus* the underside is flattened to form a solelike creeping foot, a bit like a snail. Its lower tube feet do not have an important role in locomotion. Its mouth points upward so that it can collect falling particles of food.

⊕ *The armored sea cucumber,* Psolus chitonoides, *from the Pacific Ocean around western Canada shows the vivid red color of its treelike oral tentacles.*

Underwater Adhesive

The test of sea cucumbers is often flexible and fleshy. It is not decorated with spines, but may be smooth or warty. The calcareous plates (known as ossicles) of the endoskeleton (inside the body) are not rigidly interlocked, but are loosely attached to each other to allow for movement. In some sea cucumbers, such as *Synapta* in the order Apodida, the rows of tube feet along the sides of the body have been lost altogether, and movement is achieved by waves of contractions running along the body wall. Movement of this type is known as peristalsis.

These sea cucumbers may feel sticky to the touch. They are not in fact sticky or slimy, but the "stickiness" is caused by specially shaped calcareous ossicles set in the test. They are known as "plate-and-anchor" spicules. They are typical of *Synapta* and its relatives, and the sharp points of the "anchors" are used to grip the seabed. It is also thought that wounds in the body wall can be closed by the spicules on the torn edges sticking to each other. Such a system would work like underwater Velcro™! The shape and texture of sea cucumber skeletal ossicles is a very important factor in helping identify different species.

The deep-sea sea cucumbers in the order Elasipodida are strange-looking animals. In *Molpadia* and *Pelagothuria* parts of the test are extended to form flaplike sails or webs, which probably assist in catching currents that sweep the animal up into the water column.

Burrowing forms occur in the orders Dendrochirotida, Molpadiida, and Apodida. *Cucumaria*, like most dendrochirote sea cucumbers, lives in a "u"-shaped burrow that it digs in the sand. Respiration takes place using branching respiratory organs called trees that open to the exterior via the cloaca (an opening shared with the anus). The cloaca therefore has to communicate with the outside world, so these animals need burrows with openings both at the back and the front for their tentacles to receive food. The molpadiid and apodidan cucumbers do not breathe through the cloaca, so they can manage with a burrow that has just one opening at the front end. They lack tube feet along the body radii and breathe using diffusion across the wall of the test.

Filterers and Sweepers

All sea cucumbers, even those such as *Synapta* whose tube feet have been lost from the sides of the body, have conspicuous feeding tube feet forming a ring around the mouth. They are sometimes called the oral tentacles, and they are used for collecting food. Feeding behavior varies considerably between different groups of sea cucumbers, but the oral tentacles are important in all cases and are adapted to serve different functions. Sea cucumbers feed on plankton, detritus, or on living and dead particles that cover the surfaces of rocks, sands, and gravels where they browse. They can also sweep over the sand and remove organic material from it. Sea cucumbers provide a service to the seabed much like earthworms in the garden and are often very active in rich, productive areas such as sandy terraces around coral reefs.

Sea cucumbers may select food particles according to their size and texture, or the choice may be determined by the fine

ornaments or nodules on the tips of the oral tentacles. Sea cucumbers that pick up particles of detritus have tentacle nodules—minute, sticky, padlike structures of an appropriate size—while those that filter for suspended particles have fine branches at the tips of their oral tentacles. Because the animals are particle feeders, there is no chewing apparatus. Once the tentacles have captured food particles, they bend over the mouth, which opens up to receive both the tentacle tip and the captured food particles. As the tentacle tip is removed from the mouth, the food is wiped off and swallowed.

The gut passes from the mouth through the body cavity, where it forms loops, and then to the anus. It opens either directly to the exterior or via a cloaca, an opening shared with

⬆ A sea cucumber enjoys a meal. It licks the tips of its bushy tentacles one by one to remove particles of food. This individual was photographed in the seas off California.

⬇ Synaptula species sea cucumbers are often found in their hundreds on barrel sponges such as this one in Indonesia.

Secret Weapons

Some sea cucumbers—for example, species such as *Holothuria* and *Actinopyga* in the order Aspidochirotida—have special "secret weapons" known as the Cuvierian organs, after the French naturalist Georges Cuvier. These strange defense devices can eject long, whitish threads into the seawater when the sea cucumber is disturbed by a predator—a dramatic sight! The threads are very sticky and can ensnare and confuse quite large animals. This habit has led to *Holothuria* being given the common name of cotton spinner.

Even more dramatic is the drastic, last-resort defense mechanism used by those species that do not have Cuvierian organs. It involves the spewing out of respiratory trees and part of the gut from the anus, which confuses intruders and creates a huge mess in the water. Regeneration of replacement parts takes a while, during which time the animals have to live on stored food materials.

The Cuvierian organs ejecting the sticky white threads are seen here on Holothuria forskali *in the Red Sea.*

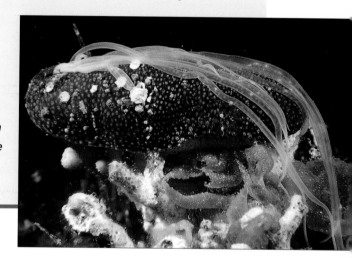

other ducts, including those of the respiratory trees and Cuvierian organs (see above).

Providing Shelter

An interesting association has developed between some species of sea cucumber and the eel-like tropical pearl fish, *Carapus*. These fish can reach up to 6 inches (15 cm) long, and they inhabit the respiratory trees of sea cucumbers such as *Holothuria* and *Stichopus*. Young pearl fish learn to stroke the sea cucumber's cloaca opening with their tail until it relaxes. They then enter the sea cucumber tail first. The fish take shelter in the sea cucumber's respiratory trees by day and leave their host to hunt for food at night.

Oriental Luxuries

Sea cucumbers are commercially important in the trepang fishery industry in the southwestern Pacific (trepang are sea cucumbers that are boiled and dried for making soup). Species such as *Holothuria scabra* are considered a delicacy and are much sought after in Asian food markets. Today sea cucumbers are fished all over the world to meet this demand. However, the demand is so great that fears are being expressed for the survival of some species, and plans are now in place to rear sea cucumbers artificially to supply the market.

Glossary

Words in SMALL CAPITALS refer to other entries in the glossary.

Abductor muscle that opens something, e.g., the jaws of a PEDICELLARIA

Adductor muscle that closes something, e.g., the shells of a clam or oyster

Ambulacrum in echinoderms usually a groove with a row of tube feet on either side; there are generally five per animal. See TUBE FOOT

Ampulla muscular bulblike sac that can hold fluid and pump it along tubes

Axons long microscopic extensions of a nerve cell along which nervous impulses are conducted. Usually minute, but some are larger and are called giant axons

Benthos community of organisms living on the seabed (adj. benthic)

Bilateral symmetry symmetry in one plane, usually longitudinal, where one side of an animal is an approximate mirror image of the other. See RADIAL SYMMETRY

Buccal cavity cavity inside the mouth where food is broken down before being swallowed

Byssus threadlike or hairlike filaments that attach some bivalves to rocks or plants

Calcareous chalky, made of calcium carbonate

Captacula club-tipped, sensory tentacles arranged round the base of the PROBOSCIS in elephant's tusk shells. Used in food selection

Cerata club-shaped, hollow protrusions, each containing a branch of the digestive gland, carried on the backs of some sea slugs

Chitin protein that forms an important component of many invertebrate bodies, e.g., the arthropod exoskeleton

Chromatophores cells in the skin of animals that can change color by contracting or expanding pigment in response to nervous stimulation

Cilium (pl. cilia) tiny hairlike projections growing from individual cells

Class biological grouping containing a number of related ORDERS

Colonial animals that either live together in a social colony, e.g., ants, bees, and termites or share a common body, e.g., hydroids, some corals, sea mats. Colony usually contains individuals with special responsibilities such as feeding or defense

Columella central pillar of the gastropod shell around which the spiral coil is arranged

Crop part of the alimentary canal where food is stored prior to digestion, e.g., in slugs and birds

Detritus an accumulation of tiny particles of dead or decomposing material in the water column—an important component of the food chain

Devonian period a geological interval that began 408 million years ago

Dorsal anatomical upper side of bilaterally symmetrical animal. See BILATERAL SYMMETRY

Epipodial lobes in elephant's tusk shells a pair of lobes arranged just behind the pointed tip of the foot

Epipodial tentacles sensory tentacles arranged on the edges of the foot of archaeogastropods such as top shells

Family a biological grouping of genera (pl. of GENUS) more closely related to one another than any other grouping of genera and always ending in -idae, e.g., the giant clam belongs to the family Tridacnidae

Fouling blocking or covering; often used when marine invertebrates block structures such as cooling ducts or encrust the bottoms of ships

Genus (pl. genera) a group of SPECIES all more closely related to one another than to any other group of SPECIES

Glochidia the larvae of some freshwater mussels. They have embryonic shells with teeth to grip onto the fins of fish. See LARVA

Hectocotylised an arm of a male squid or octopus that is specialized for transferring sperm to the female during copulation

Hermaphrodite having both female and male sex organs, not necessarily at the same time

Holdfast part of a marine animal or plant that attaches it to rocks or other structures

Homing scar round mark worn in the rocks by the shell of a limpet when it returns to rest in the same place after feeding excursions

Interambulacrum area of the TEST of an echinoderm lying between two ambulacra. See AMBULACRUM

Larva juvenile stage between egg and adult

Lunule in some bivalves a small heart-shaped depression in the shells, near the hinge

Mantle special region of the body wall, particularly of mollusks, that encloses the MANTLE CAVITY and may secrete the shell

Mantle cavity space enclosed by the MANTLE in mollusks, through which a stream of water circulates, bringing oxygen and taking away waste products. Contains the gills and the reproductive and excretory openings

Odontophore a pulleylike structure in gastropods that allows the ribbonlike RADULA to move back and forth, scraping organisms from the rocks

Operculum CALCAREOUS buttonlike plate on the foot of gastropod mollusks, used to close the shell after the body has been withdrawn

Order a biological grouping of FAMILIES more closely related to one another than to any other grouping of FAMILIES. For example, the octopuses belong to the order Octopoda

Osphradium the organ inside the MANTLE CAVITY of gastropod mollusks, such as whelks, that detects the sent of prey or predators

Palps appendages of the head that are sensory and that may assist with handling food, e.g., in worms and insects

Pedicellaria (pl. pedicellariae) minute grooming organs in starfish and sea urchins, resembling microscopic forceps, often borne on movable stalks

Pentamerism fivefold symmetry found in echinoderms

Periostracum horny, pigmented outer layer of some mollusk shells

Phylum a major group used in the classification of animals, consisting of one or more CLASSES

Phytoplankton plant PLANKTON

Pinnules branches of the arms of crinoids that also bear reproductive structures and tube feet. See TUBE FOOT

Plankton organisms, usually (but not always) small to microscopic, that drift in the surface waters of rivers, lakes, and seas

Proboscis tubelike feeding apparatus, common in insects and animals such as whelks

Purpurin poison secreted by some neogastropods to kill their prey. Also used as a purple dye in classical times

Radial symmetry symmetry in which the body consists of a central axis around which similar parts are arranged symmetrically. See BILATERAL SYMMETRY

Radula small horny tonguelike strip bearing teeth, used by many mollusks for scraping food

Ray one radius of a starfish containing one AMBULACRUM on the underside

Reefal relating to reefs, especially coral reefs

Retractor muscles muscles used to pull structures back into the shell or body, e.g., the foot of bivalves

Sediment in marine biology refers to the accumulation of muds, sands, gravels, and shingles on the seabed

Segment a section of a body part, such as the abdomen, antenna, or leg

Sinus space inside the body usually filled with blood or other fluid

Siphon tube leading into or out of the bodies of invertebrates (especially mollusks) and used for conducting water currents

Species a group of organisms that mate readily and produce healthy fertile offspring

Sphaeridium (pl. sphaeridia) microscopic club-shaped appendage of sea urchins, thought to be an organ of balance

Statocyst balance organ

Subradula organ sensory structure situated below the RADULA of chitons. Used at the start of feeding to test for presence and suitability of food

Symbiont an organism of one species that lives in close association with one of another species to their mutual advantage

Test external covering or "shell" of invertebrates, especially sea urchins. It is, in fact, an internal skeleton and lies just below the epidermis

Torsion twisting of the body applied particularly to an event in the development of certain larvae, e.g., gastropods. See LARVA

Trochophore free-swimming larval form of annelid worms and some mollusks. See LARVA

Tube foot hollow appendage of echinoderms connected to the WATER VASCULAR SYSTEM. May have suckers or carry CILIA that waft particles of food toward the mouth

Umbilicus aperture at the base of the COLUMELLA of the gastropod shell, appearing on the underside in the center of many shells

Umbo (pl. umbones) the oldest pointed part of the bivalve shell on the DORSAL side

Veliger type of microscopic marine planktonic LARVA typical of most mollusks, related in form to the TROCHOPHORE

Ventral anatomical lower side of bilaterally symmetrical animal. See BILATERAL SYMMETRY

Visceral hump part of the gastropod body containing most of the internal organs

Water vascular system hydraulic system unique to the echinoderms, made up of a system of vessels and organs such as the tube feet, and fulfilling various functions, especially locomotion and feeding

Zooplankton animal PLANKTON

Zooxanthellae minute single-celled plants that live within animal tissues and have an intimate physiological relationship with the host organism

Further Reading

General

Barnes, R. D., **Invertebrate Zoology**, Saunders College Publishing, Philadelphia, PA, 1987

Specific to this volume

Abbot, R. Tucker, **Seashells of North America: A Guide to Field Identification**, Golden Books, New York, NY, 2003

Banister, K., and Campbell, A., **The Encyclopedia of Aquatic Life**, Facts on File, New York, NY, 1985

Barker, G.M., **The Biology of Terrestrial Molluscs**, Cabi Publishing, Wallingford, U.K., 2001

Canizares, S., **What Comes in a Shell?**, Scholastic, New York, NY, 1998

Fredericks, A.D., **Slugs**, Lerner, Minneapolis, MN, 2000

Hayward, P., Nelson-Smith, Shields, C., **Sea Shores of Britain and Europe**, Harper Collins, London, U.K., 1996

Meinkoth, N. A., **National Audubon Society Field Guide to North American Seashore Creatures**, Alfred A. Knopf, New York, NY, 1998

Pascoe, E., **Snails and Slugs**, Blackbirch Press, Bellevue, WA, 1998

Wright Robinson, W., **How Shellmakers Build Their Amazing Homes**, Blackbirch Press, Bellevue, WA, 1999

Useful Websites

General

http://www.calacademy.org
Website of the California Academy of Science

http://www.tolweb.org/tree/mollusca/bilateria
The Tree of Life website includes extensive information on mollusks, snails, clams, mussels, octopuses, chitons, and elephant's tusk shells. On more than 2,600 World Wide Web pages the Tree of Life provides information about the diversity of organisms on earth, their history, and characteristics. Each page contains information about one group of organisms

Specific to this volume

http://www.amonline.net.au/invertebrates/mal/
Australian Museum online. A good section on invertebrate zoology, including snails and sea slugs

http://www.oceanicresearch.org
Oceanic Research Group, Inc. is a nonprofit environmental organization dedicated to ocean conservation. Click on Education and then Wonders of the Sea for information about echinoderms

http://www.starfish.ch/reef/echinoderms.html
A useful website containing detailed information about echinoderms and many photographs

http://www.ucmp.berkeley.edu/echinodermata
The University of Calfornia Museum of Paleontology Website provides a basic introduction to the Echinodermata

http://www.ucmp.berkeley.edu/mollusca/mollusca.html
A basic introduction to mollusks

Set Index

A **bold** number shows the volume and is followed by the relevant page numbers (e.g., **21:** 52, 74).

Common names in **bold** (e.g., **aphids**) mean that the animal has an illustrated main entry in the set. Underlined page numbers (e.g., **29:** <u>78–79</u>) refer to the main entry for that animal.

Italic page numbers (e.g., **22:** *103*) point to illustrations of animals in parts of the set other than the main entry.

Page numbers in parentheses—e.g., **21:** (24)—locate information in At-a-Glance boxes.

Animals that have main entries in the set are indexed under their common names, alternative common names, and scientific names.

A

abalones **30:** 22, 23
  red **30:** *23*
Ablattara laevigata **25:** *30*
Abraxas grossulariata
  26: 14–15
Acantharia **21:** 13
Acanthaspis **24:** *38*
Acanthaster planci
  30: (102–103)
Acanthobdellae **21:** 94
Acanthocardia echinata
  30: 66
Acanthocephala **21:** 32, 77
Acanthocirrus retrirostris
  21: *85*
Acanthoclonia paradoxa
  22: *32*
Acanthocoris sordidus
  24: (54)
Acanthophorus **25:** *8–9*
Acanthoplus armativentris
  23: *15*
Acanthops falcataria **22:** *79*
Acanthosomatidae **24:** 14,
  (71)
Acari **29:** <u>30–33</u>
Acharia **26:** *107*
  A. stimulae **26:** *106*
Achatina achatina **30:** *48*
Achias australis **23:** *87*
Acoela **21:** (81)
acraeas **26:** (55)
Acrididae **23:** *10*, <u>24–31</u>
Acrocinus longimanus
  25: *90*
Acromis sparsa
  25: *102–103*, (103)
Acronicta aceris **26:** *96*
Acrophylla titan **22:** *52, 55*
Acrothoracica **28:** 9
Acteon eloiseae **30:** 36
Actias luna **26:** *71*
Actinaria **21:** 43, <u>56–61</u>
Actinia equina **21:** *56, 59*
Actinophrys **21:** *21*
Actinote
  A. alcione **26:** *55*
  A. pellenia trinitatis
    26: *13*
Actinulida **21:** 43
Aculeata **27:** 8, 10–11
Adalia
  A. 2-punctata **25:** 54–55,
    56
  A. 10-punctata **25:** *54–55*
Adejeania vexatris
  23: *104–105*

Aegla **28:** *87*
Aeglidae **28:** 86
Aeropetes tulbaghia
  26: *46–47*
Aeshna
  A. cyanea **22:** *42, 43,*
    48
  A. juncea **22:** *51*
Aetalionidae (Aethalionidae)
  24: (95)
Aetalion reticulatum **24:** *95*
Aetheriidae **30:** 50
Agapostemon **27:** *11*
Agathemera **22:** *56–57*
Agelas conifera **21:** *36*
Agelena labyrinthica **29:** *94,*
  (96), 97
Agelenidae **29:** *40*, <u>94–97</u>
Agelenopsis aperta **29:** *95*
Aglais urticae **26:** *42–43*
Aglaophenia cupressina
  21: *46–47*
Agraulis vanillae **26:** *53*
Agrilus discolor **25:** *48*
Agriotes ustulatus **25:** *42*
Agriphila tristella **26:** *103*
Agulla **22:** *100–101*
  A. nixa **22:** *100*
alates **27:** 44
Alaus corpulentus **25:** *44*
Alcyonaria **21:** 43
Alcyonium digitatum **21:** *62*
alderflies 22: <u>98–99</u>;
  27: 26–27
  European **22:** *98*
alder psyllids **24:** *96,*
  96–97
Aleyrodidae **24:** *98–99*
Alicia mirabilis **21:** *58–59*
Alima **28:** *41*
Alleculidae **25:** (73)
Allgalathea elegans **28:** (89)
Alloeostylus diaphanus
  23: *101*
Alpaida cornuta **29:** *111*
Alydidae **24:** (56)
Amaryllis philatelica **28:** *45*
Amarynthis meneria
  26: *36–37*
Amauris ochlea **26:** *59*
Amaurobiidae **29:** <u>52–53</u>
Amaurobius similis **29:** *52,*
  52–53, 53
amberfish **30:** *110–111*
Amblyomma **29:** *31*
Amblypygi **29:** <u>26–27</u>
Ambulyx moorei **26:** *69*
Ameba proteus **21:** *13, 18,*
  19

amebas
  and allies 21: <u>18–21</u>
  reproduction **21:** *14*
  shelled, reproduction
    21: *14*
  tests (shells) **21:** 20, 21
Amitermes meridionalis
  22: (64)
Ammophila
  A. aberti **27:** *13*
  A. laevigatum **27:** *80–81*
  A. pubescens **27:** *77*
Amorena undulata **30:** *35*
Amphipoda **28:** 34,
  <u>44–45</u>
Amphitrite johnstoni **21:** *97*
Amulius longiceps **24:** *13*
Amyciaea lineatipes **29:** *69*
Amycta quadrangularis
  26: *110*
Anaea fabius **26:** *39*
Aname grandis **29:** *48–49*
Anapsidacea **28:** 34, 36
Anartia amathea **26:** *10, 44*
Anaspides tasmaniae **28:** *37*
Ancyluris aulestes **26:** *34*
Andara **30:** *53*
Andrena
  A. haemorrhoa **27:** *92–93*
  A. nigroaenea **27:** *93*
  A. nitida **27:** *94*
Andrenidae **27:** <u>92–95</u>
Anelosimus eximius
  29: (101)
Aniculus elegans **28:** *94–95*
animals
  animal kingdom
    21: <u>28–33</u>
  classification **21:** (28)
  diploblastic **21:** 30, 42
  first 21: <u>34–35</u>
  larval types **21:** 31–32
  multicellular **21:** 30–31
  spiny-skinned 30: <u>90–93</u>
  symmetry in **21:** 30
  triploblastic **21:** 30–31
Anisomorpha buprestoides
  22: *52–53, 57*
Anisoptera **22:** 42
Anisozygoptera **22:** 42
Annelida **21:** 32, 77, <u>94–97</u>
  fossils **21:** 96–97
  locomotion **21:** (96)
Anobiidae **25:** (53)
Anobium punctatum
  25: (53)
Anodonta cygnea **30:** *60*
Anomiidae **30:** 59
Anomura **28:** 56, 58
Anopheles **23:** (49)
Anopia **21:** 77
Anostraca **28:** 16–18
Antedon bifida **30:** *94*
Antheraea
  A. eucalypti **26:** *72*
  A. oculea **26:** *73*
Anthia hexasticta **25:** *18–19*
Anthocoridae **24:** (35)
Anthonomus grandis
  25: (110)
Anthophora plumipes
  27: *96–97*
Anthophoridae **27:** <u>96–101</u>

Anthozoa **21:** 43, <u>62–67</u>
anthrax **23:** 103, 108
Anthrax seriepunctata
  23: *70*
Anthrenus verbasci **25:** *53*
Anthribidae **25:** 104
Anthuridea **28:** 34
Antiantha expansa
  24: *92–93*
Antipatharia **21:** 43
ant lions **22:** 90, 95–96
ants 27: <u>8–13</u>, 40–57
  alates **27:** 44
  army **27:** 54–56
  bullet **27:** *41*, 56–57
  caterpillars and
    26: 31–33, 36–37
  cow-killer velvet
    27: 38–39
  Cremastocheilus beetles
    inhabiting ants' nests
    25: (86)
  crickets living in ants'
    nests **23:** (19)
  defense, chemical **27:** 42
  driver **27:** *45*
  green tree **27:** 48–49
  harvester **27:** 40–41, 52
  honeydew supplies
    27: (48)
  honeypot **27:** 52
  jet black **27:** *47*
  leaf-cutting **27:** *44*, 50–51
  nests **27:** 44–47, 51–52
  plants and **27:** (46)
  red **27:** *49*
  scent trails **27:** (45)
  slave-making **27:** 49–50
  sociability **27:** 40
  tandem running **27:** (45)
  termite-slaying **27:** 43
  treehoppers and **24:** (93)
  velvet **27:** <u>38–39</u>
  weaver **27:** 40–41,
    42–43, 52–54
  western harvester **27:** 52
  white *see* termites
Anyphaena accentuata
  29: *42–43*, (81)
Anyphaenidae **29:** (81)
Apaturinae **26:** 40
Aphasmida **21:** 77
Aphididae **24:** 14, <u>100–105</u>
aphids 24: 14, <u>100–105</u>;
  25: 57; **27:** *49*
  bean **24:** *102*
  cabbage **24:** *105*
  defense **24:** 103, 105
  feeding **24:** 100–101,
    102–103
  life cycle **24:** 101–102
  lupin **24:** *14*
  peach-potato **24:** *100*
  rose-root **24:** *103*
Aphis fabae **24:** *102*
  breeding **24:** 101–102
Aphonopelma seemannii **29:**
  46–47
Aphrocallistes vastus **21:** *39*
Aphrodes bifasciatus **24:** *86*
Aphrodite aculeata **21:** *99*
Apicomplexa **21:** 13, <u>26–27</u>
Apidae **27:** <u>102–113</u>
Apiomeris flaviventris
  24: *40*
Apioscelis bulbosa **23:** *33*

Apis
  A. mellifera **27:** *102, 112*
  A. mellifera scutellata
    27: (111)
Aplacophora **30:** 9
Aplysia punctata **30:** *36–37*
Aplysiomorpha **30:** 18, 37
Apocrita **27:** 8, 10–11, *12*
Apoderus coryli **25:** *109*
apollos (swallowtail
  butterflies) **26:** <u>16–21</u>
Apseudomorpha **28:** 34
Aptera fusca **22:** *70*
Apterygota **22:** 30
Arachnida **29:** 8, 9
arachnids 29: <u>14–15</u>
  anatomy **29:** 14–15
Arachnocoris **24:** *36–37*
arachnology **21:** (33)
Aradidae **24:** <u>50–51</u>
Aradus depressus **24:** 50
Araneidae **29:** <u>106–111</u>
Araneomorphae **29:** 38,
  41
Araneus **29:** *44*
  A. diadematus
    29: *110–111*
Arcas imperialis **26:** *31*
Archaeogastropoda **30:** 18,
  <u>22–25</u>
Archeognatha **22:** 30, (37)
Archiacanthocephala **21:** 77
Archiannelida **21:** 77, 94, 96
Archidoris pseudoargus
  30: *38*
Arcidae **30:** 50, 53
Arctia caja **26:** *88, 90*
Arctiidae **26:** <u>88–91</u>
  sound production **26:** (91)
Argiope
  A. argentata **29:** *106–107*
  A. bruennichi **29:** *106*
  A. versicolor **29:** *44–45*
Argonauta **30:** 72
Argonauta
  A. argo **30:** (89)
  A. nodosa **30:** *89*
argonauts **30:** 84, (89)
Argopecten irradians **30:** *8*
Argynnis paphia **26:** *12*
Argyroneta aquatica
  29: (110)
Arhynchobdellae **21:** 94
Arilus **24:** *42–43*
Ariolimax californicus **30:** *49*
Aristotle **21:** 8, (28)
Aristotle's lantern **30:** 93,
  106
Arixeniina **22:** (59)
Armadillidium vulgare
  28: *46*
Armophorea **21:** 13
Arrhenodes minutus
  25: *112*
Artemia salina **28:** *19*
Arthropoda **21:** 32
arthropods 22: <u>8–13</u>
  anatomy **22:** 9–11
  classification **22:** 8
  relatives **22:** 12
Articulata **21:** 69, 70, 71;
  30: <u>94–97</u>
Ascalopteryx **22:** *97*
Ascaris suum **21:** *90*
Asellota **28:** 34
Asilidae **23:** <u>62–67</u>

Asilus crabroniformis
23: *66–67*
Aspidomorpha punctata
25: *100*
Astacidea **28:** 56, *70–79*
Astacopis gouldi **28:** (71)
astartes **30:** 62
Asteroidea **30:** 91, 98
Asterozoa **30:** 91, 98–103
Astraea undosa **30:** *24*
Astroma **23:** (33)
Athecanephria **21:** 77
Atrax robustus **29:** 48
Atta **27:** 51
   A. *bisphearica* **27:** *51*
   A. *cephalotes* **27:** *44,*
     50–51
Attacus
   A. *atlas* **22:** *11*
   A. *edwardsi* **26:** *70*
Attelabus nitens **25:** *109*
Atteva punctella **26:** *112*
Atyidae **28:** (64)
Atypidae **29:** 50–51
Atypus affinis **29:** *50*
Auchenorrhyncha **24:** 8, 10,
   12, 13
Aurelia aurita **21:** *50*
Austrodromidia octodentata
28: *111*
Austropotamobius pallipes
28: *75*
Autographa gamma **26:** *95*
autotrophs **21:** 9

B

Baccha obscuripennis **23:** *77*
backswimmers 24: 24–27
Baetis rhodani **22:** *39*
Balanoglossus **21:** *79*
Balanus nubilis **28:** *25*
barklice 22: 86–87
barnacles 28: 10, 22–27
   acorn **22:** 8; **28:** 22
   commensal **28:** 26
   giant acorn **28:** 25
   goose **28:** 24–25, (24),
     27
   parasitic **28:** 26
   reproduction **28:** 26–27
   barnacle zone **28:** (27)
Baroniinae **26:** 16–17
basket stars 30: 98–103
Basommatophora **30:** 18,
   45–46
Batanota **25:** *101*
Batazonellus fuliginosus
27: *60–61, 61*
Bathynellacea **28:** 34, 36
Batocera parryi **25:** *90–91*
Batocnema coquereli **26:** *67*
Battus philenor **26:** *18,*
   20–21
Bdelloidea **21:** 69
beach fleas 28: 44–45
bedbugs 24: 34–35
bees 27: 8–13
   carpenter **22:** *35*
   carpenter 27: 96–101
   creeping willow **27:** *90*
   digger 27: 96–101
   and flowers **27:** (105)
   forked-tongue **27:** *89–90*
   hairy-legged mining
     27: *90–91*

bees (continued)
   honeybees and
     relatives 27: 102–113
   leaf-cutter and relatives
     27: 84–91
   leaf-cutting (leaf-cutter)
     27: 84–91
   masked **27:** 89–90
   mason **27:** 84, 87–88
   mining 27: 92–95
   orchid **27:** 102–103
   pygmy flower **27:** *11,* (95)
   red mason **27:** *85, 88*
   stingless **24:** 107–108;
     27: 102, 108–109
   wool-carder **27:** 84,
     88–89
beetles 25: 8–15
   anatomy **25:** 8–12
   antennae **25:** (10)
   asparagus **25:** *98*
   bee **25:** 86–87
   betsy (bessbugs) **25:** (75)
   blister 25: 62–67
   bombardier **25:** (18)
   brown tiger **25:** *20*
   burying (carrion)
     25: 28–31
   cardinal (fire-colored)
     25: 60–61
   carpet **25:** 53
   carrion 25: 28–31
   caterpillar hunters **25:** 16,
     17
   cellar **25:** *68*
   chafer *see* chafers
   checkered 25: 40–41
   churchyard **25:** *68*
   click 25: 42–45
   cockchafer **22:** *35*
   cock-tail (rove) **25:** *32–33*
   Colorado potato **25:** *103*
   comb-clawed **25:** (73)
   darkling 25: 68–73
   deathwatch **25:** *53,* (53)
   digestive system **25:** 12
   diving 25: 24–25
   drugstore **25:** (53)
   dung **25:** 76–77, (78), 81
   eggs **25:** 12
   elephant **25:** *87, 88–89*
   European bee-wolf **25:** *40*
   European pot-bellied
     emerald **25:** *13, 99*
   European wasp **25:** *95*
   false blister **25:** (61)
   feeding **25:** 8, 12, 13
   fire-colored 25: 60–61
   fireflies 25: 36–37
   fleet-footed tiger **25:** *12*
   flower **25:** 85–87
   forked fungus **25:** 70
   furniture **25:** (53)
   glowworms **25:** (35)
   Goliath **25:** 85–87
   green tiger **25:** *22*
   ground 25: 16–19
   hairy fungus **25:** (52)
   handsome fungus
     25: (52)
   harlequin **25:** *90;* **29:** (21)
   Hercules **25:** *76, 87*
   hide **25:** (81)
   ironclad **25:** *73*
   jewel 25: 46–49
   ladybug 25: 54–59

beetles (continued)
   ladybug **24:** *104–105*
   larder **25:** 53
   leaden tortoise **25:** *14–15*
   leaf 25: *13,* 96–103
   long-horned 25: 8–9,
     90–95
   metallic wood-boring
     (jewel) **25:** 46–49
   mint leaf **25:** *96, 97*
   museum (carpet) **25:** 53
   Neptune **25:** *86–87*
   net-winged 25: 38–39
   oil **25:** 62
   patent-leather (bessbugs)
     25: (75)
   pleasing fungus
     25: 50–53
   reproduction and growth
     25: 12–14
   rhinoceros **25:** 87
   rove 25: 32–33
   scarab 25: 76–89
   sexton (carrion) **25:** 28–31
   soldier 25: 34–35
   speckled-bellied fungus
     25: *51*
   splendor (jewel)
     25: 46–49
   stag 22: *32;* **25:** 74–75
   thick-legged flower
     25: *61*
   tiger 25: 20–23
   Titan **25:** 90
   tortoise **25:** *96, 100, 101,*
     102–103
   undertaker (carrion)
     25: 28–31
   Vedalia **25:** (56)
   waltzing (whirligig)
     25: 26–27
   warty leaf **25:** *96–97*
   water (diving) **25:** 24–25
   water scavenger **25:** (26)
   wharf borer **25:** (61)
   whirligig 25: 26–27
   see also weevils
Belonogaster juncea **27:** *11*
Belostomatidae **24:** (21)
Bembix **27:** *80*
Berytidae **24:** (49)
bessbugs **25:** (75)
Bibio
   B. *hortulanus* **23:** *54–55*
   B. *marci* **23:** 54, 55
Bibionidae **23:** 54–55
Bilateria **21:** 30, 32
bilharzia/ziasis **21:** (83);
   30: 21, 46
binary fission **21:** 14, 25
biological control *see* pest
   control
bioluminescence **28:** 29
birdwings (swallowtail
   butterflies) **26:** 16–21
   Queen Alexandra's
     26: 16, *16*
Birgus latro **28:** (100)
Biston
   B. *betularia* **26:** (75)
   B. *straria* **26:** 74
Bittacus italicus **22:** *109*
bivalves 30: 50–53
   anatomy **30:** 50–52
   attachment to surfaces
     30: (52)

bivalves (continued)
   primitive **30:** 53
   rock boring **30:** (66)
Bivalvia **30:** 9, 10, 50–53
bladderworm **21:** *84*
Blaps mucronata **25:** *68*
Blattodea **22:** 30, 68–73
bloodworms **21:** *103;* **23:** *51*
blues (gossamer-winged
   butterflies) **26:** 28, 29
   Adonis **26:** *29, 30*
   imperial **26:** *31*
   large **26:** *28*
   pygmy **26:** 28
Boisea trivittata **24:** *58,*
   58–59
Bolitotherus cornutus **25:** 70
Bombus
   B. *hortorum* **27:** *106–107*
   B. *lucorum* **29:** *33*
   B. *pascuorum* **27:** *105*
   B. *pratorum* **27:** *106*
   B. *terrestris* **27:** *104–105*
Bombycidae **26:** 78–79
Bombyliidae **23:** 68–71
Bombylius major **23:** *68*
Bombyx mori **26:** *78*
booklice 22: 86–87
   winged **22:** 86–87
Brachinus **25:** (18)
Brachionus **21:** *68*
Brachiopoda **21:** 32, 69,
   70–71
Brachycaudus cardui
   24: *100–101*
Brachycera **23:** 36, 39
Brachyomus
   octotuberculatus **25:** *106*
Brachypelma smithi **29:** *46*
Brachytrupes orientalis
   23: *19*
Brachyura **28:** 56, 58,
   102–113
Branchiopoda **28:** 9, 16–21
   feeding **28:** 19–20
   locomotion **28:** 19
Brassolidae **26:** 48–49
Brentidae **25:** 112–113
Brentus **25:** 113
   B. *anchorago* **25:** *113*
Brephidium exilis **26:** 28
Brevicoryne brassicae
   24: *105*
Brevisiana **24:** *82*
bristletails **22:** (37)
brittle stars 30: 98–103
browns (satyrs) **26:** 46–47
Bryozoa **21:** 32, 69, 72–73
bubonic plague **22:** (113)
Buccinum **30:** *32*
   B. *undatum* **30:** *19, 32*
budding **21:** 14
bugs 22: *31;* **24:** 8–15
   assassin 24: 10, 13, 14,
     15, 38–43; **27:** *39*
   backswimmers
     24: 24–27
   bark 24: 50–51
   bedbugs 24: 34–35
   box elder **24:** (59)
   broad-headed **24:** (56)
   burrower **24:** (66)
   capsid (plant) **24:** 8,
     30–33
   cochineal **24:** (109)
   cone-nose **24:** *41*

bugs (continued)
   cotton-stainers (stainers)
     24: 48–49
   creeping thistle lace
     24: 28–29
   damsel 24: 36–37
   definition **24:** 8
   eastern box elder **24:** *58,*
     59, (59)
   eggplant lace **24:** (29)
   families **24:** 8
   feeding **24:** 12–13
   fire (stainers) **24:** 48–49
   flag-footed (leaf-footed)
     24: 8–9, 14, 52–57
   flat (bark) **24:** 50–51
   flower **24:** (35)
   fulgorid (lanternflies)
     24: *12,* 72–77
   fungus (bark) **24:** 50–51
   giant shield **24:** (64)
   giant water **24:** 20–21,
     (21)
   golden egg **24:** 55–56
   green capsid **24:** 30–31
   ground (seed) **24:** *11,*
     44–47
   harlequin **24:** *70*
   lace 24: 28
   leaf (plant) **24:** 8, 30–33
   leaf-footed 24: 8–9, 14,
     52–57
   lightning (fireflies)
     25: 36–37
   litter **22:** *72*
   marsh damsel **24:** *36–37*
   Mexican bed **24:** *41*
   minute pirate **24:** (35)
   peanut **24:** 76
   peanut-head **24:** 76
   pill **28:** 46, 48
   pinching (stag beetles)
     25: 74–75
   plant 24: 8, 30–33
   plataspid stink **24:** (63)
   red (stainers) **24:** 48–49;
     29: (32)
   ripple 24: 18–19
   scentless plant
     24: 58–59
   scuttle (whirligig beetles)
     25: 26–27
   seed 24: *11,* 44–47
   shield-backed 24: 70–71
   shield (stink) **24:** 10, 14,
     60–69, (71)
   shore **24:** (23)
   short-horned **24:** *76–77,*
     (77)
   sow **28:** 46
   spider **24:** (33)
   spittlebugs 24: 78–79
   squash (leaf-footed)
     24: 8–9, 14, 52–57
   stainers 24: *11,* 48–49
   stilt **24:** (49)
   stink 24: 10, 60–69
   "Sultan" **24:** (54)
   thorn **24:** *90, 90–91,*
     93–94
   thunder (thrips)
     22: 84–85
   tip-wilter (leaf-footed)
     24: 8–9, 14, 52–57
   toad 24: 22–23
   tortoise **24:** *70*

bugs (continued)
  true *see* true bugs
  water measurers **24**: (19)
  water scorpions
    24: 20–21
  water striders 24: 16–17
  western box elder
    24: (59)
  wheel **24**: 42–43
  woundwort stink **24**: 67
Bullomorpha **30**: 18
bumblebees, white-tailed
  29: 33
bumblebees (honeybees)
  27: 102, 103–108
  buff-tailed **27**: 104–105
  carder **27**: 105
  garden **27**: 106–107
Buprestidae **25**: 46–49
buprestins **25**: 46
butterflies 26: 8–15
  African monarch **26**: 60
  alfalfa **26**: 22
  American monarch
    26: 58
  anatomy **26**: 10, 11–12
  Aracne checkerspots
    26: 44–45
  army-ant (ithomiids)
    26: 56–57
  Artemesia swallowtail
    26: 16–17
  blue morpho **26**: 50
  brimstone **26**: 22–23
  brush-footed 26: 11, 11,
    38–45
  buckeye **26**: 41
  classification example
    21: (8)
  coolie **26**: 10, 44
  eggs **26**: 12–13,
    (13)
  gossamer-winged
    26: 28–33
  green-lined charaxes
    26: 38–39
  gulf fritillary **26**: 53
  life cycle **26**: 13
  milkweed **26**: 58–61
  mimicry **22**: 34
  monarch **21**: (8); **26**: 15,
    60, 61
  owl 26: 48–49
  painted lady **26**: 38–39
  passion-flower
    (longwings) **26**: 52–55
  pipevine swallowtail
    26: 20–21
  puddling **26**: (15),
    16–17
  pupae **26**: 14–15
  red admiral **26**: 38
  silver emperor **26**: 41
  silver-washed fritillary
    26: 12
  six-tailed brush-foot
    26: 37
  swallowtail 26: 16–21
  tiger swallowtail **26**: 21
  whites *see* whites
  wing colors **26**: (11)
  see also caterpillars
butterfly lions **22**: 90,
  96
byssus threads **30**: (52), 59,
  63, (65)

C

caddisflies 22: 102–103
  great red sedge **22**: 102
Caenorhabditis elegans
  21: (90)
Caepaea nemoralis **30**: 19
Caerostris, C. mitralis
  29: 108
Calais (click beetle) **25**: 44
Calanoida **28**: 9
Calephelis perditalis **26**: 34
Caligo
  C. atreus **26**: 48
  C. memnon **26**: 49
  C. opsiphanes **26**: 48
Caligus rapax **28**: 30
Calliactis parasitica **21**: 60;
  28: (97)
Calliphora
  C. vicina **23**: 108–109
  C. vomitoria **23**: 108
Calliphoridae **23**: 108–111
Callophrys rubi **26**: 28–29
Calopteryx splendens **22**: 45
Calosoma
  C. scrutator **25**: 17
  C. sycophanta **25**: 16
Calyptocephalus gratiosus
  25: 37
Calyptraeidae **30**: 29–30
Cambaris monongalensis
  28: 58
Camponotus detritus
  27: 42–43
Camposcia retusa
  28: 110–111
Cancer gracialis **28**: 12–13
Canephora unicolor **26**: 110
cannibalism
  lobsters and crayfish
    28: 76
  mantids **22**: 77–78
  shrimps and prawns
    28: 66
  web spinners **22**: 82
Cantharidae **25**: 34–35
cantharidin **25**: 62, (63), 65
Cantharis rustica **25**: 34
Canthesancus gulo **24**: 38
Capolymma stygia **25**: 95
Caprellidae **28**: 34
Caprellidea **28**: 34
Carabidae **25**: 16–19
carcinology **21**: (33)
Carcinus maenas **28**: 102
Cardiidae **30**: 50, 65–67
Cardium edule **30**: 62–63
Caria mantinea **26**: 34–35
Caridea **28**: 56, 60–69
Casella astromarginata
  30: 20–21
Cassiopeia frondosa **21**: 53
Catacanthus anchorago
  24: 60
Catacola amatrix **26**: 92
caterpillar hunters **25**: 16,
  17
caterpillars **26**: 13–14
  Amycta quadrangularis
    26: 110
  butterfly **27**: 48–49
  California tent caterpillar
    moth **26**: 86
  Caligo opsiphanes **26**: 48
  cinnabar moth **26**: 90

caterpillars (continued)
  cloudless sulfur **26**: 24–25
  cup moth **26**: 107
  danaid **26**: 58–59
  Eucylodes **26**: (76)
  European drinker moth
    26: 85
  European feathered thorn
    26: 76
  European large elephant
    hawk moth **26**: 68
  European puss moth
    26: 82
  European sycamore moth
    26: 96
  Euthalia **26**: 42
  geometrid **26**: (76)
  gypsy moth **26**: (101)
  Heliconius sara **26**: 55
  hieroglyphic moth **26**: 97
  ithomiid **26**: 56
  lackey moth **26**: 86
  Lirimiris **26**: 82
  Lycaenidae **26**: 30–31
  monkey slug **26**: 106
  mottled umber **26**: 77
  Naprepa **26**: 82
  Narathura **26**: 32–33
  narrow-bordered five-spot
    burnet moth **26**: 109
  noctuid **26**: 95–97
  notodontids **26**: 81–83
  Oiketicus elongatus
    26: 111
  orchard swallowtail
    26: 18–19
  owlet moth **26**: 97
  pipevine swallowtail
    26: 18
  plume moths
    26: 102–103
  Prepona antimache
    26: 40
  red dagger wing
    26: 42–43
  saturniid **26**: 72–73
  silkworm moths **26**: 79
  skippers **26**: 64
  small tortoiseshell
    26: 42–43
  sphinx moth **26**: 67–69
  swallowtail **26**: (19), 20
  western tussock moth
    26: 100
  wood-boring
    26: 104–105
  yponomeutid
    26: 112–113
Cathedra serrata **24**: 72–73
Cathimeris hymenaea
  27: 36–37
Cauricara eburnea **25**: 69
Celaenia kinbergi **29**: (108)
cellulose **28**: 49
centipedes 22: 22–25
  defense **22**: (24)
  European common
    22: 22–23
  house **22**: 9, 22
Cephalocarida **28**: 9, (14)
Cephalochordata **21**: 32
Cephalopoda **30**: 9, 10
cephalopods 30: 72–73
Cerambycidae **25**: 90–95
Ceramius tuberculifer **27**: 69
Ceratitis capitata **23**: (90)

Ceratocoris cephalicus
  24: 63
Ceratopogonidae **23**: (52)
Cercopidae **24**: 78–79
Cercopis vulnerata **24**: 78
Cerianthária **21**: 43
Ceroplastes **24**: 106–107
Cerura vinula **26**: 82
Cestoda **21**: 77, 81, 82–83
Ceuthophilus brevipes
  23: 21
Chaetognatha **21**: 32, 77,
  79
Chaetonotoida **21**: 69
chafers **25**: 82, 85
  flower **25**: 85
  pine **25**: 82
Chaga's disease **21**: 17;
  24: 46
Chalcidoidea **27**: (23)
Chalicodoma
  C. parietinum, nests
    27: (88)
  C. siculum, nests **27**: (88)
Chamoideae **30**: 50
Charaxes
  C. candiope **26**: 38–39
  C. subornatus **26**: 40
  rajahs **26**: 39–40
Charis chrysus **26**: 37
Charniodiscus **21**: 35
Charonia tritonis **30**: 27
Chelicerata **22**: 9
chelicerates 29: 8–9
Chelisoches bimammatus
  22: (59)
Chelorrhina polyphemus
  25: 84–85
chemosynthesis **21**: 93
Cherax destructor **28**: 78
chiggers **29**: (32)
Chilocoris renipustlatus
  25: 58
Chilopoda **22**: 14, 22–25
Chirocephalus diaphanus
  28: 19
Chironex fleckeri **21**: 52,
  (54)
Chironomidae **23**: 50–53
Chironomus **23**: 50
  C. plumosus **23**: 51
chitons 30: 9, 14–15
  lined **30**: 15
Chlamys hastata **30**: 59
Chlorohydra viridissima
  21: 47
Choanocytes **21**: 34, 37
Choanoflagellates **21**: 34–35
Choanoflagellida **21**: 13
cholera **23**: 103
Chordata **21**: 32
Chorthippus brunneus
  23: 24–25
Chromacris colorata **23**: 9
Chromodoris **30**: 42–43
  C. quadricolor **30**: 40–41
Chrysaora fuscescens
  21: 54–55
Chrysididae **27**: 34–35
Chrysis ignita **27**: 35
Chrysochroa fulminans
  25: 46–47
Chrysolina menthastri
  25: 96, 97
Chrysomelidae **25**: 96–103

Chrysopa (Chrysoperla)
  22: 90
  C. carnea **22**: 90–91, 92
Chrysopidae **22**: 90
Chrysops caecutiens **23**: 58,
  61
Chthalamus entatus **28**: 23
Cicada orni **24**: 83
cicadas 24: 80–85
  anatomy **24**: 80
  cold-blooded **24**: 80–81
  escape behavior **24**: 80
  life cycle **24**: 83–84
  noise-producing
    24: 81–82, (82)
  periodical **24**: (84)
  warm-blooded **24**: 80–81
Cicadella viridis **24**: 86
Cicadellidae **24**: 86–89
Cicadidae **24**: 80–85
Cicindela
  C. aurulenta **25**: 23
  C. campestris **25**: 20, 22
  C. cincta **25**: 12
  C. hybrida **25**: 20–21
  C. versicolor **25**: 21
  reproduction **25**: 23
Cicindelidae **25**: 20–23
ciliates 21: 22–25
  reproduction **21**: 14
  slipper **21**: 22–23
  usefulness to humans
    21: (25)
Ciliophora **21**: 13, 22–25
Cimex lectularius **24**: 34,
  34–35
Cimicidae **24**: 34–35
Circia **22**: 53
Cirripedia **28**: 9, 22–27
clades **21**: 11
cladistics **21**: 11
clams 30: 62–71
  bean **30**: 68–69
  coral **30**: 67
  file **30**: 51
  giant **30**: 62, (65)
  hard-shelled **30**: 68
  harvesting **30**: (69)
  soft-shelled **30**: 62
  zigzag razor **30**: 71
  classification
    natural **21**: 10
    see also taxonomy
clegs (horseflies)
  23: 58–61
Cleridae **25**: 40–41
Climaciella **22**: 93
Clitellata **21**: 77, 94
clownfish **21**: (61)
Clytus arietis **25**: 95
Cnidaria **21**: 32, 42, 43
Cobanilla **26**: 98–99
Coccidae **24**: 106–111
Coccidia **21**: 13
Coccinella
  C. 7-punctata **25**: 54, 57;
    27: 29
  C. 9-notata **25**: 54–55
Coccinellidae **25**: 54–59
Coccus hesperidium **24**: 107
cochineal insects **24**: (109)
cockchafers, European
  25: 11, 83
cockles 30: 62–71
  bloody **30**: 53
  common **30**: 62–63

cockles (continued)
creeping **30:** *64*
dog **30:** *53*
prickly **30:** *66*
cockroaches 22: 68–73
American **22:** *9, 68, 69*
giant burrowing **22:** *72*
lesser **22:** *69*
reproduction **22:** 70–73
wood **22:** *71*
Coeliades keithloa **26:** *64*
Coenagrion puella
22: *44–45, 49*
Coenobita rugosus **28:** *99*
Coenothecalia **21:** 43
Coleoidea **30:** 9, 72
Coleoptera **22:** 30
see also beetles
Colias eurytheme **26:** *22*
Collembola **22:** 26, 28–29
Colletes cunicularius **27:** *90*
Colletidae **27:** 89–90
coloration, aposematic
(warning) **22:** 33–34
Colotois pennaria **26:** *76*
Colpodea **21:** 13
comb jellies 21: 42, 44–45
warty **21:** *42*
commensalism **21:** 17, 39;
28: 25–26, 65, (88),
109–112
conches **30:** 26, (27)
Conidae **30:** (33)
conjugation **21:** 25
Conopidae **23:** 82–83
Conops quadrifasciata
23: *83*
Constrictotermes
cyphergaster **22:** (64)
Conus
C. geographicus **30:** (33)
C. textilis **30:** (33)
convergence **21:** 11
Cooloola Monster **23:** (11)
Coooloolidae **23:** 11
Copepoda **28:** 9
copepods 28: 28–31
feeding **28:** 30
parasitic **28:** (30)
Copilia **28:** 28–29
Copiphora rhinoceros
23: *11, 12–13,* 14
coppers (gossamer-winged
butterflies) **26:** 28, 29
American **26:** 28
coral hopper **28:** *45*
coral reefs **21:** 64–66
Corallimorpharia **21:** 43
coral reefs **21:** 64–66
corals 21: 62–67
bleaching **21:** (66)
brain **21:** 65
coral shapes **21:** 62–64
plate **21:** 65
soft **21:** *63,* (64)
staghorn **21:** 65, 66
sunflower **21:** *62*
tube **21:** *62*
Cordulegaster boltonii
22: *46*
Cordylochernes scorpioides
29: 20–21, *21,* (21)
Coreidae **24:** 14, 52–57
Corixidae **24:** (27)
Coronatae **21:** 43
Corriola **26:** *93*
Corydalus **22:** *98–99*

Cotesia glomerata **27:** *10,*
25
Cotinus pyralis **25:** *36–37*
cotton spinners **30:** (113)
cotton-stainers (stainers)
24: 48–49
cow killers **27:** 38
cowries **30:** 26, (27)
crabs
anemone hermit **28:** *97*
arrowhead **28:** *103*
Atlantic mole **28:** *92, 93*
blue swimming **28:** *113*
Christmas Island **28:** 107
coconut **28:** (100)
decorator **28:** *110–111*
elegant hairy hermit
28: *94–95*
fiddler **28:** *112–113,*
(113)
ghost **28:** *56–57*
giant coconut
28: *100–101*
graceful **28:** *12–13*
hermit **28:** 94–101
horseshoe **29:** 8, 10–11
Japanese giant spider
28: 104
land hermit **28:** 99–100
mole **28:** 90–93
oyster **28:** 111–112
Pacific mole **28:** *90*
pea **28:** 111–112
porcelain **28:** 86–89
Puget Sound king **28:** *98*
robber **28:** *100–101*
Sally Lightfoot **28:** *103*
sand (Pacific mole) **28:** *90*
shore **22:** *8;* **28:** *102,* 108
soldier **28:** *109*
South Sea porcelain
28: *88–89*
sponge **28:** *111*
stone **28:** (98)
true *see* true crabs
Crangon crangon **28:** *60*
Craniata **21:** 32
Crassostrea virginica **30:** *56*
cray, Australian shovel-nosed
28: *12*
crayfish 28: 70–79
American spiny-cheeked
28: *75*
blue **28:** *58*
freshwater **28:** (75), *78*
Louisiana **28:** *8–9*
sense of gravity **28:** (77)
signal **28:** *72–73*
size **28:** (71)
Tasmanian **28:** (71)
white-clawed **28:** *75*
yabby **28:** *78*
Cremastocheilus **25:** (86)
Crepidula **30:** 29–30
C. fornicata **30:** *30–31*
crickets 23: 8–11, 16–19
ant-guest **23:** (19)
black **23:** *16*
bush *see* katydids
camel **23:** (21)
cave **23:** (21)
defense **23:** 19
European water **24:** *18,*
18–19
families **23:** 8
4-spotted tree **23:** *16–17*

crickets (continued)
Jerusalem (king)
23: 20–21
king 23: 20–21
leaf-rolling **23:** 21
mating **23:** 16–19
mole 23: 22–23
pygmy mole (sand)
23: (35)
sagebush **23:** (14)
sand (pygmy mole)
23: (35)
"singing" **23:** 16–17
water (ripple bugs)
24: 18–19
Crinoidea **30:** 91, 94–95
Crinozoa **30:** 91, 94
Crioceris asparagi **25:** *98*
Croesus septentrionalis
27: 20–21
Crustacea **22:** 9
crustaceans 28: 8–15
anatomy **28:** 12–14, *15*
classification **28:** 14
development **28:** 14
scientific names **28:** (11)
cryptobiosis **21:** 90; **23:** 53
Cryptocercidae **22:** 69–70
Cryptolepas rhachianecti
28: 26
Ctenidae **29:** 86–87
Ctenizidae **29:** (49)
Ctenocephalides
C. canis **22:** 110
C. felis **22:** 110, 112–113
Ctenoides ales **30:** 51
Ctenophora **21:** 32, 42, 43,
44–45
Ctenus **29:** 86
Cubozoa **21:** 43, 50–55
"cuckoo spit" **24:** (79)
cuckoo-spit insects
(spittlebugs) **24:** 78–79
Culicidae **23:** 46–49
Culiseta annulata **23:** *46, 47,*
49
Cumacea **28:** 9, 34,
50–51
Cumaceans 28: 50–51
classification **28:** 50–51
Cupiennius getazi **29:** *87*
Curculionidae **25:** 104–111
Curculio venosus **25:** *104*
Cuterebra **23:** *97*
cuttlefish 30: *73,* 76–83
giant **30:** *78*
giant Australian
30: *77*
as hunters **30:** (78)
Cyamidae **28:** 34
Cyanea capillata **21:** *50–51*
Cycliophora **21:** 32, 69
Cyclommatus tarandus
25: *74–75*
cyclomorphosis **28:** (17)
Cyclopoida **28:** 9
Cyclops **28:** *28*
Cyclosa, C. insulana
29: *106–107*
Cydnidae **24:** (66)
Cynipidae **27:** 32–33
Cynipoidea **27:** (23)
Cypridina **28:** *32*
Cysteodemus armatus
25: *62–63*

cysts **21:** 14
cytology (33)

D

Dacne bipustulata **25:** *50*
Dactylopus coccus **24:** 109
Dactylotum **23:** 24–25
daddy-longlegs 29: 22–25
crane flies 23: 42–45
defense **29:** 23–24
mating **29:** 24
pale-saddled **29:** *24*
splay-legged **29:** *23*
Damon variegatus **29:** 15
damselflies 22: 42–51
azure **22:** *44–45, 49*
demoiselle **22:** *45*
reproduction **22:** 45–51
Danaidae **26:** 58–61
Danaus
D. chrysippus **26:** *20, 60*
D. plexippus **21:** (8);
26: *15, 58, 60,* 61
Daphnia **28:** 16, 17, 21
D. magna **28:** *11*
D. reticularia **28:** 20
Dardanus
D. gemmatus **28:** *97*
D. pedunctulatus **28:** *99*
Darwin, Charles **21:** 10
Dasymutilla **27:** 38
D. occidentalis **27:** *38–39*
Dasypoda altercator
27: *90–91*
dead man's fingers **21:** *62*
Decapoda **28:** 9, 34, 56–59;
30: 72, 76–83
decapods **28:** 56–59
Decapotoma
D. catenata **25:** *65*
D. lunata **25:** *62*
Deilephila elpenor **26:** *68*
Deinacrida rugosa **23:** 20
Deinopidae **29:** 54–55
Deinopis **29:** 54–55, *55*
D. guatemalensis **29:** 54
Delias nigrina **26:** 23
Delphacidae **24:** (75)
Dendrobranchiata **28:** 56,
57–58
Dendrocoelum lacteum
21: *82*
Dendroxena maculata
25: 28
Dentalium elephantinum
30: *16, 16–17*
Deraeocoris ruber **24:** *30,*
32–33
Derbidae **24:** (77)
Dermacentor **29:** 32
Dermaptera **22:** 30, 58–61
Dermatophagoides
29: 30–31
Dermestes lardarius **25:** 53
Dermolepida albohirtum
25: *85*
deuterostomes **21:** 31
Deuterostomia **21:** 32
development stages, insects
22: 31
Diachlorus ferrugatus **23:** *61*
Diadema setosum **30:** 106
diapause **25:** (52)

diarrhea
hiker's **21:** 17
infantile **23:** 103
Dichopetala **23:** *14*
dichromatism, sexual **23:** 25
Dicksonia **21:** 34–35
Dicranopalpus ramosus
29: 23
Dictynidae **29:** (53)
Dictyoptera aurora **25:** 38
Didinium **21:** 23
digestion, external **29:** 15
Digononta **21:** 69
Diopsidae **23:** 86–87
Diopsis **23:** 86
Diphthera festiva **26:** *94–95,*
97
Diplopoda **22:** 14, 16–21
Diplostraca **28:** 9, 18
Diplura **22:** 26, (27)
Dipluridae **29:** 48–49
Diptera **22:** 30; **23:** 36–41
Dirphia **26:** *70*
Discocyrtus **29:** 23
diseases
from parasites **21:** 17
from ticks and mites
29: (32)
Dismorphia amphione
22: *34*
dobsonflies 22: 98–99
Dolatettix **23:** 34–35
Dolichoderus **24:** *108;* **27:** 9,
44
Dolichonabis limbatus
24: *36–37*
Dolichopodidae **23:** (75)
Dolichopus wahlbergi **23:** *75*
Dolichovespula media
27: *66–67*
Dolomedes **29:** 9
D. albineus **29:** *89*
D. triton **29:** *88–89*
Donacidae **30:** 68–70
Donax
D. deltoides **30:** *63*
D. gouldii **30:** *68–69*
Doratifera vulnerans **26:** *107*
Doru lineare **22:** *59*
Dorylus, D. nigricans **27:** 45
Dosidicus gigas **30:** *82*
Doxocopa laure **26:** *41*
dragonflies 22: 42–51
eastern amberwing
22: *47*
flame skimmer **22:** *42–43*
4-spotted skimmer
22: *50–51*
golden-ringed **22:** *46*
reproduction **22:** 45–51
ruddy darter **22:** *46*
southern hawker **22:** *42,*
43, 48
spangle skimmer
22: *26–27*
Drapetisca socialis **29:** 113
Dreisseniidae **30:** 60, (61)
Dromiacea **28:** 56
Drosophila melanogaster
23: 92–93
Drosophilidae **23:** 92–93
Drupa rubusidaeus **30:** *33*
Duliticola **25:** 39
Dynastes hercules **25:** *76*
Dysdera crocata **29:** *59*

Dysdercus
  D. flavidus **24:** *48–49*
  D. mimus **24:** *11*
Dysderidae **29:** 38, (59)
dysentery
  amebic **21:** 20
  bacterial **23:** 103
Dysodius lunatus **24:** *51*
Dysodonta **30:** 9, 50, <u>54–55</u>
Dysphania contraria **26:** *75*
Dytiscidae **25:** <u>24–25</u>
Dytiscus marginalis **25:** *24,*
  24–25, 25

E

earthworms 21: <u>102–105</u>
  ecological importance
    21: (104), 105
  giant Gippsland **21:** (105)
earwigs 22: <u>58–61</u>
  European **22:** *58–59,*
    60–61, 61
  linear **22:** *59*
  sand **22:** *60*
  striped **22:** *60*
  tawny **22:** *58*
Ecdysozoa **21:** 32
Ecdyzoa **21:** 69
Echinocardium caudatum
  30: *108*
Echinoderes 21: *79*
Echinodermata **21:** 32;
  30: 90, 91
echinoderms **30:** <u>90–93</u>
Echinoidea **30:** 91, <u>104–109</u>
echinoids
  camouflage **30:** *108*
  irregular **30:** 104, 108
  regular **30:** 104
Echinozoa **30:** 91
Echinus esculentus **30:** *105*
Echiura **21:** 32, 77, 78
Eciton burchelli **27:** 55, 56
ecology **21:** (33)
Ectinolobia buqueti **25:** *49*
Ectobius panzeri **22:** 69
Ectomocoris **27:** 39, (38)
ectoplasm **21:** 14
Edessa rufomarginata
  24: *60–61*
Efferia benedicti **23:** *62–63*
Eisenia foetida **21:** *105*
Elasmucha grisea **24:** *71*
Elateridae **25:** <u>42–45</u>
Eledone cirrhosa **30:** *85*
elephantiasis **21:** 91
Elphidium **21:** *21*
Elysia **30:** *42*
Embia ramburi **22:** *82–83*
Embioptera **22:** 30, <u>82–83</u>
embryology **21:** (33)
Emerita
  E. analoga **28:** *90*
  E. talpoida **28:** *92, 93*
Emersonella niveipes **27:** *29*
Empididae **23:** <u>72–75</u>
Empis
  E. livida **23:** *74*
  E. stercorea **23:** *72–73*
  E. tessellata **23:** *72*
  E. trigramma **23:** *73*
Emus hirtus **25:** *32*
Enchonopa concolor **24:** *95*
Endomychidae **25:** *52*
endoplasm **21:** 14

Endoprocta **21:** 32, 69
endoprocts **21:** (72)
Enopia **21:** 77
Enoplida **21:** 89
Enoplometopus occidentalis
  28: *58–59*
Ensis siliqua **30:** *68, 70*
Entimus granulatus **25:** *105*
entomology **21:** (33)
Eoacanthocephala **21:** 77
Eobania vermiculata **30:** *46*
Ephemera danica **22:** *39,*
  41
Ephemeroptera **22:** 30,
  <u>38–41</u>
Epibolus pulchripes
  22: *18–19, 19*
Epicaridea **28:** 34
Epicharis **27:** *97*
Epimenia **30:** *12–13*
epitokes **21:** (101)
Erannis defoliara **26:** *77*
Ercinidae **30:** 50
Erebia aethiops **26:** *46*
Eristalis
  E. nemorum **23:** *78*
  E. tenax **23:** *76, 78*
Erotylidae **25:** <u>50–53</u>
Erotylus maculiventris **25:** *51*
Eryphanis polyxena **26:** *49*
estivation **30:** 47
Ethmostigmus **22:** *24–25,*
  25
ethology **21:** (33)
Eucylodes **26:** (76)
Euglossa **27:** *102–103, 103*
Eugonycha **25:** *99*
eukaryotes **21:** 9, 10
Eulalia viridis **21:** *98*
Eulamellibranchia **30:** 9, 50,
  <u>62–71</u>
Eulophidae **27:** 25
Eulyes amaena **24:** *39*
Eumalacostraca **28:** 9, 34
Eumastacidae **23:** <u>32–33</u>
Eumenes fenestralis **27:** *64*
Eumetazoa **21:** 30, 32, 69
Eumorphus micans **25:** *52*
Eunice viridis **21:** *101*
Euphausiacea **28:** 9, 34,
  <u>52–55</u>
Euphausia superba
  28: *54–55*
Euplotes **21:** *24*
Euprymna tasmanica
  30: *80–81*
Eurota sericaria **26:** *90*
Eurygaster
  E. maura **24:** *70*
  E. testudinaria **24:** *70*
Eurytides agesilaus **26:** *18*
Euscyrtus bivittatus **23:** *18*
Eustenogaster calyptodoma
  27: *67*
Euthalia **26:** 42
Euthrix potatoria **26:** *85*
Evanioidea **27:** (23)
Evarcha arcuata **29:** *74*
Evechinus chloroticus
  30: *104*
Extatosoma tiaratum
  22: *57*
external digestion **29:** 15
Eybrachyura **28:** 56
eye diseases **23:** 103
Eysarcoris fabricii **24:** *67*

F

false heads **26:** (31), 82, 93,
  97
Fasciola hepatica **21:** *84*
feather stars 30: *92, 93,*
  94–97
Felderolia candescens
  26: *105*
filariasis **23:** (49)
Filosa **21:** 13
fire brats (silverfish)
  22: <u>36–37</u>
fireflies 25: <u>36–37</u>
  eastern **25:** *36–37*
fishflies **22:** 98
Flabellifera **28:** 34
Flabellinopsis iodinea **30:** *41*
flagellates 21: 12, 13,
  <u>16–17</u>
  commensal **21:** 17
  parasitic **21:** 16–17
  reproduction **21:** 14
Flatidae **24:** (74)
flatworms 21: <u>80–85</u>
fleas 22: <u>110–113</u>
  beach 28: <u>44–45</u>
  cat **22:** 110, *112–113*
  and disease **22:** (113)
  dog **22:** *110*
  human **22:** 111
  jumping ability **22:** (111)
  rabbit **22:** *110–111,*
    112–113, (113)
  rat **22:** *113*
  specific hosts **22:** 111
  water 28: 11, <u>16–21</u>
flies 23: <u>36–41</u>
  anatomy **23:** 36–39
  assassin (robber)
    23: <u>62–67</u>
  banana **23:** (85)
  bee 23: <u>68–71</u>
  black **23:** *52–53,* (53)
  black horsefly **23:** *60*
  "blinder" deerfly **23:** *58*
  blow 23: <u>108–111</u>
  bluebottle (blow)
    23: *36–37,* <u>108–111</u>
  bot 23: <u>96–97</u>
  cactus **23:** (85)
  crane 23: *38,* <u>42–45</u>
  dance 23: <u>72–75</u>
  dark giant horsefly **23:** *60*
  deerflies 23: <u>58–61</u>
  downlooker snipefly
    23: *59*
  drone **23:** *76, 78*
  dune bee **23:** *70*
  dung 23: <u>98–99</u>
  elephant (horseflies)
    23: <u>58–61</u>
  face (houseflies)
    23: <u>100–103</u>
  families **23:** 36
  fever (march) **23:** <u>54–55</u>
  flesh 23: <u>112–113</u>
  flower (hover) **23:** <u>76–81</u>
  fruit, large 23: <u>88–91</u>
  fruit, small 23: <u>92–93</u>
  gray (flesh) **23:** <u>112–113</u>
  greenbottle (blow)
    23: 108, *109–110*
  green colonel **23:** *57*
  hawthorn (March)
    23: <u>54–55</u>

flies (continued)
  horn (houseflies)
    23: <u>100–103</u>
  hornet robber **23:** *66–67*
  horseflies 23: *36–37,*
    <u>58–61</u>
  houseflies and relatives
    23: <u>100–103</u>
  hover 23: <u>76–81</u>
  jackal **23:** (106), *107*
  larvae **23:** 39–40
  life history **23:** 39–40
  long-horned general
    23: *57*
  long-legged **23:** (75)
  mantid **22:** 90,
    92–95
  manure **23:** *98–99,*
    (99)
  March 23: <u>54–55</u>
  marsh (snail) **23:** <u>94–95</u>
  medflies **23:** (90)
  Mediterranean fruit
    23: (90)
  Mydas **23:** (40), (63)
  noonday **23:** *100–101*
  nostril (bot) **23:** <u>96–97</u>
  parasite 23: <u>104–107</u>
  petroleum **23:** (39)
  phantom crane **23:** (45)
  picture-winged **23:** (87)
  pomace (small fruit)
    23: <u>92–93</u>
  robber 23: <u>62–67</u>
  St. Mark's (March)
    23: <u>54–55</u>
  snail 23: <u>94–95</u>
  snipe **23:** (59)
  soldier 23: <u>56–57</u>
  splayed deerfly **23:** *61*
  stable (houseflies)
    23: <u>100–103</u>
  stalk-eyed 23: <u>86–87</u>
  stiletto **23:** (65)
  stilt-legged 23: <u>84–85</u>
  suborders **23:** 39
  tangle-veined **23:** (69)
  thick-headed (wasp)
    23: <u>82–83</u>
  3-spot horsefly **23:** *58*
  tsetse **21:** (17); **23:** (103)
  vinegar (small fruit)
    23: <u>92–93</u>
  walnut husk **23:** *88*
  warble 23: <u>96–97</u>
  wasp 23: <u>82–83</u>
flight, insects **22:** (35)
flukes **21:** 80, 82–83,
  83–84
  blood **21:** *83*
  liver **21:** *84*
Flustra foliacea **21:** *72*
food, stored **25:** 71–72
forams **21:** 20–21
Forcipomyia **23:** *52*
Forficula auricularia
  22: *58–59, 60–61,*
  61
Formica rufa **27:** *49*
Formicidae **27:** <u>40–57</u>
Frankliniella occidentalis
  22: *84*
Fulcidax violacea **25:** *96–97*
Fulgora laternaria **24:** *76*
Fulgoridae **24:** <u>72–77</u>
Furcula bifida **26:** *80*

G

Galathea strigosa **28:** *86*
Galatheoidea **28:** 56, <u>86–89</u>
Galeomma turtoni **30:** *64*
Gammaroidea **28:** 34
Gammarus locusta **28:** *44*
Gargaphia solani **24:** (29)
Gasteracantha arcuata
  29: *109*
Gasteruption assectator
  27: *31*
Gastrophysa viridula **25:** *13,*
  99
Gastropoda **30:** 9, 10,
  <u>18–21</u>
gastropods 30: <u>18–21</u>
  anatomy **30:** 19–20
  coiling and torsion
    30: 19, 20–21
Gastrotricha **21:** 32, 69
Gecarcinus **28:** *109*
Gecarcoidea natalis **28:** *107*
Gelastocoridae **24:** <u>22–23</u>
Gelastocoris **24:** *22*
  G. peruensis **24:** *23*
Geometridae **26:** <u>74–77</u>
Gergarina **21:** 13
Gerridae **24:** <u>16–17</u>
Gerris
  G. lacustris **24:** 16
  G. odontogaster
    24: *16–17*
Giardia lamblia **21:** *16–17*
giardiasis **21:** 17
Gigantocypris **28:** 33
gladiators **22:** (79)
Glaucus atlanticus **30:** *38*
Glomeris marginata
  22: *20–21*
Glossina mortisans **23:** *103*
glowworms **25:** (35)
Glycimeridae **30:** 50, 53
Glypta **27:** *26*
Gnaphosidae **29:** (81)
Gnathiidea **28:** 34
Gnathobdellae **21:** 94
Gnathophausia **28:** *36–37*
Gnathostomulida **21:** 32,
  76, 77
gnats 23: <u>46–49</u>
  buffalo **23:** 52
  turkey **23:** (53)

Gnophaela vermiculata
  26: *89*
Goliathus druryi **25:** *87*
Gonepteryx rhamni
  26: *22–23*
Gordius **21:** *77*
Gorgonacea **21:** 43
Gorgonocephalus **30:** *101*
Gorgonorhynchus repens
  21: *87*
Granuloreticulosa **21:** 13
Graphium antiphates
  26: *16–17*
Graphocephala fennahi
  24: *86, 87*
Graspus graspus **28:** *103*
grasshoppers 23: <u>8–11,</u>
  <u>24–31</u>
  anatomy **22:** 11
  bladder **23:** 29–30
  eastern lubber **23:** *28–29*
  elegant **23:** *27*

grasshoppers (continued)
  families **23:** 8
  feeding **23:** 25–27
  gaudy **23:** 30–31
  gold-horned lubber
    23: 28
  horse-faced monkey
    23: 32–33
  long-horned see katydids
  lubber **23:** 28–29
  mating **23:** 27–28
  monkey 23: 32–33
  nymphs **23:** 10
  painted **23:** 24–25
  pygmy 23: 34–35
  short-horned **23:** 24
  "singing" **23:** 27–28
  slender groundhopper
    23: 34, 34–35
  stick **23:** (33)
  toad **23:** 29
Greta andromia **26:** 57
gribbles **28:** 46, 49
Gryllacrididae **23:** 21
Gryllidae **23:** 16–19
Gryllotalpa vinae **23:** 22
Gryllotalpidae **23:** 22–23
Gryllus bimaculatus
    23: 16
Gymnolaemata **21:** 69
Gymnopleurus aenescens
    25: 80
Gymnosomata **30:** 18
Gyrinidae **25:** 26–27
Gyrinus minutus **25:** 26

H

Haekel, Ernst **21:** 9
Haemopis sanguisuga
    21: 109
hairstreaks (gossamer-
    winged butterflies)
    26: 28, 29
  American gray **26:** 31
  green **26:** 28–29
  martial **26:** 28
Halesus radiatus
    22: 102–103
Halictidae **27:** (95)
Haliotis rufescens **30:** 23
Halobates **24:** (17)
Halocyprida **28:** 9
hangingflies 22: 104–109
Hapalochlaena lunulata
    30: 84, 88–89
Haplotaxida **21:** 94
Harmothoe inibricata
    21: 98
Harpa articularis **30:** 34
Harpacticoida **28:** 9
Harpobittacus **22:** 108–109
harvestfly, dogday **24:** 81
heart urchins **30:** 93, 104,
    108–109
  purple **30:** 104
Helaemyia petrolei **23:** (39)
Helicomitus **22:** 96
Heliconiidae **26:** 52–55
Heliconius
  H. erato **26:** 53,
    54–55
  H. isabella **22:** 34
  H. sara **26:** 55
Heliozoa **21:** 13
Heliozoans **21:** 21

Helix
  H. aspersa **30:** 45
  H. pomatia **30:** 46–47
Helobdella **21:** 106–107
Hemerobiidae **22:** 92
Hemichordata **21:** 32, 77,
    79
Hemimerina **22:** (59)
Hemiptera **22:** 30
  classification **24:** 8, 10
  life cycle and
    development **24:** 13–14
Hemisquilla ensigera
    californiensis **28:** 38–39
hemocoel **27:** 24–25
hemocyanin **29:** 11, 38
hemocysts **27:** 24–25
hepatitis B virus **24:** 35
Hepteronotus reticulatus
    24: 94
hermaphrodites,
    protandrous **28:** (68);
    30: 26
Hermissenda **30:** 21
  H. crassicornis **30:** 10, 41
Hermodice carunculata
    21: 99
herpetology **21:** (33)
Herpyllus blackwalli **29:** 81
Hersilia
  H. bicornutus **29:** 65
  H. savignyi **29:** 65
Hersiliidae **29:** 64–65
Hesperiidae **26:** 62–65
Heteractis magnifica **21:** 61
Heterocentrotus **30:** 105
Heteroptera **24:** 8, 10,
    11–12, 13
Heterotrichea **21:** 13
heterotrophs **21:** 9
Hexabranchus sanguineus
    30: 40, 41–42
Hexacontinium **21:** 21
Hexacorallia **21:** 43
Hexagenia **22:** 40
Hexapoda **22:** 9
hexapods **22:** 26–27
Hexodon latissimum
    25: 76–77
hibernation **30:** 47
hiker's diarrhea **21:** 17
Hippodamia convergens
    25: 58–59
Hippoidea **28:** 56,
    90–93
Hiranetis braconiformis
    24: 40–41
Hirudinea **21:** 77, 94,
    106–111
Hirudo medicinalis **21:** 106,
    (108), 108–109
Hofmannophila
    pseudospretella **26:** 111
Holconia immanis **29:** 66–67
Holopneustes inflatus
    30: 107
Holothuria forskali **30:** 113
Holothuroidea **30:** 91,
    110–113
Homalopteryx laminata
    22: 68
Homarus
  H. americanus **28:** 70–71,
    (71), 74
  H. gammarus **28:** 70, (71)
Homo sapiens **21:** 33

honeybees **27:** 12,
    110–113
  honeybee dance **27:** (113)
  **honeybees and
    relatives 27:** 102–113
  nests **27:** 110–111
honeydew **27:** (48)
hornets, giant **27:** 63
horntails (sawflies)
    27: 14–21
  giant **27:** 15
  larvae **27:** 19
hornwrack **21:** 72
Hospitalotermes **22:** 66–67
Hydatina amplustrum **30:** 37
hydras **21:** 46–47
  freshwater **21:** 46
  green freshwater **21:** 47
Hydrobia ulvae **30:** 29
hydrocorals **21:** 46
Hydrocyrius columbiae
    24: 20–21
Hydroida **21:** 43
hydroids **21:** 46, 47–48
  stalked **21:** 48
Hydrometra stagnorum
    24: (19)
Hydrometridae **24:** (19)
Hydrophilidae **25:** (26)
Hydropodura aquatica
    22: 29
Hydrozoa **21:** 43, 46–49
Hydrozoans **21:** 46–49
  life cycles **21:** (48)
Hylephila phyleus **26:** 65
Hyles lineata **26:** 69
Hyllus diardi **29:** 41
Hymenocera picta **28:** 35
Hymenoptera **22:** 30;
    27: 8–13
  anatomy **27:** 12–13
  classification **27:** 8, 9–10
  sex determination **27:** 13
  sociability **27:** 11–12
Hymenoptera neurotica
    27: 58
Hyperiidae **28:** 34
hyperparasites **27:** (27)
Hypoderma
  H. bovis **23:** 96
  H. lineatum **23:** 96–97
Hyptiotes paradoxus
    29: 56
Hystrichopsylla schefferi
    22: 111

I

Ibacus peronii **28:** 12
Icerya purchasi **24:** 106;
    25: (56)
Ichneumonidae **27:** 22–31
Ichneumonoidea **27:** (23)
ichneumons
  mating **27:** 29–30
  penetrating wood
    27: (24)
Ichneumon suspiciosus
    27: 31
icthyology **21:** (33)
Illacme plenipes **22:** 14
Illex illecebrosus **30:** 82–83
Inarticulata **21:** 69, 70, 71

infant deaths
  gaudy grasshoppers and
    23: 30
  houseflies and **23:** 103
Ingolfiellidea **28:** 34
Insecta **22:** 26, 30
insects 22: 30–35
  anatomy **22:** 30–31
  development stages
    22: 31
  flight **22:** (35)
  gender differences **22:** 32
  metamorphosis **22:** 31–32
  mimicry in **22:** 33–34
  protective resemblance
    22: 33
**invertebrates
  minor groups 21:** 68–69
    wormlike **21:** 76–79
Iphiaulax **27:** 22–23
Isopoda **28:** 9, 34, 46–49
isopods 28: 46–49
Isoptera **22:** 30, 62–67
Ithomiidae **26:** 56–57
ithomiids 26: 56–57
  mating **26:** 57
Ixodes hexagonus **29:** 30

J

Jadera obscura **24:** 58–59
Janthina **30:** 29
jelly animals 21: 42–43
jellyfish 21: 34–35, 43,
    50–55
  Australian box **21:** 52,
    (54)
  freshwater **21:** 54
  and humans **21:** 54
  jelly **21:** (52)
  lion's mane **21:** 50–51
  moon **21:** 50
  reproduction **21:** 53–54
  structure **21:** 51–52
  swimming **21:** 52–53
  upside-down **21:** 53
Jezebels (whites) **26:** 22–27
Julida **22:** 17
Junonia coenia **26:** 41

K

Karyorelicta **21:** 13
katydids 23: 8, 10, 12–15;
    29: 41, 76
  deception **23:** 15
  defense **23:** 15
  feeding **23:** 12–13
  mating **23:** 14
  rhinoceros **23:** 11, 13, 14
  singing **23:** 14
keratin **25:** 53
Kinetoplastida **21:** 13, 17
Kinorhyncha **21:** 32, 77,
    79
Kleidocerys resedae
    24: 46–47
kleptoparasitism **23:** 97,
    112
krill **28:** 52–55
  antarctic **28:** 54–55
  feeding **28:** 54
  fisheries **28:** (54)
Kristensen, Reinhardt
    21: (28)

L

Labidura riparia **22:** 58, 60
lacewings
  green **22:** 90, 92
  larvae, defense **22:** (92)
  and relatives 22: 90–97
lady beetles (ladybugs)
    25: 54–59
ladybirds (ladybugs)
    25: 54–59
ladybugs 25: 54–59
  convergent **25:** 58–59
  7-spot **25:** 54, **27:** 29
Lagoa crispata **26:** 108
Lamarckiana **23:** 29
Laminiceps **24:** 52–53
Lammellibranchiida **21:** 77
Lampyridae **25:** 36–37
Lampyris noctiluca **25:** 36
Lanice conchilega **21:** 97
lanternflies 24: 12, 72–77
Lasiocampidae **26:** 84–87
Lasioglossum calceatum
    27: 94–95
Lasius fuliginousus **27:** 47
Laternaria laternaria **24:** 76
Latrodectus bishopi **29:** 100
Lauriea siagiani **28:** 88–89
leafhoppers 24: 86–89
  feeding habits **24:** 87–88
  plant damage **24:** 87–88
  rhododendron **24:** 86, 87
  "songs" **24:** (89)
leaf insects 22: 52–57
leeches **21:** 106–111
  horse **21:** 109
  leaf **21:** 110–111
  medicinal **21:** 106, (108),
    108–109
Lepas **28:** 27
  L. anatifera **28:** 24–25
Lepidoptera **22:** 30, 30–31
  classification **26:** 8, 10–11
Leptinotarsa decemlineata
    25: 103
Leptocelis centralis **24:** 53
Leptophlebia marginata
    22: 38
Leptostraca **28:** 34, 36
Leptotarsus ducalis **23:** 43
Leucage nigrovittata **29:** 103
Libelloides
  L. coccajus **22:** 90
  L. longicornis **22:** 96
Libellula
  L. cyanea **22:** 26–27
  L. quadrimaculata
    22: 50–51
  L. saturata **22:** 42–43
Libyaspis coccinelloides
    24: 63
lice 22: 88–89
  body **22:** (89)
  crab **22:** 88–89
  cymothoid fish **28:** 30
  dog **22:** 88
  head **22:** 88–89
  on humans **22:** (89)
  **jumping plant
    24:** 96–97
    marine fish **28:** 30
Ligia oceanica **28:** 46, 49
Limacodidae **26:** 106–109
Limax maximus **30:** 48–49

Limidae **30:** 59
Limnephilus flavicornis
22: *103*
limpets 30: 22–25
blue **30:** *25*
common **30:** *22*
giant keyhole **30:** *24*
keyhole **30:** *22*
shimmering **30:** *22–23*
slipper **30:** *26, 30–31*
Limulus polyphemus **29:** *10, 10–11*
linalool **27:** *90*
Lineus **21:** *86–87*
L. longissimus **21:** *86*
Lingula anatina **21:** *70*
Linn (Linnaeus), Carolus
(Carl) **21:** 9
Linyphia triangularis **29:** *112, 113*
Linyphiidae **29:** 112–113
Liothyrella uva **21:** *70–71*
Liposcelis terricolis **22:** *86*
Lirimiris **26:** *82*
Lissocarcinus **28:** *112*
Lissocarpa vespiformis
24: *86–87*
Lithobius forficatus
22: *22–23*
Lithodidae **28:** (98)
Litostomatea **21:** 13
Littorina
L. obtusata **30:** *26*
L. peruviana **30:** *28–29*
L. saxatilis **30:** *28*
"littorinid zone" **30:** (28)
Loboza **21:** 13
lobster, spiny squat **22:** *8*
lobsters 28: 70–79
American **28:** *70–71, (71)*
Atlantic squat **28:** *86–87*
Caribbean spiny **28:** *82, 84–85*
common **28:** *70*
as human food **28:** *78*
migration **28:** *77–78*
overfishing **28:** *83*
pink squat **28:** *88–89*
pistol **28:** *76*
"red whalefeed" **28:** *87*
reef **28:** *58–59*
ridgeback slipper **28:** *83*
sense of gravity **28:** (77)
slipper 28: 82–85
spiny 28: 82–85
spiny squat **28:** *86*
squat 28: *14–15,* 86–89
traps for **28:** (78), *79*
locusts **23:** 24, (26)
Loliginidae **30:** 72
Loligo **30:** *76*
L. opalescens **30:** *83*
longwings 26: 52–55
Lopha cristagalli **30:** *71*
Lophia folium **30:** *56–57*
Lophodes sinistraria **26:** *74*
Lophogastrida **28:** 34, 37
Lopholithodes mandtii
28: *98*
lophophorates **21:** 68
Lophotrochozoa **21:** 32, 69
Loricella angasi **30:** *14*
Loricifera **21:** 32, 69
louse *see* lice
lovebugs (March flies)
23: 54–55

Loxosceles, L. rufescens
29: *58–59*
Loxoscelidae **29:** (59)
Lucanidae **25:** 74–75
Lucanus cervus **22:** *32;*
25: *74*
lucines **30:** 62, 63
Lucinidae **30:** 50, 63
Lumbriculida **21:** 94
Lumbricus terrestris **21:** *102, 104–105*
luminous crustaceans
28: 29, 53
luminous insects **25:** (35),
36–37, 43, (44)
Lutraria **30:** *70–71*
L. lutraria **30:** *71*
Lutraridae **30:** 50
Lycaena phlaeas **26:** *28*
Lycaenidae **26:** 28–33
Lycaeninae **26:** 29
Lycidae **25:** 38–39
Lycosa **29:** *84*
L. narbonensis **29:** *82–83*
Lycosidae **29:** 82–85
Lycus
L. constrictus **25:** *11*
L. vittatus **25:** 38–39
Lygaeidae **24:** 44–47
Lygaeus kalmii **24:** *44*
Lygocoris pabulinus
24: *30–31*
Lygus rugulipennis **24:** *30*
Lymantria
L. dispar **26:** (101)
L. monacha **26:** *98*
Lymantriidae **26:** 98–101
Lyme disease **29:** (32)
Lymnaea
L. peregra **30:** *45*
L. stagnalis **30:** *44*
Lyothyrella uva **21:** *70–71*
Lyramorpha **24:** *64–65*
Lyrognathus robustus **29:** *47*
Lysandra bellargus **26:** *29, 30*
Lysiosquilla **28:** *41*

M

Machimus atricapillus **23:** *62*
Machtima crucigera **24:** *52–53*
Macraspis lucida **25:** *80*
Macrobrachium **28:** *62, 64*
Macrocheira kaempferi
28: *104*
Macrodasyoidea **21:** 69
Macropanesthia rhinoceros
22: *72*
Macrosiphum
M. albifrons **24:** *14*
M. cholodkovskyi **24:** *103*
Macrotermes **22:** *67*
Macrothylacia rubi
26: *84–85*
Maculinea arion **26:** *28*
Maculolachnus submacula
24: *103*
maggots **23:** (110)
Malacosoma
M. californicum **26:** *86*
M. neustria **26:** *84, 86*
Malacostraca **28:** 9, 34
malacostracans 28: 34–37

malaria **21:** 26–27, **23:** (49)
life cycles **21:** (27)
malaxation **27:** 70
Malaza empyreus **26:** *63*
mammalogy **21:** (33)
Manomera tenuescens
22: *52–53*
mantid flies **22:** 90, 92–95
mantis, praying (mantids)
22: 9, 74–79
Mantispidae **22:** 92
Mantis religiosa **22:** *74*
Mantodea **22:** 30, 74–79
Mantophasmatodea **22:** (79)
Margaritiferidae **30:** 50
Margulis, Lynn **21:** 10
Marpesia
M berania **26:** *15*
M petreus **26:** *42–43*
Marphysa sanguinea **21:** *98*
Marpissa muscosa
29: *74–75*
Mastigias **21:** *43*
Mastigophora **21:** 13, 16–17
Mastigoproctus giganteus
29: *28*
Maxillopoda **28:** 9
mayflies 22: 38–41
dark olive **22:** *39*
green drake **22:** *39, 41*
mealybugs 24: 112–113
long-tailed **24:** *112*
Mechanitis lysimnia **26:** *56*
meconium **27:** *172*
Mecoptera **22:** 30, 104–109
Mecopus torquis **25:** *107*
medical applications,
cantharidin **25:** (63)
Megachile
M. centuncularis
27: *84–85*
M. willughbiella
27: *86, 87*
Megachilidae **27:** 84–91
Megaloptera **22:** 30, 98–99
Megalopygidae **26:** 108
Megascolides australis
21: (105)
Megasoma elephas
25: *88–89*
Megathura crenulata **30:** *24*
Melanargia galathea **26:** *47*
Meliponinae **27:** 108
Melittidae **27:** 90–91
Meloe proscarabaeus **25:** *62*
Meloidae **25:** 62–67
Melolontha melolontha
22: *35;* **25:** *11, 83*
Membracidae **24:** 90–95
Membracis foliata **24:** *15*
Membranipora **21:** 72–73
Mercenaria mercenaria
30: *68*
Merostomata **29:** 8, 10–11
Mesembrina meridiana
23: *100–101*
Mesogastropoda **30:** 18,
26–31
Mesozoa **21:** 32, 34, 35
Messor **27:** *40–41*
metalmarks 26: 34–37
blue doctor **26:** *35*
Meta segmentata **29:** *105*
Metasyrphus luniger
23: *80–81*

metazoans **21:** 30–31
Metellina segmentata
29: *105*
methyl palmitate **27:** *67*
Metridium senile **21:** *56*
Miagrammopes **29:** *57*
Micrathena sagittata
29: *109*
Microcerberidea **28:** 34
Micrommata virescens
29: *66*
Micropeza corriziolata
23: *84*
Micropezidae **23:** 84–85
microscopes **21:** (12)
Microspora **21:** 13
Microstigmus comes **27:** *77*
Microstylum **23:** *64–65*
Mictacea **28:** 34, 37
Mictyris longicarpus **28:** *109*
midges
biting **23:** (52)
nonbiting 23: 50–53
seashore **23:** 50–51
migration
monarch butterflies
26: (61)
noctuids **26:** 94
skippers **26:** 63–64
Milesia crabroniformis
23: *76*
Milichiidae **23:** (106)
Milleporina **21:** 43
millipedes 22: 14–15,
16–21
breeding **22:** 18–20
cyclindrical **22:** *17*
defense **22:** (21)
flat-backed **22:** *17, 21*
giant **22:** *16, 18–19, 19*
pill **22:** *20–21*
sound production **22:** 18
walking movement
22: (17)
Mimallonidae **26:** (86)
mimicry
Batesian **22:** 34
by bugs **24:** 31, 37,
40–41, 56, 86–87, 95
by butterflies **22:** 34;
26: 19–21, 44
by cockroaches **22:** 68
by flies **23:** 79–80, 84, 88
in insects **22:** 33–34
by long-horned beetles
25: 95
by mantid flies **22:** 93
by mantids **22:** 79
by moths **26:** 80–82
Müllerian **22:** 34
by octopuses **30:** 87
by zebra flatworms
21: 81
**minor invertebrate
groups 21:** 68–69
Miridae **24:** 30–33
Miris striatus **24:** *31*
Mirperus jaculus **24:** *56–57*
*Mischocyttarus
immarginatus* **27:** *67*
Misophrioida **28:** 9
Misumena vatia **29:** *68, 72–73*
mites 29: 30–33
animal hosts **29:** 33
diseases **29:** (32)

mites (continued)
house-dust **29:** *30–31, (32)*
scabies **29:** (32)
size **29:** 32
velvet **29:** *31*
Mnemiopsis mccradyi **21:** *42*
Moducia typicalis **28:** *12*
Mollusca **21:** 32
mollusks 30: 8–11
anatomy **30:** 8
shell **30:** 9, (10)
Monogenea **21:** 77, 81, 82
Monogononta **21:** 69
Monoplacophora **30:** 9,
12–13
Monstrilioida **28:** 9
Morphidae **26:** 50–51
Morpho
M. menelaus **26:** *50, 51*
M. peleides **26:** *50–51*
morphos 26: 50–51
mosquitoes 21: (27), 91;
23: 46–49
blood feeding **23:** 48,
(49)
disease and **23:** (49)
egg-laying **23:** 46–48
feeding **23:** 48, 49
head **23:** *37*
ring-legged **23:** *46, 47, 49*
moss animals 21: 72–73
moths 26: 8–15
ailanthus webworm
26: *112*
anatomy **26:** *10, 11–12*
angle-shades **22:** *32–33*
atlas **26:** *70*
bagworm 26: 110–111
black arches **26:** *98*
black-waved flannel
26: *108*
borer (clearwinged)
26: 104–105
brown house **26:** *111*
carpenter **26:** (105)
Chinese oak silk **26:** *8–9*
**clearwinged
26:** 104–105
eggar (tent caterpillar)
26: 84–87
eggs **26:** *12–13, (13)*
emperor (giant silkworm)
26: 70–73
ermine 26: 112–113
European fox **26:** *84–85*
European silver Y **26:** *95*
fairy **26:** *112–113, (113)*
flannel **26:** 108
flower **26:** 94
garden tiger (great tiger)
26: *88, 90*
geometer
(measuringworm)
26: 74–77
giant agrippa **26:** *93*
giant saturniid **22:** *11*
**giant silkworm
26:** 70–73
great tiger **26:** *88*
gypsy **26:** (101)
hawk (sphinx) **26:** 66–69
hieroglyphic **26:** *94–95*
hornet **26:** *104*

moths (continued)
inchworm
(measuringworm)
26: 74–77
lackey **26:** *84*
lappet (tent caterpillar)
26: 84–87
looper (measuringworm)
26: 74–77
luna **26:** *71*
Madagascan hawk **26:** *66*
magpie **26:** *14*
measuringworm
26: 74–77
micro **26:** 111
oak beauty **26:** *74*
owlet 26: 92–97
pepper **26:** (75)
plume 26: 102–103
poplar kitten **26:** *80*
processionary **26:** (83)
puddling **26:** (15)
pupae **26:** 14–15
royal (giant silkworm)
26: 70–73
sack-bearers **26:** (86)
silkworm 26: 78–79
slug-caterpillar
26: 106–109
smoky **26:** 108–109
sphinx 26: 66–69; **27:** *30*
sweetheart underwing
26: *92*
tent caterpillar
26: 84–87
tiger 26: 88–91
tussock 26: 98–101
white plume **26:** *102,
102–103*
yucca **26:** (113)
see also caterpillars
Munida
M. gregaria **28:** *14–15,
87*
M. rugosa **28:** *86–87*
Muricidae **30:** 34–35
Musca domesticus **23:** *100,
102*
Muscidae **23:** 100–103
mussels 30: 54–55
brown **30:** *54*
common **30:** *55*
date **30:** *54*
edible **30:** *54*
fan **30:** *54, 58, 59*
freshwater **30:** 60–61
horse **30:** *54–55*
marine **30:** *54*
orb **30:** *61*
southern rainbow
30: *60–61*
swan **30:** *60*
Mutillidae **27:** 38–39
Mya arenaria **30:** *62*
Mycetophagidae **25:** (52)
Mydaidae **23:** (63)
Mydas **23:** (63)
M. fulvifrons **23:** *63*
Mygalomorphae **29:** *38, 41*
myiasis **23:** *108*
Myidae **30:** *70*
Mylabris tiflensis **25:** *64*
Myodocopa **28:** *9*
Myopa testacea **25:** *82–83*
Myriapoda **22:** *9*
myriapods 22: 14–15

Myrmaridae **22:** (86)
Mysida **28:** *34*
Mysidacea **28:** *9,* 42–43
Mysidia **24:** *76–77*
Mysis relicta **28:** *42*
Mytilidae **30:** *50*
Mytilus edulis **30:** *55*
myxomatosis **22:** *110,* (113)
Myzostomaria **21:** *77, 94,
96*
Myzus persicae **24:** *100*

N

Nabidae **24:** 36–37
Nabis feras **24:** *36*
Nacerdes melanura **25:** (61)
nagana **23:** (103)
Namib Desert **25:** *68–70,
71;* **29:** *67*
Nanoloricus mysticus **21:** *69*
Naprepa **26:** *82*
Narnia inornata **24:** *52*
Nassophorea **21:** *13*
Nasutitermes **22:** *62*
N. corniger **22:** *66*
N. ephratae **22:** *65*
Natantia **28:** *56*
Nautilidae **30:** *72*
Nautiloidea **30:** *9, 72*
nautiluses 30: 74–75
eyes **30:** (86)
paper **30:** (89)
pearly **30:** *74*
Nautilus pompilus **30:** *74, 75*
Neacoryphus bicrucis
24: *44–45*
Nebaliopsis **28:** *36*
Necrosia **22:** *32*
Nemaster rubiginosa **30:** *96*
Nematocera **23:** *36, 38*
nematocysts **21:** *43, 58, 60*
Nematoda **21:** *32, 77,*
88–91
Nematomorpha **21:** *32,
77–78*
*Nematopogon
swanmerdamella*
26: *112–113*
Nembrotha rutilans **30:** *39*
Nemertea **21:** *32, 77,*
86–87
Nemestrinidae **23:** (69)
Neobisium muscorum **29:** *20*
Neogastropoda **30:** *18,*
32–35
Neopetrolisthes maculatus
28: *88–89*
***Neopilina* 30:** 12–13
N. galatheae **30:** *12–13*
Neotanaidomorpha **28:** *34*
Neothyonidium magnum
30: *92–93*
Neotrypaea californiensis
28: *80–81*
Nepa cinerea **24:** *20*
Nephila maculata **23:** *52*
Nephrotoma **23:** *44*
Nephtys caeca **21:** *97*
Nepidae **24:** 20–21
Neptunides polychromus
25: *86–87*
Nereis
N. diversicolor **21:** *97*
N. virens **21:** *95*
Neriidae **23:** (85)

nerites **30:** *26–27*
Nerthra **24:** *22*
Neuroptera **22:** *30,* 90–97
Neuroterus
N. numismalis **27:** *33*
N. quercus-baccarum
27: *32*
Nicrophorus **25:** *28, 30*
N. vespillo **25:** *29*
Nigma puella **29:** *53*
Nilio testaceus **25:** *70*
Nisitrus **23:** *19*
Noctuidae **26:** 92–97
feeding **26:** (96)
Noroma nigrolunata **26:** *99*
Notodontidae **26:** 80–83
Notodoris gardineri **30:** *39*
Notonecta glauca **24:** *24,
24–25, 25, 26*
Notonectidae **24:** 24–27
Notostraca **28:** *18*
Nucella lapillus **30:** *32,
34–35*
Nuculidae **30:** *50*
Nuda **21:** *43*
nudibranch
aeolid **30:** *41*
black-lined **30:** *20–21*
defense **30:** (41)
Nudibranchia **30:** *18,* 38–43
Nymphalidae **26:** *11,* 38–45
Nymphalinae **26:** *40–43*

O

Obelia geniculata **21:** *46*
Ochlodes venata **26:** *62*
Octocorallia **21:** *43*
Octopoda **30:** *72,* 84–89
Octopodidae **30:** *72*
Octopus
O. bimaculoides **30:** *88*
O. cyanea **30:** *73*
O. maorum **30:** *84–85*
octopuses 30: 84–89
blue-ringed **30:** *84*
day **30:** *73*
eyes **30:** (86)
lesser **30:** *85*
Maori **30:** *84–85*
mimic **30:** *87*
poison **30:** *88–89*
in shells **30:** (89)
two-spotted **30:** *88*
Ocypode quadrata
28: *56–57*
Odonata **22:** *30,* 42–51
Odontochila **25:** *22*
Odontodactylus scyllarus
28: *38, 40*
Odontomyia viridula **23:** *57*
Odontotaenius disjunctus
25: *75*
Odontotermes obesus
22: *62–63*
Oecanthus quadripunctatus
23: *16–17*
Oecophylla
O. longinoda **27:** *40–41*
O. smaragdina **27:** *42,
48–49, 52–53, 54–55*
Oedemera nobilis **25:** *61*
Oedemeridae **25:** (61)
Oedipoda miniata **23:** *24*
Oestridae **23:** 96–97
Ogdoecosta **25:** *101*

Oiketicus elongatus **26:** *111*
Oligobrachia ivanovi **21:** *92*
Oligochaeta **21:** *77, 94,*
102–105
Oligohymenophorea **21:** *13*
Olyras crathis **26:** *56–57*
Ommatopia pictifolia **23:** *12*
Oncea **28:** *31*
Oncomeris flavicornis **24:** *64*
Oniscoidea **28:** *34*
Onophas columbaria
26: *62–63*
Onychophora **21:** *32;* **22:** *13*
Onymacris rugatipennis
25: *69–70, 71*
Oonopidae **29:** *38*
Opalinata **21:** *13*
Ophiarachnella incrassata
30: *98*
Ophioderma wahlbergi
30: *92*
Ophiotrix fragilis **30:** *98–99*
Ophiuroidea **30:** *91, 98*
Opiliones **29:** 22–25
Opisthobranchia **30:** *9, 10,
18,* 36–37
Oplomus dichrous **24:** *62*
orange-tips (whites)
26: 22–27
Orconectes limosus **28:** *75*
Orgyia vetusta **26:** *100*
ornithology **21:** (33)
Ornithoptera alexandrae
26: *16, 16*
Orthonectida **21:** *32, 35*
Orthoptera **22:** *30;* **23:** 8–11
anatomy **23:** *8–10*
life cycle **23:** *10–11*
osmeteria **26:** *18–19,* (19),
20
Osmia rufa **27:** *85, 88*
osmoconformers **28:** (105)
osmotic stress **21:** *14*
Ostracoda **28:** *9,* 32–33
Ostreidae **30:** *50*
Ostreiformes **30:** *9, 50,*
56–57
Otiorhynchus singularis
25: *110*
oviparity **27:** *13*
ovoviviparity **25:** *19, 99*
owlflies **22:** *90, 96–97*
Oxycomanthus bennetti
30: *95*
Oxyopes
O. heterophthalmus
29: *78*
O. schenkeli **29:** *79, 80*
O. superbus **29:** *78–79*
Oxyopidae **29:** 78–81
Oxyrrhachis versicolor **24:** *93*
Oxythyrea funesta **25:** *85*
oysters 30: 56–57
eastern **30:** *56*
Pacific **30:** *52–53*
pearls **30:** *56–57, 61*
saddle **30:** *58, 59*
spiny **30:** *52*
wing **30:** *58, 59*

P

*Pachycerianthus
multiplicatus* **21:** *57*
Pachycondyla commutata
27: *43*

Pachypoda guatemalensis
24: *32–33*
Pacifastacus lenuisculus
28: *72–73*
Pagarus prideauxi **28:** *76–77*
Paguroidea **28:** *56,* 94–101
Pagurus bernhardus **28:** *94*
Palaeacanthocephala **21:** *77*
paleozoology **21:** (33)
Palinura **28:** *56,* 82–85
Palpares **22:** *95, 94–95*
Palpigradi **29:** (29)
Pandalus
P. borealis **28:** *60, 68*
P. platyceros **28:** *60–61*
Pandinus imperator **29:** *16*
Panorpa
P. communis
22: *104–105, 106–107*
P. nuptialis **22:** *104*
Pantophthalmus tabaninus
23: *40–41*
Panulirus
P. argus **28:** *82, 84–85*
P. marginatus **28:** *83*
Papilio **22:** *31*
P. aegeus **26:** *18–19*
P. glaucus **26:** *21*
P. machaon **26:** *16–17*
Papilionidae **26:** 16–21
Papilioninae **26:** *17–18*
Parabuthus **29:** 18–19
P. capensis **29:** *16–17*
Paragnathobdellae **21:** *94*
Parajalysus nigrescens **24:** *49*
Paramastax nigra **23:** *32*
Paramecium **21:** *22, 22–23*
Paramesopodopsis rufa
28: *43*
Paraphrynus **29:** *26–27*
Paraponera clavata **27:** *41,
56–57*
Parasitellus fucorum **29:** *33*
parasites **21:** *17,* (25), *26–27*
host-parasite relationship
21: (85)
see also tapeworms
Parasitica **27:** *8, 10, 23*
parasitoids **27:** 22–31
finding hosts **27:** *25–26*
parasitology **21:** (33)
Parasphendale agrionina
22: *75*
Parawixia bistriata **29:** *43*
Parazoa **21:** *32, 34*
Parcoblatta **22:** *71*
Pardosa
P. amentata **29:** *82*
P. nigriceps **29:** *84–85*
Parnasiinae **26:** *18*
Paroliogolophus agrestis
29: *22*
parthenogenesis
in beetles **25:** *97, 107*
in bugs **24:** *101, 108, 112*
in crustaceans **28:** *20, 33*
in insects **25:** *41, 55, 81,
87*
in scorpions **29:** *19*
Passalidae **25:** (75)
Patella
P. coerulea **30:** *25*
P. vulgata **30:** *22, 22–23*
pathology **21:** (33)
Pauropoda **22:** *14*
pauropods **22:** (14), *15*

pearls **30:** 56–57, 61
Pecten maximus **30:** *58*
Pectinidae **30:** 50
Pedicillina **21:** *68*
Pediculus
  P. humanus **22:** (89)
  P. humanus capitis **22:** *89*
Pedum spondyloidum **30:** *67*
Pelatachina tibialis **23:** *105*
Peltocheirus **24:** *86*
Penaeidea **28:** 56, 60–69
Penaeus meruguiensis
  28: *63*
Pennatulacea **21:** 43
pentamerism **30:** 90,
  110
Pentatomidae **24:** 60–69
Peracarida **28:** 9, 34
Perga affinis **27:** *19*
Periclemenes **28:** 67, 69
  P. colemani **28:** *65*
  P. imperator **28:** *57*
Peripatus acacioi **22:** *12–13*
Periplaneta americana
  22: 68, 69
Perithemis tenera **22:** *47*
periwinkles **30:** 26, 27, (28)
  flat **30:** *26*
  rough **30:** (28)
Perla bipunctata **22:** *80*
Perna perna **30:** *54*
Peromatus **24:** 60–61,
  68–69
pest control (biological
  control)
  by ants **24:** 54; **27:** 39
  by blow flies **23:** 111
  by bugs **24:** 36–37,
    45–46, (49), 62–64,
    (75)
  by ladybugs **25:** (56)
  by moths **26:** (103)
  by parasitoids **27:** 30–31
  by parasitic flies
    23: 106–107
  by weevils **25:** 110
Petrobius maritimus **22:** *37*
Peucetia viridans **29:** *80–81*
Phaeodaria **21:** 13
Phalera sundana **26:** *81*
phasma, great brown **22:** *52*
Phasmatodea **22:** 30, 52–57
Phasmida **21:** 77
Phelypera distigma
  25: *108–109*
Phenax variegata **24:** *72*
Phengodidae **25:** (35)
pheromones **22:** 11; **27:** 43,
  (45), (65), 69, 73, 75,
  111–112
Phiale tristis **29:** *75*
Philaenus spumarius **24:** 78,
  78, 78–79
Philipomyia **23:** *58–59*
Philoscia muscorum
  28: *46–47, 48–49*
Phlaeothripidae **22:** 85
Phlogophora meticulosa
  22: *32–33*
Phlyctenanthus australis
  21: *60*
Phobetron **26:** *106*
Phoebis sennae **26:** *24–25*
Pholadidae **30:** 71
Pholcidae **29:** 60–63

Pholcus phalangioides
  29: *60, 61, 62–63*
Phoneutria **29:** *87*
phoresy **29:** (21), 33
Phoronida **21:** 32, 68, 69,
  74–75
Phoronis **21:** *75*
Phoronopsis viridis **21:** *74*
photosynthesis **21:** 9, 60,
  (65), (66), 93
Phreatoicidea **28:** 34
Phrictus quinquepartilus
  24: *12*
Phromnia rosea **24:** *74–75*
Phrynarachne tuberosa
  29: *70*
Phthiraptera **22:** 30, 88–89
Phthirus pubis **22:** 88–89
Phyllium **22:** *54–55*
Phyllocarida **28:** 9, 34
Phyllomorpha laciniata
  24: *55, 55–56*
Phyllopharyngea **21:** 13
Phylolaemata **21:** 69
Phymateus **21:** *30–31*
Phyrinus **29:** *26*
Physonota alutacea
  25: *14–15*
Phytomastigophora **21:** 13,
  16
Phytonomus nigrirostris
  25: *104*
piddocks **30:** 62, 71
Pieridae **26:** 22–27
Pieris
  P. brassicae **26:** *24–25*
  P. rapae **26:** (24)
Pinnidae **30:** 59
Pinnotheres ostreum
  28: *111–112*
Pinnotheridae **28:** 111–112
pipi **30:** *63*
Pirata piraticus **29:** *83*
Piroplasmea **21:** 13
Pisaura mirabilis **29:** *42, 88,*
  (91), 92–93
Pisauridae **29:** 88–93
Pisilus tipuliformis **24:** *42*
Placozoa **21:** 32, 35
Plagiopylea **21:** 13
Plagiostoma giganteum
  30: *53*
Plagiotryptus hippiscus
  23: *32–33*
plague, bubonic **22:** (113)
Planaria **21:** *80–81, 81–82*
plant control **24:** 54–55, 91
planthoppers
  delphacid **24:** (75)
  flatid **24:** (74)
  fulgorid (lanternflies)
    24: *12, 72–77*
plants
  and ants **27:** (46)
  Hymenoptera and **27:** 8–9
Plasmodium **21:** 26, 26–27
Plataspidae **24:** (63)
Platycpoida **28:** 9
Platydesmida **22:** 14–15
Platyhelminthes **21:** 32, 77,
  80–85
Platyptilia gouodactyla
  26: *102*
Plebeia **27:** *109*
Plecoptera **22:** 30, 80–81

Pleocyemata **28:** 56, 58
Pleurobrachia **21:** *44–45*
  P. pileus **21:** *44*
Pleurobranchomorpha
  30: 37
Plexippus paykulli **29:** *76*
Poecilostomatoida **28:** 9
Pogonomyrmex **27:** 52
  P. occidentalis **27:** *52*
Pogonophora **21:** 32, 77,
  92–93
Poladryas minuta **26:** *44–45*
Polistes
  nest organization
    27: 70–72
  P. cinerascens **27:** *73*
  P. fastidiosus **27:** *68–69*
  P. instabilis **27:** *62–63,*
    70–71
Pollenia rudis **23:** *111*
Polybia occidentalis
  27: *66–67*
Polychaeta **21:** 77, 94,
  98–101
Polycirrus caliendrum **21:** *28*
Polycystina **21:** 13
polyembryony **27:** 23–24
polymorphism **22:** 33
Polyommatinae **26:** 29
polyphenism **22:** 33
Polyphylla fullo **25:** *82*
Polyplacophora **30:** 9, 14–15
Polyspilota aeruginosa
  22: *74–75, 77*
Pompilidae **27:** 58–61
pondskaters (water striders)
  24: 16–17
Popricopida **28:** 9
Porcellanidae **28:** 86
Porcellio scaber **28:** *48–49*
Porifera **21:** 32, 34, 36–41
Portia labiata **29:** (77)
Portuguese man-of-war
  21: 46, 48–49, 49
Portunus **28:** *104*
  P. pelagicus **28:** *113*
Potamon fluviatilis **28:** *105*
prawns 28: 60–69
  hinge-beak **28:** 66–67
  or shrimps **28:** (60)
  spotted Pacific **28:** 60–61
  tiger **28:** 62
praying mantis **22:** 9, 74–79
Prepona antimache **26:** *40*
Priapulida **21:** 32, 77, 78
Priapulus caudatus **21:** *78*
Prionyx kirbyi **27:** *81*
Procambarus clarki **28:** *8–9*
Proconia marmorata
  24: *88–89*
Proctotrupoidea **27:** (23)
prokaryotes **21:** 9
prominents 26: 80–83
  coxcomb **26:** 80–81
  defense **26:** 82–83
Prosobranchia **30:** 9, 10, 18
Prostheceraeus vittatus
  21: *80*
Prostomata **21:** 13
Protista **21:** 12, 13
Protobranchia **30:** 50
Protophormia **23:** *36–37*
protoplasm **21:** 13–14
Protoreaster nodosus **30:** *91*
protostomes **21:** 31
Protostomia **21:** 32, 69

protozoans **21:** 12–15
  reproduction **21:** 14
Protula magnifica
  21: *100–101*
Protura **22:** 26, (26–27)
provisioning
  mass **27:** 66, 79
  progressive **27:** 66, 79
Pselaphacus giganteus
  25: *50–51*
Pseudoceros zebra **21:** *81*
Pseudococcidae
  24: 112–113
Pseudococcus
  P. adonidum **24:** *112*
  P. affinis **24:** *113*
Pseudocolochirus axiologus
  30: *110*
Pseudocreobotra ocellata
  22: *78–79*
Pseudocuma cercaria **28:** *50*
Pseudolamellibranchia **30:** 9,
  50, 58–59
Pseudomeloe collegialis
  25: *64*
Pseudomops **22:** *70–71*
Pseudomyrmex ferruginea
  27: *46*
Pseudopallene ambigua
  29: *12–13*
pseudopods **21:** 18–19
Pseudoscorpiones **29:** 20–21
pseudoscorpions
  29: 20–21
Psilopa petrolei **23:** (39)
Psocoptera **22:** 30, 86–87
Psolus chitonoides **30:** *111*
Psychidae **26:** 110–111
Psylla alni **24:** *96–97*
Psyllidae **24:** 96–97
Pteriidae **30:** 59
Pterinochilus junodi
  29: *36–37*
Pteronarcyidae **22:** 80–81
Pterophoridae **26:** 102–103
Pterophorus pentadactyla
  26: 102, *102–103*
Pteroplatus **25:** *90–91*
Pterostichus madidus **25:** *17*
Pterygota **22:** 30
Ptilodon capucina **26:** *80–81*
Ptiloglossa guinnae, nests
  27: 90
Ptilosphen insignis
  23: *84–85*
Ptomaphila lacrymosa **25:** *31*
Ptychoptera contaminata
  23: *45*
Ptychopteridae **23:** (45)
puddling **26:** (15), 16–17
Pulex irritans **22:** 111
Pulmonata **30:** 9, 10, 18,
  44–49
Pulvinaria regalis **24:** *107*
punkies **23:** (52)
purpurin **30:** 35
Pycnogonida **22:** 9
Pycnogonum littorale **29:** *12*
Pyralidae **26:** (103)
Pyrochroa
  P. coccinea **25:** *60*
  P. serraticornis **25:** *60–61*
Pyrochroidae **25:** 60–61
Pyrops **25:** *72–73*
Pyrrhocoridae **24:** 48–49
Pyrrhocoris apterus **24:** *48*

Q

quinones **25:** 73

R

Radiata **21:** 30, 32
radiolarians **21:** 14–15
ragworms 21: 97
  and allies 21: 98–101
Ralpharia magnifica **21:** *48*
Ranatra linearis **24:** *20*
Ranzovius **24:** (33)
Raphidioptera **22:** 30,
  100–101
Reduviidae **24:** 38–43
reflex bleeding **25:** 58
Remipedia **28:** 9, (14)
Reptantia **28:** 56
Rhadinoceraea micans
  27: *18*
Rhagionidae **23:** (59)
Rhagio scolopaceus **23:** *59*
Rhagoletis completa **23:** *88*
Rhagonycha fulva **25:** *34–35*
Rhaphidophoridae **23:** (21)
Rhaphirrhinus phosphoreus
  24: *89*
Rhetus periander **26:** *35*
Rhicnogryllus lepidus **23:** *17*
Rhigus horridus
  25: *110–111*
Rhinastus latesternus
  25: *104–105*
Rhingia campestris
  23: *76–77, 78*
Rhinocoris
  R. albopilosus **24:** *14*
  R. tristis **24:** *42*
Rhizostomae **21:** 43
Rhodogastria **26:** *89*
Rhombozoa **21:** 32, 35
Rhopalidae **24:** 58–59
Rhopalus subrufus **24:** *58*
Rhynchobdellae **21:** 94
Rhynchocinetes **28:** 11
  R. durbanensis **28:** *66–67*
Rhysella approximator
  27: *24–25*
Riftrida **21:** 77
Riodinidae **26:** 34–37
Rizocephala **28:** 9
Rocky Mountain spotted
  fever **29:** 32, (32)
Rodalia cardinalis **25:** (56)
roller, bean-leaf (long-tailed
  skipper) **26:** *62*
Romalea microptera **23:** *28*
Rosema **26:** *80*
Rotifera **21:** 32, 68–69

S

Sabella pavonina **21:** *97*
sabellids **21:** *34–35*
Sacculina carcini **28:** *26*
Sacoglossa **30:** 18, (43)
sacoglossans **30:** (43)
Sacoglossus **21:** *79*
Sagitta elegans **21:** *79*
Saldidae **24:** (23)
Salmonella **23:** 108
Salticidae **29:** 39, 74–77
sand dollars **30:** 93, 104,
  108, 109
sand gaper **30:** 62

sand hoppers 28: 44–45
Sarcodina **21:** 13, 18–21
Sarcomastigophora **21:** 13
Sarcophaga carnaria
 23: *112, 112–113*
Sarcophagidae **23:** 112–113
Saturniidae **26:** 9–10, 70–73
 defense **26:** (72)
Satyridae **26:** 46–47
satyrs 26: 46–47
 marbled whites **26:** 47
 mating **26:** 47
 mountain beauty
 26: 46–47
 scotch argus **26:** 46
sawflies 27: 12
 and allies 27: 14–21
 colon **27:** 9
 defensive measures
 27: 19–20
 European iris **27:** 18
 feeding **27:** 17–18
 hazel **27:** 20–21
 and humans **27:** 20
 larvae **27:** 18–19
 lime-green **27:** 16
 maternal care **27:** (17)
 as pests **27:** 20
 spitfire **27:** 19
 striped bracken **27:** 17
scale insects **24:** 106–111
 cottony cushion **24:** 106;
 25: (56)
 as pests **24:** 109–110
 soft **24:** 106, 107
 tortoise **24:** 106
 wax **24:** 106
 woolly insects **24:** 110
scallops
 and allies 30: 58–59
 Atlantic bay **30:** 58
Scaphopoda **30:** 9, 10,
 16–17
Scaphura **23:** 15
Scapteriscus vicinus **23:** 23
Scarabaeidae **25:** 76–89
Scathophagidae **23:** 98–99
Scathophaga stercoraria
 23: 98, 98–99
Sceliphron
 S. fistularum **27:** 78–79
 S. fuscum **27:** 79
Schinia masoni **26:** 94
Schistosoma mansoni **21:** 83
schistosomiasis **21:** (83),
 (85); **30:** 46
Schizodonta **30:** 9, 50,
 60–61
schizogony **21:** 14
Sciomyzidae **23:** 94–95
Scleractinia **21:** 43
Scoliidae **27:** 36–37
Scolopendra cingulatus
 22: 22–23
Scolopostethus affinis
 24: (45)
Scorpiones **29:** 16–19
scorpionflies 22: 104–108
 common **22:** 106–107
 snow **22:** 104–108
scorpions 29: 8, 9, 16–19
 African emperor **29:** 16
 anatomy **29:** 16–17
 body **29:** 17
 false **29:** 20
 mating **29:** 18–19

scorpions (continued)
 microwhip **29:** (29)
 stings **29:** (18)
 tailed whip 29: 28–29
 tailless whip 29: 15,
 26–27
 water **24:** 20–21
 wind (sun spiders)
 29: 34–35
scrub typhus **29:** (32)
Scudderia **23:** 12–13
Scutelleridae **24:** 70–71
Scutigera coleoptrata **22:** 22
Scutigerella immaculata
 22: (15)
scuttle bugs (whirligig
 beetles) **25:** 26–27
Scyllarides haanii **28:** 83
Scyphozoa **21:** 43, 50–55
Scytodes
 S. globula **29:** 58–59
 S. thoracica **29:** 58
Scytodidae **29:** 58–59
sea anemones 21: *34–35,
 42,* 56–61; **28:** (97), 99
 aggression **21:** (59)
 anatomy **21:** 57
 beadlet **21:** *56, 59*
 burrowing **21:** (58)
 and clownfish **21:** (61)
 fireworks **21:** 57
 frilled **21:** 56
 magnificent **21:** 61
sea butterflies **30:** 36, 37
sea cucumbers **30:** 91,
 92–93, 93, 110–113
 armored **30:** 111
 Cuvierian organs
 30: (113)
 defense **30:** (113)
 plate and anchor spicules
 30: (111)
sea fans **21:** 66–67
sea hares **30:** 36, 36–37, 37
sea lemon **30:** 38
sea lilies 30: 92, 94–97
 orange **30:** 96
sea monkeys **28:** (20)
sea mouse **21:** 99
sea nettles **21:** 55
sea potato **30:** 108–109
sea roach **28:** 46
sea slater **22:** 9; **28:** 46, 49
sea slugs 30: 38–43
 nudibranch **30:** 21
 opalescent **30:** 10–11
 pyjama **30:** 40–41
 seasnails **30:** 26
 violet **30:** 29
sea spider **22:** 8
seastar, horned **30:** 91
sea urchins 30: 91, 93,
 104–109
 Aristotle's lantern **30:** 93,
 106
 common **30:** 105
 hatpin **30:** 106
 pedicellariae **30:** (107)
 regular (rounded) **30:** 104
 slate pencil **30:** 105
 spines **30:** 104–106
sea wasp **21:** 52
sedge darner **30:** 51
Segestria senoculata **29:** 63
Segestriidae **29:** (63)
Sehirus bicolor **24:** 66–67

Semaeostomae **21:** 43
Semibalanus balanoides
 28: 22
Semicassis labiata **30:** 30
Semiotus insignis **25:** 43
Senoculidae **29:** 93
Sepia **30:** 77–78
 S. apama **30:** 77
 S. latimanus **30:** 78
 S. officinalis **30:** (78)
 S. pharaonis **30:** 76–77
sepia dun **22:** 38
Sepiidae **30:** 72
Sepsidae **23:** (99)
Sepsis fulgens **23:** 98–99,
 (99)
Sepidium tricuspidatum
 25: 72–73
Sepsidae **23:** (99)
Sesia apiformis **26:** 104
Sesiidae **26:** 104–105
sexual dichromatism **23:** 25
sheep strike **23:** 109–110
shells 30: (93)
 ark, and relatives **30:** 53
 auger **30:** 35
 bubble, and allies
 30: 36–37
 burrowing razor **30:** (70)
 carpet **30:** 62, 67–68
 coat-of-mail *see* chitons
 coin **30:** 63–64
 cone 30: 32–35
 elephant's tusk
 30: 16–17
 file **30:** 58, 59
 harp **30:** 34, 35
 hatchet **30:** 62, 63
 helmet **30:** 26, 30
 jewel box **30:** 62, 67
 laver spire **30:** 29
 miter **30:** 35
 mollusk **30:** 9, (10)
 olive **30:** 35
 otter **30:** 70–71
 pullet carpet **30:** 67
 razor 30: 62–71
 textile cone **30:** 33
 top 30: 22–25
 turban **30:** 22, 25
 venus **30:** 62, 67–68
 wavy top **30:** 24
 wedge **30:** 62, 68–70
shipworms **30:** 71
shovelheads **28:** 84
shrimps 28: 60–69
 Baikal **28:** 44–45
 banana **28:** 63
 boxer **28:** 63, 64, 64, 65,
 67–68
 brine (fairy) **28:** 16–21
 brown **28:** 60
 California mantis
 28: 38–39
 clam (fairy) **28:** 16–21
 cleaner **28:** (67)
 clown mantis **28:** 38
 Coleman **28:** 65
 common **28:** 60
 emperor **28:** 57
 fairy 28: 16–21, 42–43
 flat-browed mud **28:** 80
 freshwater **28:** (64)
 ghost 28: 80–81
 giant deep-water
 opossum **28:** 36–37
 glass (ghost) **28:** 80–81

shrimps (continued)
 harlequin **28:** 35
 harlequin mantis **28:** 38
 helmeted **28:** (17)
 hingebeak **28:** 11
 mantis 28: 38–41
 Mono Lake **28:** (19)
 mountain **28:** 37
 mud 28: 80–81
 mussel 28: 32–33
 northern **28:** 60, 68
 opossum 28: 42–43
 pink possum **28:** 43
 pistol **28:** 63, (63)
 or prawns **28:** (60)
 sex-change **28:** (68)
 snapping **28:** (63)
 tadpole (fairy) **28:** 16–21
 vibrant Indonesian mantis
 28: 40
Sialis lutaria **22:** 98, 98–99
Sibine see *Acharia*
Sicus ferrugineus **23:** 82
Sigmoria aberrans **22:** 21
silk
 casting **29:** (101)
 production **29:** 43, (44)
 spiders' use of **29:** 45
Silpha **25:** 31
 S. tristis **25:** 28
Silphidae **25:** 28–31
silverfish 22: 31, 36–37
Simuliidae **23:** (53)
Simulium **23:** 52
single-celled life 21: 12–15
Siphonaptera **22:** 30,
 110–113
Siphonophora **21:** 43
Siphonostomatoida **28:** 9
Sipuncula **21:** 32, 77, 78
skipjacks (click beetles)
 25: 42–45
skippers 26: 62–65
 long-tailed **26:** 62
sleeping sickness **21:** (17);
 23: (103)
slugs 30: 44–49
 banana **30:** 49
 great gray **30:** 48–49
 terrestrial **30:** 44, 45,
 48–49
 see also sea slugs
snails 30: 44–49
 dune **30:** 46
 European grove
 30: 18–19
 freshwater **30:** 19, 44
 garden **30:** 45
 giant African land **30:** 48
 great pond **30:** 44
 South Pacific **30:** (48)
 terrestrial **30:** 44, 45,
 46–48
 wandering **30:** 45
 water **30:** 45–46
 see also seasnails
snakeflies 22: 100–101
 Texas **22:** 100
sociability
 ants **27:** 40
 Hymenoptera **27:** 11–12
Solaster papposus **30:** 98
Solenidae **30:** 50, 68
solenogasters **30:** (13)
Solifugae **29:** 34–35
Solpuga **29:** 34

Someticus bohemani **25:** 19
sound production **22:** 30
 millipedes **22:** 18
 spiny lobsters **28:** (84)
Spanish dancer **30:** 40
Sparassidae **29:** 66–67
Spartocera fusca **24:** 54
Spatangus purpureus
 30: 104
Spelaeogriphacea **28:** 34, 37
spermatophore **22:** 11
sperm competition **22:** 48
Sphaerium **30:** 61
Sphecidae **27:** 76–83
Sphecius speciosus **27:** (82),
 82–83
Sphingidae 26: 66–69
Sphodrolestes **24:** 15
Sphodros **29:** 50, 51
 S. atlanticus **29:** 50–51
Sphongophorus guerini
 24: 90
spiders 29: 8, 9, 36–45
 anatomy **29:** 35–36,
 38–42
 anemone sea **29:** 12
 aquatic **29:** (110)
 arrow-shaped thorn
 29: 109
 Asian bird-dropping
 29: 70
 banana **29:** 111
 bark **29:** 108
 bird-eating (tarantulas)
 29: 46–47
 black-lined orchard
 29: 103
 brown **29:** (59)
 bugs living with **24:** (33)
 bull's horn **29:** 109
 buzzing **29:** (81)
 cellar **29:** 60, 99
 classification **29:** 38
 cobweb **29:** 40
 comb-footed
 29: 89–101
 crab 29: 68–73
 daddy-longlegs
 29: 60–63
 dead-leaf jumpers
 29: (77)
 death's head **29:** (108)
 decoy **29:** 106–107
 Diard's heavy jumper
 29: 41
 European buzzing
 29: 42–43
 European water **29:** (110)
 false wolf **29:** 93
 feather-footed
 29: 56–57
 fence-post jumper
 29: 74–75
 fisher **29:** 89
 flat wolf **29:** 93
 flower **29:** 71–72
 funnel-web 29: 48–49
 garden **29:** 110–111
 giant crab (huntsman)
 29: 66–67
 gladiator (net-casting)
 29: 54–55
 goldenrod **29:** 71–72
 gossamer 29: 112–113
 grass (sheet-web weavers)
 29: 94–97

spiders (continued)
green lynx **29:** *80–81*
hammock-web (gossamer) **29:** 112–113
house **29:** *95*
huntsman 29: 66–67
jumping 29: *39,* 74–77
lynx 29: 78–81
mating **29:** *42–43*
meadow stilt **29:** *103, 104*
money (gossamer) **29:** 112–113
mothercare **29:** *98, (99)*
mouse **29:** *(81)*
net-casting 29: 54–55
nursery web 29: 88–93
ogre-faced (net-casting) **29:** 54–55
pirate **29:** *83*
purse-web 29: 50–51
rafter **29:** *60, 61, 62–63*
red widow **29:** *100*
rusty wandering **29:** *87*
sea **22:** *8;* **29:** *8,* 12–13
silk-city **29:** *(101)*
silk production and use **29:** *43, (44), 45*
six-spotted fisher **29:** 88–89
snake's back **29:** *63*
spear-fanged **29:** *(59)*
sperm induction **29:** *(42)*
spider families **29:** *36*
spiny **29:** *108–109*
spiny flag **29:** *111*
spitting 29: 58–59
stick **29:** *57*
sun 29: 34–35
trap-door **29:** *(49)*
tube-web **29:** *(63)*
two-tailed 29: 64–65
wandering 29: 86–87
wasp **29:** *106*
wedding-present **29:** *42, 88, (91)*
whip (tailless whip scorpions) **29:** 26–27
widow **29:** *100–101*
wind (sun) **29:** 34–35
wolf 27: *(61);* **29:** 82–85
see also silk; tarantulas; weavers
Spilopsyllus cuniculi **22:** *110–111*
Spilostethus pandurus **24:** *11*
spiny-skinned animals 30: 90–93
Spirobranchus giganteus **21:** *98–99*
Spirostreptida **22:** *16*
Spirotrichea **21:** *13*
spirula **30:** *(80)*
Spirula spirula **30:** *(80)*
spittlebugs (froghoppers) **24:** 78–79
Spondylus **30:** *52*
sponges 21: *28–29, 34–35,* 36–41
azure vase **21:** *36–37*
barrel **21:** *40*
body forms **21:** *36–38*
brown tube **21:** *36*
classes of **21:** *35*

sponges (continued)
cloud **21:** *39*
coralline **21:** *(40)*
orange puffball **21:** *37*
red **21:** *39*
reproduction **21:** *39–40*
structure **21:** *(38)*
yellow tube **21:** *40–41*
Sporozoa **21:** *13*
Spriggina **21:** *35*
springtails 22: 28–29
squids 30: 76–83
California market **30:** *83*
dumpling **30:** *80–81*
eyes **30:** *(86)*
giant **30:** *(82)*
Mexican giant Humboldt **30:** *82*
ram's horn *see Spirula spirula*
short-finned **30:** *82–83*
Squilla **28:** *38*
stabilimenta **29:** *107–108*
Stagmatoptera septrionalis **22:** *76–77*
stainers 24: *11,* 48–49
Staphylinidae **25:** 32–33
Staphylinus olens **25:** *32–33*
starfish 30: *91, 92,* 98–103
candy cane **21:** *64*
crown-of-thorns **30:** *(102–103)*
stomach eversion **30:** *92, 100, 102*
stars
basket 30: 98–103
brittle 30: 98–103
feather 30: *93,* 94–97
rosy feather **30:** *94*
Stauromedusae **21:** *43*
Steatoda grossa **29:** *99*
Stegobium paniceum **25:** *(53)*
Stelopolybia pallipes **27:** *72*
Stenocara gracilipes **25:** *68–69*
Stenolaemata **21:** *69*
Stenopalmatus fuscus **23:** *20*
Stenopelmatidae **23:** 20–21
Stenopodidea **28:** *56,* 60–69
Stenopus **28:** *64*
Stenorhynchus seticornis **28:** *103*
Stephanitis pyri **24:** *28*
Sternorrhyncha **24:** *8, 10, 12, 13, 15*
Sternotomus variablis **25:** *92*
stick insects (walkingsticks) **22:** 52–57
giant **22:** *55*
titan **22:** *52*
Stigmodera rufolimbata **25:** *47*
Stolonifera **21:** *43*
Stomatopoda **28:** *34,* 38–41
stoneflies 22: 80–81
European **22:** *80*
giant **22:** *80–81*
Stratiomyidae **23:** 56–57
Stratiomys
S. longicornis **23:** *57*
S. potamida **23:** *56–57*
Strepsiptera **22:** *30;* **25:** *(14)*
stridulation **22:** *18, 30, 87*
Strongylogaster lineata **27:** *17*

Strongyloides **21:** *88*
Strymon
S. martialis **26:** *28*
S. melinus **26:** *31*
Stylasterina **21:** *43*
Stylommatophora **30:** *18, 45, 47*
sulfurs (whites) **26:** 22–27
mass migration **26:** *26*
orange **26:** *22*
ultraviolet markings **26:** *25*
sun stars **30:** *98*
sweet-oils (ithomiids) **26:** 56–57
swordtails (swallowtail butterflies) **26:** 16–21
fivebar **26:** *16–17*
Symbion pandora **21:** *69*
symmetry, pentameric **30:** *90, 110*
Sympetrum sanguineum **22:** *46*
Symphoromyia **23:** *(59)*
Symphyla **22:** *14, 15*
symphylans **22:** *(15)*
Symphyta **27:** *8, 9–10, 12, 14–21*
Synaptula **30:** *112–113*
Syncarida **28:** *9, 34*
Synodus variegatus **28:** *30*
Syrphidae **23:** 76–81
Systelommatophora **30:** *18, 45*
Systoechus **23:** *71*

T

Tabanidae **23:** 58–61
tabanids **23:** 58–61
blood feeding **23:** *61*
feeding **23:** *61*
larvae **23:** *61*
mating **23:** *58–60*
Tabanus
T. atratus **23:** *60*
T. sudeticus **23:** *60*
T. trimaculatus **23:** *58*
Tachina fera **23:** *104, 106*
Tachinidae **23:** 104–107
Taeniopoda auricornis **23:** *28*
Tanaidacea **28:** *9, 34, (51)*
Tanaidomorpha **28:** *34*
tanaids **28:** *(51)*
tapeworms 21: 80–85
tarantulas 29: 46–47
red-knee **22:** *9*
Mexican red-knee **29:** *46*
Tardigrada **21:** *32;* **22:** *12–13*
Tauroma auricornis **25:** *97*
Taxodonta **30:** *50*
taxonomy **21:** 8–11
Tealia lofotensis **21:** *56–57*
Tectocoris diophthalmus **24:** *70–71*
Tegenaria duellica **29:** *95*
Telestacea **21:** *43*
tellins (wedge shells) **30:** *62, 68–70*
Telostylinus **23:** *85, (85)*
Tenebrionidae **25:** 68–73
Tentaculata **21:** *43*
Tenthredo **27:** *9*
T. mesomelas **27:** *16*
Tephritidae **23:** 88–91

Teredinidae **30:** *71*
termitaria **22:** *(64)*
termites 22: 62–67; **27:** *11, 40, 41*
colonies **22:** *63–65*
compass **22:** *(64)*
defense **22:** *(67)*
feeding **22:** *65–66*
fungus gardens **22:** *(64), 65, 67*
nasute soldier **22:** *62*
nests **22:** *(64)*
western subterranean **22:** *62–63*
Tessaratomidae **24:** *(64)*
Tetanocera **23:** *94*
T. assogans **23:** *95*
Tethya aurantia **21:** *37*
Tetrabranchia **30:** 74–75
Tetragnatha
T. extensa **29:** *103, 104*
T. montana **29:** *102*
Tetragnathidae **29:** 102–105
Tetrastichus galactopus **27:** *25*
Tetrigidae **23:** 34–35
Tetrix subulata **23:** *34, 34–35*
Tettigoniidae **23:** 12–15
Tevniida **21:** *77*
Thalassema neptuni **21:** *78*
Thalassinidea **28:** *56,* 80–81
Thalassius **29:** *92*
Thanasimus formicarius **25:** *40*
Thecanephria **21:** *77*
Theclinae **26:** *29*
Thecosomata **30:** *18*
Thecostraca **28:** *9*
Thelenota anax **30:** *110–111*
Themos olfersii **27:** *17*
Theraphosidae **29:** 46–47
Thereva annulata **23:** *65*
Therevidae **23:** *(65)*
Theridiidae **29:** 98–101
Theridion
T. impressum **29:** *(99)*
T. sisyphium **29:** *98, (99)*
Thermobia domestica **22:** *36*
Thermosbaenacea **28:** *34, 37*
Theromyzon tessulatum **21:** *110–111*
Thetetra japonica **26:** *66–67*
Thomisidae **29:** 68–73
Thoracica **28:** *9*
thrips 22: 84–85
tube-tailed **22:** *84*
western flower **22:** *84*
thunder bugs (thrips) **22:** 84–85
Thyrsopsocus **22:** *86–87*
Thysania agrippina **26:** *93*
Thysanoptera **22:** *30,* 84–85
Thysanura **22:** *30,* 36–37
Tibicen
T. canicularis **24:** *81*
T. plebejus **24:** *80*
Tibificida **21:** *94*
tick-bite fever **29:** *(32)*
ticks 29: 30–33
diseases **29:** *(32)*
hard **29:** *31*
hedgehog **29:** *30*
wood **29:** *32*

tigers
ithomiids **26:** 56–57
plain **26:** *60*
timemas **22:** *52, (55)*
Tingidae **24:** 28
Tingis ampliata **24:** *28–29*
Tipula
T. maxima **23:** *42*
T. oleracea **23:** *39*
T. paludosa **23:** *38, 42–43*
Tipulidae **23:** 42–45
Titanus giganteus **25:** *90*
Tomaspis inca **24:** *79*
Tonicella lineata **30:** *15*
Tonna perdrix **30:** 26–27
Toxocara vitellorum **21:** *91*
Toxorhynchites moctezuma **23:** *48*
Trachelophorus giraffa **25:** *106–107*
transparents (ithomiids) **26:** 56–57
Trachylina **21:** *43*
Trapezonotus arenarius **24:** *44*
Trechalea **29:** *93*
Trechaleidae **29:** *93*
treehoppers 24: *15,* 90–95
ants and **24:** *(93)*
mating **24:** *94*
Mexican **24:** *92–93*
parental care **24:** *93–94, 94, (95)*
pronotum **24:** *(91)*
Trematoda **21:** *77, 81, 82–83*
Trialeurodes vaporariorum **24:** *98, 99*
Triatoma sanguisuga **24:** *41*
Triatominae **24:** *(41)*
Trichinella spiralis **21:** *88–89*
Trichius fasciatus **25:** *86*
Trichochermes walkeri **24:** *96–97*
Trichodectes canis **22:** *88*
Trichodes
T. apiarius **25:** *40–41*
T. ornatus bonnevillensis **25:** *41*
Trichogramma semblidis **27:** *26–27*
Trichomonadida **21:** *13*
Trichophthalma jaffueli **23:** *69*
Trichoptera **22:** *30,* 102–103
Tridacna **30:** *(65)*
T. crocea **30:** *(65), 66*
Tridacnidae **30:** *50*
Tridactylidae **23:** *35*
Trigona fulviventris **27:** *108–109*
Trigonalyoidea **27:** *(23)*
trilobites **28:** *(13)*
triungulins **25:** *(14), 65–66*
trochophore larva **21:** *(76), 101*
Trochozoa **21:** *32, (76)*
Troginae **25:** *(81)*
trophallaxis **27:** *41–42, (42), 56, 70*
true bugs 24: 8–15
anatomy **24:** *10–11*
defense **24:** *14–15*

true bugs (continued)
development **24:** 13–14
families **24:** 8
life cycle **24:** 13–14
see also bugs
true crabs 28: 102–113
anatomy **28:** 102–104
communication **28:** 113, (113)
feeding **28:** 108
as human food **28:** 113
land crabs **28:** 105–106
larvae **28:** (108)
migrations **28:** 106–108
mineral supplements **28:** (105)
predator avoidance **28:** 108–109
reproduction **28:** 112–113
swimming **28:** 102–104
walking sideways **28:** (104)
see also crabs
trumpet, triton **30:** 27
trypanosomes **21:** 17
Trypeta serratulae **23:** 89
tsetse flies **21:** (17)
Tubastrea **21:** 64
T. faulkneri **21:** 62
tubeworm **21:** 28
tumblebugs **25:** 76, 78
tuns **30:** 26
Pacific partridge **30:** 26–27
Turbellaria **21:** 81–82, (81)
twighoppers, net-winged **24:** 95
twisted-winged insects **25:** (14)
Tylos granulatus **28:** 49
typhoid **23:** 103
Tyria jacobaeae **26:** 90

U

Uca **28:** (113)
U. annulipes **28:** 112–113
Uloboridae **29:** 56–57
Umbonia spinosa **24:** 90, 90–91
Unionidae **30:** 50, 60, (61)
Upogebia affinis **28:** 80
Urbanus proteus **26:** 62
Urocerus gigas **27:** 15
Urochordata **21:** 32
Uropygi **29:** 28–29

V

Vaejovis boreas **29:** 19
Valvifera **28:** 34
Vampyromorpha **30:** 72, (75)
Vampyroteuthis infernalis **30:** (75)
Vanessa
V. atalanta **26:** 38
V. cardui **26:** 38–39

Van Leeuwenhoek, Antonie **21:** 9, (12)
Velia caprai **24:** 18, 18–19
Veliidae **24:** 18–19
Vema **30:** 13
Veneridae **30:** 50, 67–68
Venerupis senegalensis **30:** 67
Venustria superba **24:** 84–85
Vespa crabro **27:** 63
Vespidae **27:** 62–75
Vespula
V. germanica **27:** 74–75
V. vulgaris 68, 73
Vestimentifera **21:** 77
Villa modesta **23:** 70
Villosa vibex **30:** 60–61
vinegaroons (tailed whip scorpions) **29:** 28–29
giant **29:** 28
virgin birth *see* parthenogenesis
viviparity **25:** 99
Volucella bombylans **23:** 79
volutes **30:** 35, 35
Vorticella **21:** 24–25

W

walkingsticks 22: 52–57
defense **22:** 56–57
giant thorny **22:** 57
Macleay's specter **22:** 57
slender-bodied **22:** 52–53
2-striped **22:** 52–53
wasps 27: 8–13
alder wood **27:** 14–15
cicada-killer **27:** (82)
cuckoo 27: 34–37
digger 27: 36–37
feeding **27:** (73)
fig **27:** (33)
gall 27: 32–33
German **27:** 73, 74–75
hornets **27:** 63
horse guards **27:** 79–80
hunting (solitary) **27:** 76–83
ichneumon 27: 22–31
jewel (cuckoo) **27:** 34–35
mason **27:** 64
mass provisioning **27:** 66, 79
nectar-gathering **27:** 69
nest cooling **27:** (69)
nest defense **27:** 75
nests **27:** 66–69
paper (social) **27:** 11, 62–75
parasitic (parasitoids) **27:** 22–31
potter (social) **27:** 62, 64–66
progressive provisioning **27:** 66, 79
ruby-tailed (cuckoo) **27:** 34–35

wasps (continued)
slender digger **27:** (37)
social 27: 62–75
solitary 27: 76–83
spider 27: 58–61
spider-hunting (spider) **27:** 58–61
thread-waisted sand **27:** 13, 77, 80–81
wild carrot **27:** 31
wood (sawflies) **27:** 14–21
yellow jacket **27:** 66–67, 72–73
water bears **22:** 12–13
water boatmen (backswimmers) **24:** 24–27
lesser **24:** (27)
waterbug **22:** 68
water fleas 28: 11, 16–21
water measurers **24:** (19)
water scorpions 24: 20–21
water stick insects (water scorpions) **24:** 20–21
water striders 24: 16–17
small (ripple bugs) **24:** 18–19
water vascular system **30:** 91–92, 96
weavers
cobweb (comb-footed spiders) **29:** 98–101
funnel (sheet-web) **29:** 94–97
grass funnel **29:** 97
lace **29:** 52–53
large-jawed orb **29:** 102–105
leaf lace **29:** 53
orb **29:** 43, 106–111
pygmy hackled-web **29:** (53)
sheet-web **29:** 94–97
web spinners 22: 82–83
weevils 25: 104–111
acorn **25:** 104
big-foot **25:** 104–105
boll **25:** (110)
clay-colored **25:** 110
cloverleaf **25:** 104
destructive habits **25:** 109–110, (110)
eight-humped **25:** 106
emerald **25:** 105
fungus **25:** 104
giraffe-necked **25:** 106–107
hazel leaf-rolling **25:** 109
larvae **25:** 109
oak leaf-rolling **25:** 109
pest control **25:** 110
primitive **25:** 112–113
reactions to danger **25:** 110
reproduction **25:** 105–109

weevils (continued)
toothpick (primitive) **25:** 112–113
twelve-spined **25:** 110–111
zygopine **25:** 107
wetas (king crickets) **23:** 20–21
whelks 30: 32–35
common **30:** 32
common northern Atlantic **30:** 19
dog **30:** 32, 34–35
waved **30:** 32
whiteflies **24:** 98–99
greenhouse **24:** 98
rain-forest **24:** 98
whites 26: 22–27
cabbage whites **26:** (24)
Whittaker, Robert **21:** 9
winkles, and relatives 30: 26–31
wireworms (click beetles) **25:** 42–45
false **25:** 71
woodlice **28:** 46–47
common **28:** 48–49
common striped **28:** 46–47
wormlike invertebrates 21: 76–79
worms
acoelomate **21:** 77
acorn **21:** 30–31, 79
annual festival **21:** (104)
arrowworms **21:** 79
beard 21: 92–93
bootlace **21:** 86
bristleworms **21:** 99
candystripe flatworms **21:** 80
Christmas tree **21:** 98–99
coelomate **21:** 77
deuterostomian coelomate **21:** 77
earthworms *see* earthworms
feather-duster **21:** 100–101
fire (bristleworms) **21:** 99
flatworms 21: 80–85
gordian (horsehair) **21:** 77–78, 77
green phoronid **21:** 74
horsehair **21:** 77–78, 77
horseshoe 21: 74–75
innkeeper **21:** 78
palolo **21:** 101
peacock **21:** 97
polychaete **21:** 97
proboscis (ribbon) **21:** 86–87
pseudocoelomate **21:** 77

worms (continued)
ragworms *see* ragworms
ribbon 21: 86–87
roundworms 21: 88–91
sand mason **21:** 97
scale **21:** 98
segmented 21: 94–97
spiny headed **21:** 76, 77
spoonworms **21:** 78
tapeworms 21: 80–85
threadworms (roundworms) **21:** 88–91
velvet **22:** 13
wireworms (click beetles) **25:** 42–45
zebra flatworms **21:** 81
Wyeomyia **23:** 48

X

Xanthopan morgani praedicta **26:** 55
Xenopsylla cheapis **22:** 113
Xestobium rufovillosum **25:** 53, (53)
Xestospongia testudinaria **21:** 40
Xiphydria camelus **27:** 14–15
Xyleutes ceramicus **26:** 105
Xylocopa **22:** 35; **27:** 100–101
X. nigra **27:** 101
Xyphosia miliaria **23:** 89, 90
Xysticus cristatus **29:** 68–69, 70–71

Y

Yponomeuta padella **26:** 112–113
Yponomeutidae **26:** 112–113

Z

Zaphobas **25:** 71
Zoantharia **21:** 43
Zoanthidea **21:** 43
Zonitis sayi **25:** 66–67
Zonocerus elegans **23:** 27
zoogeography **21:** (33)
zoology **21:** (33)
Zoomastigophora **21:** 13, 16–17
Zopheridae **25:** 73
Zopherus nodulosus **25:** 73
Zoraptera **22:** 30, (83)
Zorotypus hubbardi **22:** (83)
Zosis geniculatus **29:** 56–57
Zygaena
Z. graslini **26:** 109
Z. lonicerae **26:** 109
Zygaenidae **26:** 108–109
Zygoptera **22:** 42

Picture Credits

Abbreviations

A Ardea London; C Corbis; FLPA Frank Lane Picture Agency; NHPA Natural History Photographic Agency; NPL naturepl.com; OSF Oxford Scientific Films; SPL Science Photo Library

t = top; **b** = bottom; **c** = center; **l** = left; **r** = right

Jacket

tl, tr, br Ken Preston-Mafham/Premaphotos Wildlife; **bl** John Mason/Ardea London

8 Eye of Science/SPL; **8–9** Stephen Frink/C; **11** Rodger Jackman/OSF; **12–13** Karen Gowlett-Holmes/OSF; **14** Becca Saunders/A; **14–15** David Hall/NPL; **16–17** Kjell Sandved/OSF; **18–19** Konrad Wothe/Minden Pictures/FLPA; **19** Ken Preston-Mafham/Premaphotos Wildlife; **20–21** Mark Webster/OSF; **21** Michael Fogden; **22–23** Anthony Bannister/NHPA; **23, 24t, 24b** Ken Lucas–Photo/A; **25** B. Borrell/FLPA; **26–27** Jurgen Freund/NPL; **27** Gerard Soury/OSF; **28** N.R. Coulton/NHPA; **28–29** Ken Preston-Mafham/Premaphotos Wildlife; **29** imagequestmarine.com/NHPA; **30** Karen Gowlett-Holmes/OSF; **30–31** OSF; **32** Pat Morris/A; **32–33** Scott Johnson/NHPA; **34** B. Jones & M. Shimlock/NHPA; **34–35** Geoff Trinder/A; **35** A.N.T./NHPA; **36–37** OSF; **37t** Kathie Atkinson/OSF; **37c** David Shale/NPL; **38** OSF; **38–39** Constantinos Petrinos/NPL; **39** Jurgen Freund/NPL; **40** Mark Deeble & Victoria Stone/OSF; **40–41** Peter Scoones/NPL; **41t** Norbert Wu/NHPA; **41b** Jurgen Freund/NPL; **42–43** B. Jones & M. Shimlock/NHPA; **43** Pam Kemp/OSF; **44** Clouds Hill Imaging Ltd./SPL; **44–45** Ken Preston-Mafham/Premaphotos Wildlife; **45** G.I. Bernard/NHPA; **46** Jose B. Ruiz/NPL; **46–47** Premaphotos Wildlife/NPL; **47** Raymond Blythe/OSF; **48** Rob Nunnington/OSF; **48–49** OSF; **49** Karl Switak/NHPA; **50–51** F. Bavendam/Minden Pictures/FLPA; **52t** Pat Morris/A; **52b** James King-Holmes/SPL; **52–53** C. & S. Hood/Bruce Coleman Collection; **53** Sinclair Stammers/SPL; **54–55c** Jeffrey L. Rotman/C; **54–55b** Laurie Campbell/NHPA; **56–57** Jurgen Freund/NPL; **57t** Robert Holmes/C; **57c** Kenneth W. Fink/A; **58** John Lythgoe/Seaphot; **58–59** David Fleetham/OSF; **60–61t** Lynda Richardson/C; **60–61b** Colin Milkins/OSF; **62** Gerard Lacz/NHPA; **62–63** Kathie Atkinson/OSF; **64** Karen Gowlett-Holmes/OSF; **64–65** Stephen Frink/C; **66t** D.P. Wilson/FLPA; **66b** A.N.T./NHPA; **67t** Jurgen Freund/NPL; **67b** Ken Preston-Mafham/Premaphotos Wildlife; **68c** Alan James/NPL; **68r** Roy Waller/NHPA; **68–69** Richard Herrmann/OSF; **70** John Mason/A; **70–71** B. Jones & M. Shimlock/NHPA; **71** D.W. Greenslade/A; **72–73** Pacific Stock/Bruce Coleman Collection; **74** W.T. Miller/FLPA; **74–75** Ken Lucas–Photo/A; **76–77** Peter Scoones/NPL; **77** Brent Hedges/NPL; **78c** Linda Pitkin/NHPA; **78b** Constantinos Petrinos/NPL; **79** Linda Pitkin/NHPA; **80** D. Roberts/SPL; **80–81** Rudie Kuiter/OSF; **81** Peter David/FLPA; **82c** Norbert Wu/NHPA; **82b** Bettmann/C; **82–83** Jeffrey L. Rotman/SPL; **83** C; **84–85** F. Bavendam/Minden Pictures/FLPA; **85** OSF; **86** Jeff Rotman/NPL; **87t** David Hall/NPL; **87b** B. Jones & M. Shimlock/NHPA; **88** Norbert Wu/OSF; **88–89** Norbert Wu/NHPA; **89** Rudie Kuiter/OSF; **90–91** Georgette Douwma/NPL; **92** Anthony Bannister/NHPA; **92–93** Colin Marshall/FLPA; **93** Franco Banfi/Bruce Coleman Collection; **94** Sinclair Stammers/SPL; **94–95** David Fleetham/OSF; **96** Trevor McDonald/NHPA; **97** Georgette Douwma/NPL; **98–99** Roy Waller/NHPA; **99** David Hall/NPL; **100c** Jeff Rotman/NPL; **100b** Jurgen Freund/NPL; **101t** David Hall/NPL; **101b** Florian Graner/NPL; **102** Valerie Taylor/A; **102–103** Georgette Douwma/NPL; **104–105** B. Jones & M. Shimlock/NHPA; **105** Laurie Campbell/NHPA; **106–107** Robert Yin/C; **107** Karen Gowlett-Holmes/OSF; **108t** Norbert Wu/NHPA; **108b** Dr. Rod Preston-Mafham/Premaphotos Wildlife; **108–109** Norbert Wu/NHPA; **110–111t** Rodger Jackman/OSF; **110–111b** Jurgen Freund/NPL; **112–113** Norbert Wu/NHPA; **113c** Dr. F. Ehrenstrom & L. Beyer/OSF; **113b** Becca Saunders/A